0 416 964 00 34

INDUSTRIALIZATION POLICIES AND REGIONAL ECONOMIC DEVELOPMENT IN MALAYSIA

INDUSTRIALIZATION POLICIES AND REGIONAL ECONOMIC DEVELOPMENT IN MALAYSIA

Dean Spinanger

SINGAPORE
OXFORD UNIVERSITY PRESS
OXFORD NEW YORK
1986

Oxford University Press
Oxford London New York Toronto
Petaling Jaya Singapore Hong Kong Tokyo
Delhi Bombay Calcutta Madras Karachi
Nairobi Dar es Salaam Cape Town
Melbourne Auckland
and associates in
Beirut Berlin Ibadan Nicosia

ISBN 0 19 582659 0

Printed in Singapore by Koon Wah Printing Pte. Ltd.
Published by Oxford University Press Pte. Ltd.,
Unit 221, Ubi Avenue 4, Singapore 1440

Preface

MANY studies on industrialization policies in Malaysia and other successful developing countries have been carried out and published in the past. What most of these studies ignore is the regional impact and ramifications of such policies. This study attempts to make a contribution in this direction. Its specific purpose is to help understand the influence of industrialization policies on regional economic development in Malaysia, particularly with respect to the declared goal of reducing regional development disparities. The relevance of this topic for Malaysia is underlined by the statement in the Mid-Term Review of the Fourth Malaysia Plan (p. 21). "The marginal success in reducing inter-state imbalances requires a review and redirection of the strategy for regional and urban development."

The approach taken in this study is based on the assumption that just as the structuring of industrialization policies in line with international comparative advantages contributed to the economic success of those countries which followed such a path, an analogous approach in a regional context can produce a similar success. The study itself is written in a manner that should allow informed readers as well as economists to profit from it. In the former case it may prove advisable to read only the introduction and the last two sections of Chapter 2 in order not to be burdened by theoretical technicalities.

This study would not have been possible without the assistance and encouragement of many people in both Malaysia and the Federal Republic of Germany. Without implying anything through the order listed about the importance of the individual contributions nor without implying that all those not mentioned were not helpful, the following persons I should like to mention specifically. In Malaysia: Paul Chan, Chee Peng Lim (both University of Malaya) and Khoo Teik Huat (Department of Statistics) all provided assistance for which the author is extremely grateful. Likewise numerous people at MIDA in Kuala Lumpur and the branch office in Cologne, the EPU, MIDF and the Penang Economic Development Corporation provided me with data and information, from which the study greatly profitted. In Germany: particular gratitude must be expressed to my colleagues Mathias Bruch, Juergen Donges, Egbert Gerken und Ulrich Hiemenz as well as to Prof. Manfred Willms for their comments and criticism. The author applies, however, the usual waiver. The study would not have been produced without the untiring efforts of Christiane Schröder in deciphering my scribblings in the original manuscript and the revisions. Michaela Rank provided with considerable patience the statistical support necessary to allow the study to be written in the first place. Finally I am indebted to my wife who not only persevered at home during two two-month trips to South-East Asia, but who also had to accept a larger share of the family burdens than would have been dictated by interpersonal comparative advantages.

Gratitude is also due to the Volkswagen Foundation, which funded the project on 'Firm Size and Locational Factors in Employment and Growth-Oriented Industrialization Policies: the Experience of Selected South-East Asian Countries', from which this study evolved.

Kiel, Germany Dean Spinanger

September 1985

Contents

Tables

Appendix Tables

Diagrams

Maps

Appendix

Abbreviations

CIC	Capital Investment Committee
CMI	Census of Manufacturing Industries
CAC	Directory of Approved Companies
FIDA[1]	Federal Industrial Development Authority
FTZ	Free Trade Zone
ICA	Industrial Coordination Act
IE	Industrial Estate
IIA	Investment Incentives Act
ITC	Investment Tax Credit
LDR	Less Developed Region
LI	Location Incentive
LUR	Labor Utilization Relief
MARA	Majlis Amanah Ra'ayat
MDR	More Developed Region
MIDF	Malaysian Industrial Development Finance Ltd.
MIEL	Malaysian Industrial Estate Ltd.
NEP	New Economic Policy
OI	Other Incentives
PI	Pioneer Industry/Incentive
PIO	Pioneer Industries Ordinance
SEDC	State (Economic) Development Corporation
WI	Without Incentive

[1]Note: FIDA was renamed to Malaysian Industrial Development Authority (MIDA) in 1978. With the exception of mentioning FIDA's creation MIDA was otherwise used throughout the study.

1
Introduction

THE PROBLEM AND ITS RELEVANCE

INDUSTRIALIZATION policies in developing countries during the last thirty years were imprinted for a long time by the intent to achieve primarily a rapid increase in the production of goods and services. As growth in production and production facilities was equated with an appropriate improvement in the welfare of all members of society, there seemed to be little reason to direct special attention to either the distribution of income or the spread of economic activities. Since the late 1960s, however, when it was perceived that the pressing employment and distribution problems facing the developing countries were not being adequately solved by such macro-oriented growth strategies, increasing criticism has been voiced and interest in alternative approaches evoked.

With a shift of industrialization policies away from a basically macro-oriented growth approach to strategies incorporating regional aspects, the question arises as to how to best formulate policies, given socio-political parameters, to ensure an exploitation of economic resources in line with employment and growth goals. In light of the convincing evidence that those countries whose economic growth performances were stronger were also the same countries where a more convincing attempt was made to allow comparative advantages to be exploited, it would seem to follow that the same criteria should apply to regions within a country. This study thus takes this approach and based on the experience in Malaysia[1] attempts to provide some evidence on the workings and regional impact of industrialization policies in order to determine their efficiency and effectiveness. Malaysia represents an almost ideal country for carrying out such a study, as numerous policies together with reliable data permit a rather direct examination of industrialization policies on regional economic development in Malaysia.

The neglect of the ramifications of regional industrialization aspects in general basically resulted from a failure to recognize the actual and/or potential problems (be they of economic, social or political nature) accruing from regional development disparities. Thus the adjustment processes initiated by growth-oriented policies proved to be slow in bringing about a decrease in regional disparities and the apparent evidence, in the form of a human exodus out of the peripheral (low income) and into the core (high income) areas, that the market was actually working seemed neither persuasive nor adequate. Furthermore, in many cases the human exodus was considered to be mounting at such a rate that deep concern developed about the future economic viability of both the in-migration as well as the out-migration areas.

Given this constellation, it would seem that basic to solving or at least mitigating regional development disparities, thereby reducing disequilibrating migration flows, would be to explicitly introduce measures aimed at the creation of adequate and appropriate employment opportunities in outlying areas. Since manufacturing industry in almost all developing countries can be regarded as the motor of development (engine of growth)[2], attempts to formulate policies aimed at production and employment growth on a macro and regional level need to place particular stress, in line with comparative advantages, on this sector.

In the past, empirical studies on industrialization strategies have approached the issue from a macro-level, with the manufacturing industry being disaggregated into branches[3]. A large number of these studies have concentrated on those countries which have been particularly successful in industrializing – i.e. the newly industrializing countries (NICs) – with the intention of using them as a reference base for further economic research. The dissatisfaction with macro-oriented policies has led in more recent times to an investigation of problems of income distribution[4] and the regional or spatial distribution of economic activities[5]. In the latter case (i.e. as concerns the spatial distribution of economic activities) the treatment has often tended to remain general or concentrated on specific regions within a country and the presentation of policy measures has been basically carried out without being interfaced with an empirical analysis. It is the purpose of this study to attempt to at least partially fill this gap by examining in detail for one of the NICs, Malaysia[5], some of the industrialization policies, particularly with respect to their impact on reducing regional development disparities. Aside from extensive agricultural policies, the promotion of regional industrialization received high priority in the Malaysian regional policy mix. The subsequent analysis focuses on such industrialization policies, thereby keeping in mind that one goal of such policies is to increase the level of employment.

It should perhaps be noted at this point that while economists in general are not certain about the extent to which there exist trade-offs between widening the spatial distribution of economic activities, i.e. reducing regional development disparities, and increasing overall growth rates, the regional imbalances in developing countries and the myriad of problems resulting therefrom create a situation in which time often seems to work against first best solutions. Thus in most cases the question is not whether regional policies should be instituted, but rather which regional policies can be implemented to help ensure that current imbalances are at least kept from worsening in the short run and corrected in the long run. Given such conditions, economic efficiency criteria are then assumed to be relevant in determining the structure of the policies to be instituted.

This means, in other words, given the aim to reduce regional development inequalities within a country – whatever the reasons behind this decision[6] – those tools should be employed which efficiently exploit the respective given/potential comparative advantages. It can be argued that just as the newly industrializing countries (and for that matter any number of developed countries) have been able to employ an array of measures to allow their economies to grow more rapidly and to reduce or even close the gap between themselves and the leading countries, it is equally possible for the lagging regions in a country to be successfully assisted by measures analogous to those derived from neoclassical international trade theory and applied by the NICs.

For the LDCs as a whole, the relevance of trying to determine how well certain industrialization measures worked towards reducing regional development disparities follows not only from the above-mentioned criticism and the lack or inadequacy of other studies, but in particular from the awareness of the problems associated with the expected rapid and massive increase in urban population in the coming years[7].

THE STRUCTURE AND THRUST OF THIS STUDY

The study itself concentrates basically on that sector which has served as the driving force of economic growth in all newly industrializing countries, namely the manufacturing sector. This does not mean, however, that this is done in an isolated fashion, forgetting that comparative advantages of a given region may well lie in either the primary or tertiary sector or that the manufacturing industry places certain demands on backward or forward linkages to other sectors. Rather the thrust of the presentation covers the manufacturing sector, overlapping into other sectors wherever necessary, but with the empirical analysis almost entirely limited to this sector where data demands can be most easily met.

To begin with this chapter completes the introductory remarks by putting the choice of Malaysia into a proper perspective with other NICs and presenting a brief overview of the macro and regional economic setting in Malaysia. After this background has been provided, Chapter 2 commences with a discussion of the theoretical underpinnings of development strategies based on the premise that an optimal allocation of resources can only be achieved via an exploitation of inter- as well as intranational comparative advantages. In this section attention is drawn to the basic issues involved in correctly specifying the structure of comparative advantages in the course of development as well as their application to questions of regional economics, not neglecting thereby the impact of certain distortions such as agglomeration economies. Fundamental to this approach is the realization that those instruments used in international trade policies to promote trade and development (e.g. exchange rates and tariffs) have their counterparts in intranational/interregional development policies (e.g. subsidies, taxes and infrastructure).

This is followed in Chapter 3 by a presentation of the thrust and structure of macro and regional economic policies in Malaysia over the last twenty-five years. In Chapter 4 an initial quantitative evaluation of the regional impact of industrialization policies is undertaken and in Chapter 5 an analysis is made of the use of industrial estates as a policy measure. This is then followed by a chapter in which a more rigorous econometric assessment of the impact of regional industrialization measures is attempted[8].

Throughout the three empirical chapters answers to two key questions are sought. First of all, did Malaysian industrialization policies, in their entirety, influence the spread and structure of economic activities in accordance with the assumed criteria? Secondly, did Malaysian industrialization policies exert an impact on the factor intensity of new investments in a manner that could be considered as corresponding to the assumed principles? In rounding out the study, a brief summary and some concluding remarks on the overall 'correctness' of policies practised in Malaysia are presented in Chapter 7.

MALAYSIA IN RELATION TO OTHER NICS

In selecting a country that would lend itself to the above-stated objectives with respect to analysing the regional impact of industrialization policies, it was felt that one of the NICs, i.e. one of those countries which clearly exhibited the success with which comparative advantages could be exploited to achieve high rates of economic growth, would be appropriate[9]. Within this group of NICs those were eliminated in the first place where an empirical analysis of regional problems would not have been possible (i.e. Hong Kong and Singapore). The final specification of the countries was then based on the availability and quality of the data and in particular on the extent to which a wide range of regional industrialization policy measures had been instituted, i.e. not only fiscal incentives but also a variety of measures aimed at improving the industrial infrastructure, such as the regional spread of industrial estates (IEs) and free trade zones (FTZs). After applying these criteria[10] and taking into account research already carried out[11], Malaysia seemed to be a logical choice.

In comparing Malaysia with other NICs and developing countries it can be seen (in Diagram 1.1) that Malaysia (depicted by 0) has not only outperformed most other countries in recent years; it has also considerably improved its position over the course of the last twenty years.

Focusing more closely on key economic indicators (Table 1.1), Malaysia's performance (compared with other Asian countries and the whole of middle income developing countries) can be determined to be above average. While developments in Singapore and Taiwan were positively affected by special factors (respectively, by being a point economy and by the influx of human capital from the mainland), Malaysia was basically free of such influences. Thus the results of a study of the regional impact of industrialization policies in Malaysia could be well be considered relevant for other developing countries confronted with the problem of reducing regional development disparities.

DEVELOPMENT IN MALAYSIA - SOME BACKGROUND INFORMATION

Malaysia upon becoming independent in 1957 was in many ways similar to other developing countries at such a point in time. It had, for instance, a dualistic society, stemming on the one hand from the role Malaysia played in supplying its mother country, as well as the rest of the world, with tin and then rubber and, on the other hand, from the entrepôt trade which thrived particularly in

DIAGRAM 1.1

Economic Performance of Selected Developing Countries, 1960-1980*

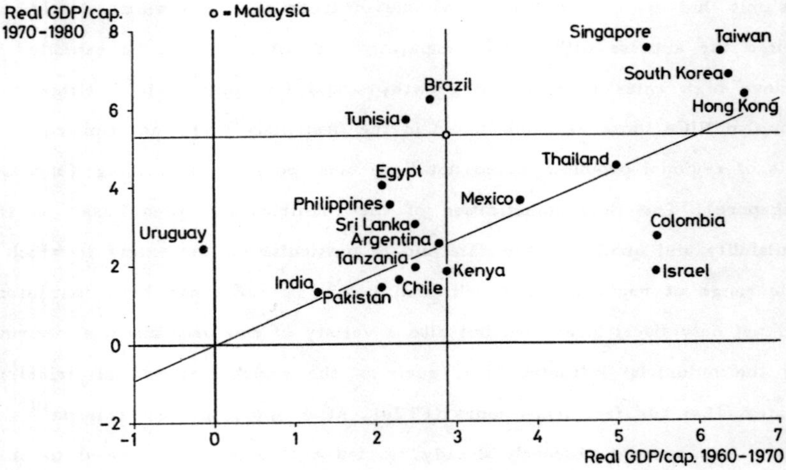

Source: Own calculations based on World Bank data.

*Annual rate of growth of real GDP/capita in per cent.

the Straits Settlements, especially in Penang (excluding the Province Wellesley on the mainland) - see Map 1.1 for regional breakdown.

Thus, those regions in which these activities were located – mainly along the western coast of the Malay Peninsula (and its hinterland) – were inevitably at a more advanced stage of development than those in the north and along the eastern coast (see Table A1 for regional distribution of agricultural, mining and manufacturing activities). Coinciding with this concentration of economic activities on the west coast was the concentration of the population in the same areas. In the other parts of Malaysia, that is on the east coast, the settlements were widely scattered; as a matter of fact over half of the entire territory of Malaysia was virtually uninhabited[12] (see area and population concentration in Table 1.2)[13].

To classify Malaysia as a simple dualistic society, however, would be incomplete or even incorrect and would ignore the rationale behind one important thrust of economic policy measures introduced in the last ten years. That is to say, the indigenous population of Malaysia (in recent years referred to as *bumiputra)* was not only concentrated in the rural/less developed areas[14], it also dominated occupations on the lower level of the income ladder (partly, of

TABLE 1.1

Development Indicators for Selected East and Southeast Asian Countries, 1960-1982[a,b]

	Indonesia		Malaysia		Philippines		Singapore		Thailand		Taiwan		Middle Income Countries	
	60-70	70-82	60-70	70-82	60-70	70-82	60-70	70-82	60-70	70-82	60-70	70-82	60-70	70-82
GDP/Capita	1.7	6.8	3.5	5.1	2.0	3.6	6.3	8.5	4.9	4.1	6.7	6.6	3.6	3.6
GDP by sector														
Agriculture	2.7	3.8	6.8	5.1	4.3	4.8	5.0	1.6	5.6	4.4	3.4	1.3	3.5	3.0
Industry	5.2	10.7	6.4	9.2	6.0	8.0	12.5	8.9	11.9	9.3	16.4	11.6	7.4	5.8
Services	4.8	9.3	6.2	8.4	5.2	5.2	7.7	8.6	9.1	7.4	7.8	9.5	5.5	5.5
Private consum.	4.1	9.0	4.2	7.2	4.7	4.3	5.4	6.2	7.0	6.1	8.2	7.2	5.2	5.2
GD investment	4.6	13.7	7.5	11.4	8.2	9.3	20.5	8.7	15.8	6.4	14.7	10.7	7.6	6.6
Exports	3.5	4.4	6.1	3.8	2.3	7.9	4.2	..	5.2	9.1	21.6	14.0	5.4	2.6
Imports	1.9	12.3	2.4	7.3	7.2	2.1	5.9	..	11.3	4.3	16.8	11.8	5.9	3.9
Inflation rate	-	19.9	-3.0	7.2	5.8	12.8	1.1	5.4	1.8	9.7	4.1	10.3	3.0	12.8
Money supply	-	32.2	5.9	16.1	10.0	15.2	9.9[c]	14.4	6.7	12.4	18.0	25.2	-	-
Population														
Total	2.1	2.3	2.8	2.5	3.0	2.7	2.3	1.5	3.1	2.4	2.9	1.9	2.6	2.4
Urban	3.6	4.5	3.5	3.4	3.8	3.8	2.3	1.5	3.6	4.3	3.3	4.2	4.4	4.2
Labour force	1.7	2.5	2.7	2.9	2.1	2.5	2.7	2.6	2.1	2.8	2.6	3.4	2.1	2.4

Sources: Own calculations based on: World Tables (1980), National Statistics (various issues), International Financial Statistics (various issues), World Development Report 1984.

[a]Annual average growth rates; wherever applicable in real terms.

[b]The underlined figures are above average for middle income countries.

[c]1963-70.

MAP 1.1

Malaysian Regional and State Divisions

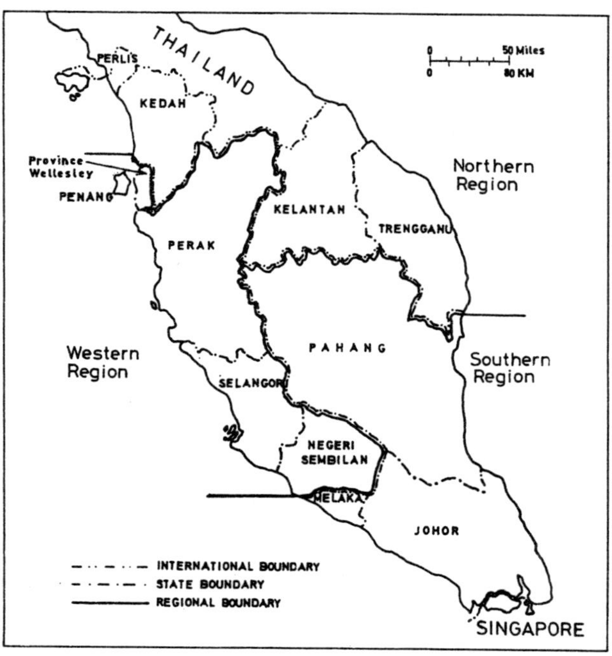

course, reflecting their rural location) and shared only to a very small per cent in the wealth of the country. The rural aspect can be seen in Table 1.2 where the concentration ratios are far higher for the Malays in the northern states; the occupational pattern (Table 1.2) shows quite clearly the predominance of the traditional sectors for the Malay population.

The reasons for these lopsided ethnic group distributions lie mainly in the development and exploitation of the Malaysian resource base, as the Chinese initially immigrated in greater numbers to work in the tin mines and the Indians immigrated largely in connection with the plantations[15]. In addition to these areas of activity the Chinese and Indian immigrants also became, as was the case elsewhere (see Wu, Wu, 1980), heavily involved in banking, trading and other services, whereas the Malays remained almost entirely in the traditional sectors[16].

In other words, there was actually little overlapping in the distribution of the immigrant peoples and the Malays (Ooi, 1976, p. 127). Since there have been no large inflows of either Chinese of Indians since the Second World War, the structure of the population living in West Malaysia has remained relatively constant[17]. The shifts which did occur were caused by the higher birth rates of the Malays (as could be expected by their heavy concentration in rural areas) and the internal migration flows into the more developed areas (which were actually quite moderate).

At the time Malaysia became a sovereign nation, it could therefore be described as a doubly dualistic country; i.e. a rural/urban dualism on the one hand and a native/non-native dualism on the other hand (Tables 1.2 and A1). Malaysia was nonetheless at that time very atypical for an LDC in many other respects. It had, for instance, a reasonably high level of infrastructure, communication services, utilities and other social-capital installations (see IBRD, 1955, p. 13; this in-depth World Bank mission report exerted a strong influence on economic policies during Malaysia's formative years). These facilities, in particular the transportation infrastructure, had been necessary for the exploitation of the resource base (see, for instance, Leinbach, 1975)[18]. It might be added that while it was tin mining which gave the Malaysian economy its first big push during the nineteenth century, it was the cultivation of rubber beginning near the railway lines about the turn of the century that spread economic development beyond its footholds on the coast and the mine fields. But just as important as the physical infrastructure was the human capital potential left behind in the form of a fairly well-functioning public administra-

TABLE 1.2
Distribution[a] and Concentration Ratios for Population and Labour Force by Ethnic Groups in West Malaysia: 1947, 1957, 1970 and 1980

Region/Industry	Area[a]	Total[a] (per cent)				Malays[b]				Chinese[b]				Indians and Others[b]			
		1947	1957	1970	1980	1947	1957	1970	1980	1947	1957	1970	1980	1947	1957	1970	1980
Population by States																	
Northern states	29.2	26.4	25.1	24.6	23.9	1.64	1.61	1.55	1.54	.33	.36	.34	.34	.43	.45	.39	.47
Trengganu	9.9	4.6	4.4	4.6	4.7	1.87	1.86	1.76	1.74	.17	.18	.15	.15	.09	.09	.04	.09
Kelantan	11.4	9.1	8.1	7.7	7.4	1.87	1.83	1.77	1.73	.13	.15	.16	.16	.10	.11	.07	.16
Perlis	.7	1.4	1.4	1.4	1.3	1.64	1.64	1.43	1.46	.43	.50	.43	.46	.29	.21	.14	.16
Kedah	7.2	11.3	11.2	10.9	10.5	1.37	1.36	1.32	1.32	.54	.55	.54	.53	.85	.86	.79	.87
Southern states	43.0	25.0	24.4	24.9	25.6	.95	1.00	1.03	1.04	1.16	1.09	1.06	1.05	.64	.67	.67	.67
Pahang	27.3	5.1	5.0	5.7	6.5	1.10	1.14	1.16	1.15	1.00	.92	.90	.86	.55	.70	.70	.68
Melaka	1.3	4.9	4.7	4.7	4.5	1.00	.98	.96	1.00	1.04	1.11	1.09	1.11	.78	.70	.72	.82
Johor	14.4	15.0	14.7	14.5	14.6	.89	.97	1.01	1.00	1.25	1.14	1.11	1.12	.69	.69	.63	.62
Western states	28.1	48.4	50.5	50.6	50.6	.68	.69	.74	.73	1.28	1.28	1.29	1.28	1.47	1.43	1.46	1.41
Perak	16.0	19.4	19.5	17.8	16.9	.77	.80	.81	.81	1.22	1.19	1.20	1.20	1.36	1.32	1.34	1.30
Selangor	6.2	14.5	16.1	18.5	19.8	.53	.58	.65	.68	1.33	1.30	1.31	1.29	1.88	1.80	1.73	1.59
Negeri Sembilan	5.1	5.4	5.8	5.5	5.5	.85	.83	.86	.87	1.11	1.10	1.07	1.02	1.33	1.35	1.53	1.47
Penang	.8	9.1	9.1	8.8	8.4	.62	.58	.58	.56	1.44	1.54	1.58	1.60	1.18	1.09	1.08	1.19
Labour Force by Industry																	
Agriculture																	
Rubber cultivation		25.9	28.4	23.5	16.7	.77	.90	1.08	1.11	.90	.92	.75	.68	1.82	1.46	1.42	1.46
Padi cultivation		24.7	18.4	16.2	9.2	1.96	2.03	1.81	1.62	.25	.07	.08	.24	.11	.11	.18	.37
Other activities		10.7	7.7	5.5	8.1	.63	.82	.73	1.18	1.57	.97	1.33	.67	.75	.74	1.16	1.15
Fishing and hunting		3.1	2.8	2.1	1.8	1.55	1.46	1.24	1.17	.81	.89	1.00	1.02	.07	.07	.10	.13
Mining and quarrying		2.1	2.7	1.9	1.2	.24	.37	.47	.56	2.05	1.93	1.89	1.66	.67	.82	.79	1.06
Manufacturing/construction		7.8	9.4	10.9	19.0	.65	.50	.52	.74	1.65	1.79	1.84	1.53	.51	.72	.50	.60
Transport/communication		3.6	3.5	3.4	3.7	.83	.74	.82	.78	.92	1.09	1.12	1.26	1.56	1.46	1.53	1.23
Commercial/financial services[c]		8.0	9.0	9.6	14.1	.38	.34	.45	.57	1.80	1.82	1.81	1.73	.91	1.09	.96	.81
Public sector/other services[c]		14.1	18.1	26.9	26.3	.60	.85	.93	1.11	1.15	.98	1.00	.72	1.68	1.48	1.34	1.31

Source: Own calculations based on data from Dept. of Statistics (General Report of the Population Census, 1970 and 1980; Preliminary Report, 1980).

[a] Percentage distribution with respect to total area of West Malaysia and total population/labour force in respective years. For regional distributional of ethnic groups see Table A2; for industrial shares see Table A3.

[b] Concentration ratios calculated by dividing share of specific ethnic group (out of total population/labour force of given ethnic groups in West Malaysia) in a given region/industry by share of region's/industry's total population/labour force in Malayisa's total population/labour force.

[c] Includes also persons seeking first employment.

tion and government officials responsive to constructive criticism[19].

The extent to which the government adopted and successfully instituted a wide variety of the outside recommendations (e.g. from IBRD, 1955) would seem generally to testify to the openness and capability of the government institutions – traits of eminent importance in providing an environment in which development can succeed. Likewise the free-trade philosophy (adopted from the British) proved to be engrained deep enough so as to largely withstand the pressure from those groups which would have chosen a basically inward-oriented (import substitution) development policy, rather than the outward-looking (export diversification) approach[20].

Naturally, the mere existence of a relatively well-functioning administrative system as well as a belief in free trade would not have produced the development results if the educational facilities and institutions aimed at improving labour/entrepreneurial skills (i.e. all those facilities responsible for upgrading human capital) had not been adequate; and in this aspect Malaysia was also atypical for an LDC. First of all, Malaysia's education system was generally speaking one of the best in South-East Asia and the developing world. Not only were enrollment and retention rates through the primary and lower secondary cycles high, but compared with other developing countries, teacher quality was high and the system was well organized as well as fairly well equipped (McMeekin jr., 1975, p. 142)[21]. Secondly, while the formal education system was generally considered to be quite good[22], the level of vocational education might seem to have been rather poor since only very limited school facilities for technical and vocational training were provided in the Federation (IBRD, 1955, p. 460). Such an assessment, however, fails to acknowledge the contribution made by companies in providing on-the-job training. This is of particular importance in the case of the Chinese, where, in their relatively self-contained society, it was common practice for children to be fully incorporated into the family business (or the business of relatives or friends) and thereby receive the necessary general and/or specific training. Thus, although formal vocational training facilities were initially lacking – this of course mainly put the Malays at a disadvantage – there was at least an informal system which worked well enough so as not to really hinder the development process[23]. Thirdly, entrepreneurial skills in Malaysia were definitely available, particularly among the non-indigenous population groups (which comprised about 50 per cent of the population) and despite the relative dominance of the British in many areas after independence. As a matter of fact, the differential between

TABLE 1.3
Indicators of Malaysian Regional Development Disparities

Region/State	Per Capita Income (National Average = 100)				Manufacturing Share (Per Cent of GDP)				Percentage of Population in Towns with >15,000 Inhabitants		Net Migration (Per Cent of Population)	
	1965	1970	1975	1978	1965	1970	1975	1978	1970	1980	1970	1980
Northern states												
Trengganu	61.79	59.62	51.55	59.82	3.0	4.9	6.5	4.0	17.5	42.8	1.5	- .6
Kelantan	49.17	46.64	38.07	37.45	4.5	5.4	6.4	6.7	8.1	23.3	-4.7	-3.7
Perlis }	65.33	67.04	54.82	53.57	5.2	6.3	6.9	16.4	.0	.0	1.0	- .1
Kedah									12.6	14.1	-2.3	-5.3
Southern states												
Pahang	116.04	98.26	88.11	103.53	6.4	7.5	13.0	12.3	16.8	23.2	9.6	13.2
Melaka	76.65	80.43	80.17	72.46	6.7	5.9	11.2	7.5	21.4	23.3	-2.9	-7.2
Johor	92.22	90.73	94.62	93.55	10.4	13.9	18.5	37.8	24.4	32.1	- .6	-0.6
Western states												
Perak	101.77	98.85	85.60	84.12	6.3	8.9	13.2	35.8	26.3	30.9	-4.5	-5.8
Selangor	166.27	162.87	185.95	183.40	15.9	21.4	24.4	57.8	43.4	58.0	6.0	8.2
Negeri Sembilan	108.14	98.68	91.01	88.19	14.3	15.5	16.0	11.2	16.7	28.4	-2.6	-3.8
Penang	96.34	99.47	115.84	113.06	11.7	12.7	23.4	25.3	49.4	43.0	.4	.3
National	848	994	1431	1681	10.2	13.3	18.2	21.5	26.2	35.0	-	-

Sources: Own calculations based on: Per capita income and manufacturing share, 1965: Lim Lin Lean (1971, Table III.1); 1970: Malaysia Plan (1976, Table 10-1; 1975 and 1978: Malaysia Plan (1979, Tables, Tables 5-1 and 5-2); Population: Dept. of Statistics (Field Count Summary, 1971, Tables 16-26; Local Authority Areas: Population, Households and Living Quarters, 1982, Tables 1-12); Net migration: Dept. of Statistics (The Population of Malaysia, 1975, Table 3.2; and General Report on the Population Census, 1982, Vol. 1, Table 5.10).

the indigenous and non-indigenous groups was even reinforced by certain development policies which embodied a greater degree of direct government intervention in rural areas, thereby leaving industrialization in the urban areas to be promoted by private enterprises[24].

ECONOMIC DEVELOPMENT AND REGIONAL DEVELOPMENT DISPARITIES IN MALAYSIA

Given the above conditions, Malaysian industrialization strategies were initially more concerned with strengthening the overall industrial base[25] than with reducing regional development disparities. This was manifested in policies, the basic framework of which was of free-market natûre. The government's rôle thereby centred around infrastructure investments and the creation of an economic environment (via investment incentives and tariffs) conducive to entrepreneurial development[26]. The goal of this approach was to reduce dependency on rubber and tin which accounted for almost 30 per cent of GDP and 75 per cent of exports around 1960. The manufacturing sector, on the other hand, accounted for a mere 5 per cent of GDP and 3 per cent of exports.

Thus the government did not initially institute explicit regional industrialization policies. Restraint on the government's part would seem to have been well founded as an analysis of regional development differentials (see Tables 1.3 and A1 as well) reveals that severe regional development disparities (common to many LDCs) actually did not (and even still do not) exist [27]. Nonetheless, notable differences between the key indicators of Malaysian regional development levels can be determined, and hence allow Malaysia to be divided into three regions: the northern states (low income), the southern states (middle income) and the western states (high income).

In light of such relatively nominal regional development disparities the question might be raised as to the necessity of introducing and carrying out regional development policies. One basic reason can be seen in the intention to improve the lot of the Malays (i.e. *bumiputra),* whose share of population in the LDRs far exceeds the share of the non-Malays (Table 1.2). In other words, policy-makers perceived the nature of the underlying economic structure as not interfacing with national aims. However, the main thrust of their activities (as incorporated into development plans) was directed towards sectors other than the industrial sector (Table 1.4), in particular the primary sector.

Behind these development/industrialization policies lay a framework of macro-economic policies which was already seen (in Table 1.1) as being successful in keeping inflation down to relatively low levels. Monetary policies, for instance, were rarely more than accommodating and budget deficits did not arise as tax receipts were quite elastic[28]. All these (and other) factors taken together led over the two decades up to the early 1980s to a more competitive economy with larger trade balance surpluses, increasing direct foreign investment and higher growth rates of GDP (see Diagram 1.2).

TABLE 1.4

West Malaysia - Public Development Expenditure, 1956-1985 (Per Cent)

Sector	*First Malaya Plan 1956-1960*	*Second Malaya Plan 1961-1965*	*First Malaysia Plan 1966-1970*	*Second Malaysia Plan 1971-1975*	*Third Malaysia Plan 1976-1980*	*Fourth Malaysia Plan 1981-1985*
Agriculture and rural development	23.61	17.53	30.74	24.50	29.11	29.74
Mining	n.a.	.03	.01	.01	.01	.16
Industrial development	1.26	2.52	4.62	21.63	11.94	20.41
Transport	23.88	25.10	12.00	17.04	15.45	11.26
Communications	5.35	4.83	5.38	6.55	7.84	5.00
Utilities	24.76	22.49	21.82	10.80	13.60	8.66
Social services	14.40	22.22	21.75	15.88	18.73	21.91
Government administration	6.74	5.27	3.68	3.19	3.12	2.72
Total development expenditures (M$m.)	963.7	2,344.4	2,964.5	7,131.9[a]	13,405.7[a]	25,738.2[a]

Sources: Own calculations from Malaysia Plan (1965, pp. 28ff., 69ff.; 1971, pp. 68-71; 1976, pp. 240ff.; 1981, pp. 393ff.). For actual figures see Table A4.

n.a. = not available.

[a]Includes M$28.9 m. and M$36.0 m. respectively for feasibility studies.

Despite such a positive retrospective overview of development trends, there were times when developments failed to coincide with expectations, such as in the second half of the 1960s when fixed capital investment had begun to stagnate. In an attempt to correct this trend and the overall slackening off of GDP growth rates, industrialization policies were revamped and government involvement in the workings of the market in the second decade after independence (1968-78) exhibited a noticeable increase[29]. An additional impetus was given by worries about stagnating long-term demand for the natural resource-based products (rubber and tin) which were still a mainstay of the economy. But perhaps government activities were shaped the most by the 1969 race riots, after which they were directed toward promoting more participation of the *bumiputra* in all areas of economic activity.

The shift to more wide-sweeping policies (beginning in 1968) incorporated

DIAGRAM 1.2

Malaysian Economic Development Indicators

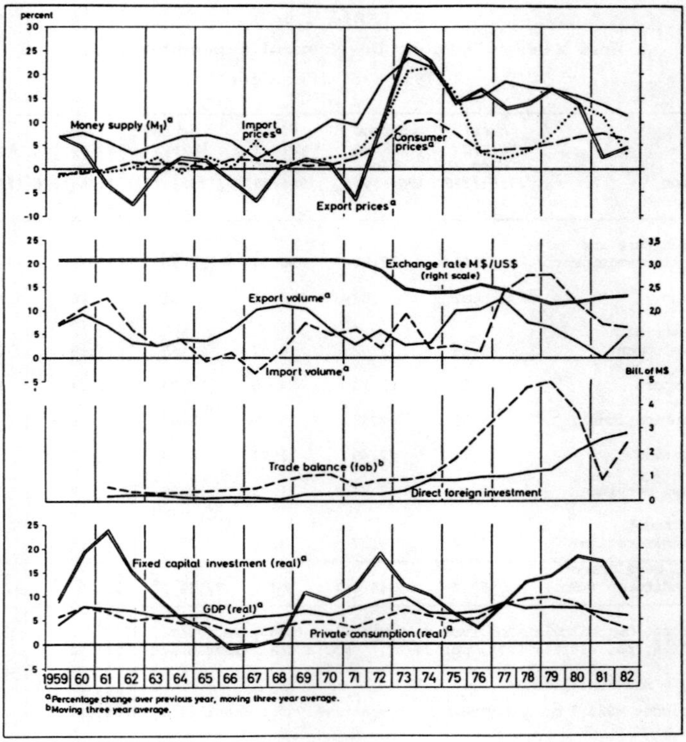

above all broader-based investment incentives. While an increased application of tariffs was not specifically included in such measures, it has been noted that they were often either implemented or increased with less respect to comparative advantage arguments[30].

CONCLUDING REMARKS

The fact that in the years following the Second World War development economists paid little attention to the problem of inequality within developing countries (Arndt, 1983, p. 8) was reflected in industrialization policies, which were primarily aimed at reducing inequalities between developing and developed countries. To the extent that certain developing countries succeeded in decreasing the income level gap between themselves and developed countries, it was pointed out above that this could be attributed to policies stressing comparative advantages. Knowing that comparative advantages of individual countries reflect nothing more than an aggregate of intracountry comparative advantages, an analogous examination of intracountry or regional economic development should yield that successful industrialization policies at this level incorporated measures which encouraged an efficient allocation of resources. In other words, policies were effected to promote a factor intensity of production in the regions of a country in line with the given factor endowment.

While most of the studies on efficient industrialization strategies remain on a macro-level, this study moves into a relatively unresearched area and deals with explicit and implicit implications of such strategies in a regional context. For the country studied, Malaysia, it was shown that the development path over the last quarter century was one of the most successful in moving it into the ranks of those countries on the threshold of becoming an industrialized country. While well endowed with natural resources and released from a colonial status with relatively high levels of infrastructure and human capital, the essential ingredient for its success would seem to have been the policy package and the overall economic environment.

Given such a background, the ensuing ramifications of the manifold industrialization policies, which were directly or indirectly aimed towards reducing regional development disparities, lend themselves quite well to an analysis, because the relatively small size of such disparities would seem to permit measures to be introduced which could compensate for barriers keeping comparative advantages from being exploited.

1 Unless otherwise noted the term Malaysia used in this study refers to West Malaysia.

2 The term engine of growth can be attributed to Dennis H. Robertson (1938).

3 These in-depth studies, carried out by the Kiel Institute of World Economics, The National Bureau of Economic Research (NBER), The OECD Development Center and the World Bank, cover in the meantime two dozen countries: in Africa (5), Asia (10), Europe (3) and Latin America (6). The largest of these projects was carried out by the Kiel Institute and encompassed 15 countries (Brazil, Colombia, Egypt, Hong Kong, India, Israel, Malaysia, Mexico, Pakistan, Singapore, South Korea, Spain, Taiwan, Turkey and Yugoslavia). An extensive review and synthesis of the results of these studies is presented in Donges, Müller-Ohlsen (1978). A distillation of the results and summarizing remarks are provided in Donges (1976) and Donges, Riedel (1977). In the NBER project 10 countries were dealt with (Brazil, Chile, Colombia, Egypt, Ghana, India, Israel, the Philippines, Korea and Turkey); the results are summarized in Krueger (1978b), Bhagwati (1978) and Krueger *et al.* (1981). The earliest study was prepared for

the OECD Development Center in 1970 (see Little *et al.*, 1970). The World Bank project is in the process of being completed (Balassa *et al.*, 1982). For a report on initial results see Balassa (1978). For a description of other World Bank work investigating the impact of industrialization see Hollis B. Chenery (1980, pp. 281-7). For a recent overview of many of the above studies see Donges (1981).

4 The joint study by the World Bank and the Institute of Development Studies at the University of Sussex (see Chenery *et al.*, 1974; Adelman, Morris, 1973) represents a major attempt of cross-sectional nature to grasp the complexities and inter-relationships between growth and interpersonal income distribution. For a recent study see Chow, Papanek (1981). On a country level, the studies by D.C. Rao (1978), Ranis (1978) and Fei *et al.* (1979) are in-depth attempts which extend the analysis into the urban-rural dimensions. A wide variety of studies has also been made in connection with the World Employment project of the ILO.

5 With respect to a spatial distribution of economic activities - which in a larger sense can be assumed to deal with regional development disparities - one of the most recent publications, Fischer *et al.* (1982) analyses (among other things) the regional impact of various policy measures, using for this purpose a full-blown general-equilibrium model of the Johnson type. Lo, Salih (1978) treat the structuring and impact of various policies to a large extent on a verbal level; Mathur (1978), however, does tread softly in an empirical direction. An earlier attempt, in a voluminous project sponsored by the U.N. Research Institute for Social Development, also contains little direct integration of policies in an empirical analysis (see for instance, Lefeber, Datta-Chaudhuri (1971)). For a review of the literature and a sample of the approaches see Gilbert (1976) and Hoyle (1974). In a relatively comprehensive study of regional policies in a wide range of countries the difficulty involved in trying to separate out regional policy factors from other aspects is noted (see Stöhr, Tödtling (1978). For a work on a specific country, see, for instance, Hiemenz (1979), where econometric techniques are neatly applied, but, due to the lack of data, the impact of policies could only be verbalized.

6 Such a decision might well be prompted by pressing non-economic factors (e.g. racial or religious differences) where a non-solution or even a market solution with long adjustment processes could well mean civil war or even a dissolution of a nation. It is accordingly assumed here that the preservation of a national entity, regardless of how it came to be, is one of those foremost goals not subordinated to any other goal. This assumption, however, should not be misconstrued as being anything else but an assumption.

7 See, for instance, World Bank (1979).

8 The author would like to express his sincere gratitude to the Malaysian Investment Centre in Düsseldorf as well as to the Malaysian Industrial Development Authority and the Statistical Department (both in Kuala Lumpur) for supplying data without which this study would have suffered.

9 Since the main impetus in these cases stemmed from the expansion of the manufacturing industry, particular attention was paid to whether the manufacturing industry was well established by the mid-1970s. Likewise the degree to which social and industrial infrastructure investment had already been erected was also taken into account.

10 While these criteria would seem to fit for both Taiwan and South Korea the variety of measures, particularly of regional nature, as well as the availability of essential data make Malaysia a more worthwhile country to investigate.

11 The most recent in-depth studies on Malaysian general development/industrialization policies and performance have been carried out by Hoffmann and Tan (1980), Snodgrass (1980) and Young *et al.* (1980); an earlier study by Lim (1973) should also be mentioned. As concerns regional aspects of development in Malaysia only Spinanger (1980) has gone into greater depth; Zehender *et al.* (1978) have also investigated this area, but with more limited aims. General readings as well as references to other literature have been edited by Lim (1975), Chee and Mun (1975) and Cheong *et al.* (1979).

12 See, for example, IBRD (1955, p. 13). This east-west differential was all the more pronounced because of the mountain range which runs down the

middle of the peninsula.

13 For population distribution see Table A2.

14 The change in the regional distribution of the various ethnic groups between 1947 and 1957 was influenced to some extent by the (to a large degree) forced resettlement of almost one million persons (mainly rural Chinese) between 1948 and 1960 into more than 600 resettlement projects. The major component of this massive reshuffling of the population was the establishment of so-called new villages which were self-contained and defensible, and which allowed the population to be efficiently cut off from communist insurgents, thereby robbing the insurgents of possible support and supplies. Aside from the strategic success of the new villages they also served to increase the degree of urbanization of the population (particularly the Chinese) and thus spread the development deeper into the countryside. Unfortunately, however, most of these new villages were not in the less developed states. See Kühne (1976, pp. 80-2, 122-5).

15 Drabble (1974) points out that the British even took the view that the Malays were the only permanent agricultural population of the Peninsula, on whom would devolve the main task of food production. Hence, the official policy of encouraging them in rice farming, and to a lesser extent vegetables, poultry, etc. ... It has been frequently said that British policies were governed by a concept of the Malays as essentially non-commercial people (p. 207).

16 For an opinion of how the various ethnic groups view each other (in order to better appreciate certain important underlying problems in Malaysian society) see Ness (1967, pp. 45-7).

17 McTaggart (1968, p. 81) even notes that it is quite evident that despite changes in Malaysian population patterns, certain basic patterns of ethnic distribution became established at an early stage of development, chiefly in the first three decades of the twentieth century.

18 It is interesting to note that although initially the rural/urban dichotomy was to a large extent a product of the above-mentioned colonial rôle, the necessary infrastructure served to facilitate the spread of development later on. Thoburn (1977, p. 60) mentions that an improvement of the transportation system came about via an event normally considered to have been merely very trying: the so-called 'Emergency' (the name given to the communist-led rebellion of 1948-60). That is, in those areas of the country where it was the worst, the infrastructure (in particular the roads) was greatly improved upon. Since these areas were generally speaking located in lesser developed regions, the implementation of development plans in such areas later did not first require a substantial amount of spending for such essentials.

19 See, for instance, the comment in Robinson (1977, p. 30) on the integrity of public officials and the absence of an ideological commitment in respect to the rôles of public and private enterprise. As refers to developments in most recent times, however, the impact of the worldwide spread of Islamic activism remains an open question.

20 This, of course, is not to say that import substitution did not exist, but rather that the bulk of the policy rested on improving Malaysia's competitive position in the world.

21 Meerman (1980, pp. 131-8), while basically pointing out the quality of the Malaysian educational system, notes two crucial problem areas. First of all, although the primary level is 'free' (but not compulsory) the cost of retaining children in schools, instead of having them earn money, represents a severe burden for poorer families. This burden is hardly mitigated by federal subsidies as these are directed towards post-secondary education. Secondly, the formal education system as it stands is producing a mismatch between societal demands and individual desires, i.e. more job-specific training is necessary. This is a problem which Malaysia shares with industrial countries (see Soltwedel and Spinanger, 1976).

22 It should be noted, however, that the formal school system was not without the general problem stemming from the main ethnic groups. Thus there were primary schools for Malays, Chinese and Indians, each being taught in their own language – the only link between them took place in the fourth type of

school where English was the working language. Now Bahasa Malaysia is required in all schools.

23 In the past, i.e. before the Second World War, important skills were acquired through the immigration of Chinese and Indians – in other words in the form of imported human capital.

24 See, for instance, Sundrum's comments on Chai's paper on 'Apprenticeship and Entrepreneurs in Malaysia' (Sundrum, 1971, pp. 82 ff.). Chai's designation of the system of training in companies as haphazard and inefficient would, however, seem incorrect. What he possibly means is that the firms emphasize specific as opposed to general training, so that possible external benefits are reduced to a minimum.

25 For an in-depth analysis of these strategies see Hoffmann, Tan (1980).

26 One ingredient in the policy mix to provide a conducive environment, tariffs, were initially structured so as to incorporate the imperial preferences (IPs), but these were almost entirely phased out by 1970. Their abolition, however, did not lead to massive across-the-board increases. As a matter of fact the integration of tariffs into the industrialization policy framework was viewed with a considerable amount of caution, as it was fully realized that an unwise use of tariffs can distort development and bring in industries which have no real economic basis. Thus only those industries which were deemed to have chances to prosper after a reasonable period of time were given tariff protection to stimulate further industrial development (Malaysia Plan, 1963, p. 49). Tariffs were accordingly reviewed by the Tariff Advisory Board (after being disbanded in 1969, by the Capital Investment Committee and the subordinate Action Committee on Tariffs and Industrial Development – ACTID). During its existence the number of tariffs increased from 811 to 1,207. Of the initial 811 there were 274 increases and 92 decreases (Lee, 1978, p. 481). The nominal (effective) tariff rate increased from 27.4 (28) per cent to 33.6 (38) per cent in the period 1962-70 (1964-74) (Lee, 1978, p. 483; Donges, Müller-Ohlsen, 1978, p. 61).

27 In Malaysia the difference between the highest and the lowest income regions was only roughly 3 to 1, in Brazil it amounted to as much as 8 to 1 and in Mexico it even exceeded 10 to 1. The nominal income disparities no doubt help explain to a large degree why migration rates were relatively low. In some cases the migration pattern – for instance, for Pahang – was strongly influenced by government-sponsored settlement programmes. See, for instance, Hawley *et al.* (1979).

28 The main source of revenue was from direct (income) taxes, followed by import duties (including a 2 per cent surtax introduced in 1967), consumption taxes (excise and road transport fees as well as a sales tax beginning in 1972) and export duties (mainly on tin and rubber, but since 1968 also on palm oil and timber).

29 Again, in the 1970s investment activity slackened considerably, this time, however, to a large extent because of government legislation to register companies. This downturn has in the meantime been turned around, but only after a watering down of strongly stated intentions. In most recent times the government has been cracking down very hard on corruption to ensure that the overall business environment remains, relative to other Asian countries, conducive. Malaysia's position was aptly revealed in a survey of over 400 organizations concerned with West Germany's trade and investment activities in Asia (Far Eastern Economic Review, 4 July 1980, p. 51). Malaysia and Hong Kong shared the top position. This corresponds to the results of another survey carried out among foreign-owned companies in Asia (Kapoor, 1973). In this publication the integrity of Malaysian institutions was underlined.

30 It should be mentioned, however, that often at least an attempt was made to measure the amount of protection needed by comparing landed import prices with the price of domestically produced goods.

2
Developing a Theoretical Framework

INTRODUCTION

STRUCTURING a theoretical framework within which industrialization policies and regional economic development can be appropriately analysed implies that the fundamental issues involved in specifying development/industrialization policies must first be developed. These having been clarified, a review of the role a given country (in this case Malaysia) can play in an interdependent world is presented, following thereby the principles laid down by international trade theory and paying special attention to delineating factor intensities of industries of inherent interest to this study. Given this framework a more consistent and specific treatment of regional aspects can then be undertaken[1].

Before the above is incorrectly interpreted, it must be recalled that (as was pointed out in the opening chapter) in this study aspects relevant to an economically efficient division of labour between countries are deemed to apply basically to those relevant between regions within countries[2]. That is, fundamental to the approach taken here is the premise that international trade theory is also widely applicable to intranational aspects[3]. Such an approach is in general agreement with the foundations of mainstream theory. To be sure it can even be stated that 'the distinction between trade theory and the general theory of location and space economy is one of definition only. Trade theory can be broadly conceived as synonymous with the general theory of location and space'[4]; this then represents the approach taken in this study.

ESTABLISHING A THEORY OF ECONOMIC DEVELOPMENT

With the advent of theories applicable to those countries whose level of economic development was relatively low, the teachings of mainstream economics[5] were often neglected, as developing countries were considered to be a special case[6]. Common to the various approaches was the belief that mainstream economic thought was actually not relevant for developing countries or, because of the fact that many of these countries were former colonies, that they had to be treated in a different fashion. In other words up to the end of the 1950s, policies towards developing countries were often aimed at solving problems perceived to be inherent in those countries rather than viewing them within the broader economic context as part of a failure to be integrated into the international division of labour and seeking therein a solution[7].

While it cannot be denied that the role played by former colonies or other less developed countries up till the 1940s did engender distortions, to conclude that these distortions meant that LDCs deserved special treatment and special theories would be overlooking the historical evidence. Nonetheless, one of the overriding doctrines stemming from this period is that of Prebisch (1950), whose plea for import substitution policies left a mark on development strategies which is still visible today[8]. However, beginning roughly with the 1964 UNCTAD Conference it came to be realized that import substitution policies beyond a certain, albeit difficult to define threshold where infant industry arguments based on the exploitation of domestic demand potential become weaker, did not lead to a rapid or at least sustained improvement in the well-being of a country in general. An adequate solution to improve the relative lot of the developing countries was then perceived in a strategy embodying an expansion of the manufacturing industry via the export sector. While scepticism about the ability of the less developed countries to actually be able to extradite themselves from their low income levels[9] still existed, evidence from a number of countries as well as the upsurge in public discussion regarding the gains in welfare from increased economic integration[10] could not help but to redirect attention to the basic premises upon which neo-classical economic theory rests. Here the proposition is put forth that, *ceteris paribus,* to the extent to which countries specialize in the production of those goods in which they have comparative advantages, world/country income will be maximized. It follows herefrom that any attempt to restrict trade means a reduction in the world's income and a less efficient allocation of resources. In this simplistic form international trade theory merely indicates in what direction trade and thus development strategies should be heading – a delineation by sectors, factor intensities or scale of production is not indicated.

INTERNATIONAL TRADE THEORY AND THE SPECIFICATION OF INDUSTRIAL DEVELOPMENT

Trade theory in the form presented by Adam Smith merely dealt with the 'natural advantages' which one country has over another in producing particular commodities; these being sometimes so great that it would be a 'manifest absurdity' to redirect employment and capital in excess of the amount which would be necessary to purchase from foreign countries an equal quantity of the commodities wanted (p. 458)[11]. The basic principles of contemporary international trade theory, down to thinking in opportunity costs, are quite visible. It was, however, David Ricardo who formalized the argumentation, based on the labour theory of value[12] in a precise manner, making his prime contribution by couching it in terms of comparative costs/advantages. Later on this was reinterpreted in terms of opportunity costs so that the theory achieved a more general level of application[13]. As it then stood it stated that out of the entire set of relative opportunity costs, given full employment and the well-known conditions pertaining to perfect competition, those goods would be imported which cannot be domestically produced at lower costs. Nonetheless this theory was still wanting, in that the factor intensity of production was left unspecifieid – a definite weakness if the theory is to offer a framework for concrete policies.

A major respecification of the theory in terms of relative factor intensities was consequently undertaken independently of one another by Heckscher and Ohlin and it provided a more firm basis for conclusions on the structure of trade, and thus the structure of production as well[14]. Briefly stated, a country would tend to export (import) the commodity embodying that factor with which it is relatively heavily (weakly) endowed. Factor prices were seen (by Ohlin) as tending towards equalization. In a further rigorous refinement Stolper and Samuelson[15], and Samuelson[16], extended the arguments to show that under the specified conditions factor prices would be equalized. Given this rough theoretical framework, abstracted from observed trade patterns, the first straightforward attempt to test its empirical relevance by Leontief[17] produced results which shook the foundations upon which the two-factor (labour and capital) international trade theory was based. He had set out to investigate the widely shared view that the nature of trade between a highly developed country, like the United States, and the rest of the world, is derived from the assumption that the United States has a comparative advantage in the production of commodities requiring large inputs of capital and relatively small amounts of labour (Leontief, 1953, p. 69). The United States was thus assumed to be an exporter of capital-intensive goods and an importer of labour-intensive products[18]. Leontief's results, however, contradicted the predictions derived from the contemporary interpretation of international trade theory: exports for a country supposedly heavily endowed with capital were shown to be labour-intensive and imports capital-intensive. Analogously, had such an analysis been carried out for a developing country, with labour being an abundant factor, then exports would have been shown to be capital-intensive.

This evidence, which revealed weaknesses in the state of the art, engendered a wealth of articles not only offering explanations for the supposed lack of coherence between theory and reality, but also advancing theoretical insights into the workings of the international economy. In particular the degree to which it has become possible to delineate between the factor intensity of production of various types of products is helpful in specifying in an a priori manner the structure of international as well as intranational trade, given assumptions on factor endowment.

While various attempts to classify the numerous approaches have been made, they are discretionary and subjected to the aims of the specific studies. In this case the following classification has been applied here[19]:

Ricardo goods,

Heckscher-Ohlin-Stolper-Samuelson goods,

Product-cycle goods,

Policy-induced goods.

Ricardo goods are those products which can be attributed to a comparative advantage originating from the 'natural' production conditions given in each country: in the widest sense they are natural endowment parameters represented by agricultural, mineral and environmental resources[20]. While it seems almost superfluous to state that a country or region rich in a given natural resource will tend to export it, an investigation of the factor intensity of such exports could well reveal that they are capital-intensive[21].

In the case of an LDC like Malaysia this could mean that exports are more capital-intensive than imports due to the capital-intensive nature of the extractive industries (tin mining and oil production[22]) and possibly the downstream processing of such natural resources. As a matter of fact, this was actually the case when Hoffmann and Tan (1974, p. 410) found that Malaysia had indeed developed its comparative advantage in the resource based industries and its imports were more labour-intensive than domestically produced exports would have been. However, in a refinement later on (1980, pp. 194-202)[23], a substantiation of the assumption that relatively labour-intensive products were exported by Malaysia, could be shown. Of particular relevance to the analysis of regional industrialization in this study is the attempt to explain production patterns between regions of the United States[24]. There it is concluded that the concentration of resource-intensive manufacturing in the South is systematically related to southern endowments of primary natural resource products. Furthermore, the complementarity between natural resource and reproducible capital-intensity explains the capital-intensive slant given to production, as opposed to earlier hypotheses that the South only had comparative advantage in labour-intensive industries. A word of caution is necessary should the conclusion be drawn that resource-intensity automatically means capital-intensity, since Donges and Riedel (1977) have pointed out that, downstream from initial extraction, there are certain processing industries where (unskilled) labour-intensive production seemed able to prevail[25].

Heckscher-Ohlin-Stolper-Samuelson (HOSS) goods fit into the basic interpretation of the theorem, where it is assumed that like goods are produced with the same combinations of production factors with internationally available technology in all countries and that the marginal productivity of the individual factors is strictly a function of the ratios in which they are combined in a production process. The factors of production are not, however, limited to labour and physical capital[26], but rather extended to cover various types of human capital[27]. This was necessary, for instance, in trying to explain the Leontief paradox (Leontief, 1953 and 1956), where it was hypothesized that the greater labour productivity of US workers was an underlying reason explaining why the US seemed to be a net importer of physical capital in the form of goods[28]. However, it is not merely the investment in the education of human resources as such which matters, but rather the skill with which such investment is employed. Given this approach it can be determined that US exports were indeed far more skill intensive than imports[29]. On an intranational basis (for the USA) Horriba, Kirkpatrick (1981) showed how very well the factor intensity of trade between regions conforms to the relative factor endowments of the regions (including thereby human capital as well).

All these attempts to determine whether a country or a region is specializing in products in agreement with its assumed comparative advantages have dwelt on conventional delineations of factor intensity. Recent evidence, however, tends to suggest that such a breakdown is insufficient as it neglects the size factor in trade (Banerji, 1977; Bruch, 1980, 1983). That is, if production functions across countries differ to the extent that an expansion path of production differs according to the relative factor intensity of production methods in the various countries concerned, then in a given industry optimal plant size will be higher in the capital-intensive country than in the labour-intensive one[30].

With respect to an industrializing country like Malaysia this means that, given its level of development and relative to industrialized countries, imports would tend to be relatively human capital intensive as well as stemming from relatively large-scale firms. Analogously on a regional level it could be expected that the less developed regions would be specializing in products of relatively low human capital intensity as well as such produced by smaller size firms. In the former case Bruch (1980, 1983) has produced some tentative evidence on firm size and exports for Malaysia; Sanguanruang (1978) came to similar conclusions for Thailand[31]. Lim (1981) also touches implicitly on the human capital aspects of production in the less developed regions of Malaysia.

With the term product-cycle goods[32] an attempt has been made to fill in the gap where technology used is not universally available; in essence trying to fit into trade theory the cropping up of new products and their subsequent absorption into the international division of labour. Initially these goods, which are perceived as embodying a high degree of research and development inputs, are usually produced with physical and skilled human capital-intensive methods. Later on standardized techniques become available, and a high degree of lower skilled or unskilled labour can be used[33]. An obvious outcropping of this theory was the explanation of the phenomenon of intraindustry trade (Kojima, 1964 and Grubel, 1967), for in those cases where products had reached the standardized stage of the cycle, firms would shift production of such products to countries whose advantage lay in the labour-intensive area[34]. Perhaps it would not be incorrect to hypothesize that behind the entire process of producing new products is the ability of a country to produce innovators or entrepreneurs.

With regard to countries like Malaysia many of the products already existing today as new products and being produced in high income countries will, given today's technology, eventually (i.e. in increasingly shorter periods of time) be produced there or in other developing countries[35]. This means that the conditions prevailing for HOSS products would dictate the factor intensity of production of product cycle goods in Malaysia *vis-à-vis* inter- as well as intranational trade.

In the final category, that of policy-induced products, those distortions are introduced which result from man-made intervention and induce trade and production patterns not otherwise in agreement with the above-mentioned mainstream thinking (see e.g., Krueger (1977)). Beginning with tariffs, the spectrum of such distortions has gone beyond the initial effective tariff protection stage[36] and include in particular the wide range of non-tariff barriers (NTBs) – see, for example, Baldwin (1970) as well as socio-economic/political features[37]. Despite the obvious lure to include quantitatively all these items influencing trade and production patterns, difficulties abound and results have not always met a priori expectations. Nonetheless the necessity to include such aspects has been realized and in essence the approach taken by Olsen (1979) represents an attempt to come to grips with this area.

However, it can be concluded from the wealth of other empirical evidence available on industrialization policies in developing countries that as far as the social net benefits stemming from manufacturing activities are concerned, government officials did not prove to be more knowledgeable than the market (Donges, 1976) and the greater their misjudgement the more trade patterns deviated from what comparative advantages would have engendered.

While the posited global impact of such measures on world welfare is well known, since they induce deviations from an optimal allocation of resources, the position of a given country like Malaysia and the resulting conclusions for the impact of industrialization policies on its welfare must remain somewhat cloudy. That is, since the real world comprises many countries with such distortions, an individual country not applying them (so as not to induce investments with incorrect factor intensities) might be considered to be less attractive for investments from abroad. On the other hand, being aware of this, once restrictions begin or incentives are introduced they have a tendency to become very resistant to changes and often induce other measures to be enacted. Thus retreating behind barriers is at best a non-solution. The more efficient way is to promote flexibility *vis-à-vis* new output and technologies mixes in line with the changing factor endowment of the economy; ergo such development policies should be instituted which permit these changes to be transmitted via factor price adjustment (Fei and Ranis (1971, p. 116)).

The gist of this section is obvious: to be efficiently integrated into the international division of labour the role which a country like Malaysia plays *vis-à-vis* industrialized countries or rather the role played by less developed regions within a country, embodies the production of resource, labour-intensive and small-establishment size goods. Such an approach can be said to be in agreement with its comparative advantages.

INTERNATIONAL TRADE AND REGIONAL ECONOMIC DEVELOPMENT: SOME KEY ISSUES

Distilled from the above discussion of the determinants of inter- or intranational trade and production, where countries or regions are treated as point economies, the essence for a discussion of purely regional aspects is in its simplified version quite clear. Indeed, it can be shown with contemporary neoclassic trade theory that the location of production, first of all assuming zero transportation costs and given fixed production techniques, will be determined by the relative prices of the inputs. The relative prices on the other hand are determined by the factor endowment in each given region. Thus, assuming that products can be classified according to their degree of factor intensity (factor reversals excluded), then industries will be distributed between regions according to the correspondence between the relative availability of factors in a region and the specific production mix of each industry[38].

Given this basic framework with which to approach regional development issues, the next step, after delineating the given/potential comparative advantages the LDRs and MDRs, is to specify the distinguishing characteristics of the LDRs and postulate which factors have allowed regional development disparities to occur or rather keep comparative advantages from being exploited.

TABLE 2.1

Posited Comparative Advantages between LDRs and MDRs

	Labour	*Physical Capital*	*Human Capital*	*Natural Resources*	*Small Scale*
LDRs	+	-	-	+	+
MDRs	-	+	+	-	-

For the purpose of this study and based on the theoretical discussion (thereby keeping in mind the overview of Malaysia's situation in Chapter 1) the posited comparative advantages (designated with a +) are presented in Table 2.1.

With regard to the distinguishing characteristics of the LDRs, for the

TABLE 2.2

Posited Assessment of Some Regional Development Indicators

Indicator	*Assessment*
Population	LDR: low density, mainly in smaller towns or rural areas. MDR: medium density, larger cities dominate.
Transportation	International: direct links limited to MDRs. Interregional: less than adequate; costs often increase non-linearly.
Non-conventional inputs	Concentrated in larger towns, mainly in MDRs.

purpose of this study it is posited that, *inter alia*, they have lower population densities, lower levels of human capital and industrial infrastructure as well as a lack of agglomeration economies (see Table 2.2). It is assumed that the extent to which cost differentials[39] between LDRs and MDRs are engendered by factors like agglomeration economies it is usually possible to compensate for them by enacting specific measures. Such measures are considered as allowing the given/potential comparative advantages to be exploited in accordance with economic efficiency criteria[40]. That is, analogous to the battery of measures applied to international trade in a manner to ensure that distortions are overcome and comparative advantages can be tapped[41], there exist similar measures to be used in an intranational context.

In light of the above it becomes evident that the usual assumptions made in connection with international trade theory exclude aspects important to an investigation of regional problems. While the simplifying assumption that trade takes place between point economies is helpful in generally portraying the workings of international trade theory when dealing with relations between countries[42], its adaptation to an analysis of intranational/regional aspects of development requires that certain adjustments be made. First of all, regions within countries are usually intended to be developed on an area-wide basis and not just as a point or a specific core area. Secondly, the regions themselves neither exhibit an equal distribution of population nor do they reveal an internally constant economic environment. It is thus necessary to take such differences into consideration when aiming at reducing regional development disparities.

In the case of transportation costs, their inclusion drives a wedge between the degree of specialization that could take place between two regions.

As a matter of fact when transportation costs equal comparative production cost differences between two regions, trade, *ceteris paribus*, will not take place. Those products for which this occurs are termed, *ceteris paribus*, non-tradables. But the set of goods classified as non-tradables is not permanently fixed, as technological change in transportation methods can easily turn non-tradable into tradable goods. To be sure, the technological gains made in the area of transportation since the beginning of the last century and leading to a reduction in transportation costs have been just as responsible for the expansion in world trade as tariff reductions were[43], not only by allowing existing trade to expand but, perhaps more important, allowing non-tradeables to be traded and unexploited resources to be tapped[44].

If the problem could be limited to tariffs and transportation costs then conclusions drawn from Deardorff (1980) could be interfaced with posited entrepreneurial behaviour to produce an appropriate delineation of the structure of the economy. However, such an approach is pre-empted, given the distinguishing factors and their impact on the decision-making process of entrepreneurs to invest in a specific location. It is accordingly assumed that the outcome of this process has allowed development disparities[45] between LDRs and MDRs to evolve. Such decisions are considered to have been made based on attempting to maximize profits[46], given cost differentials[47], due to differing endowments, for the factors of production as well as for procurement and distribution costs.

In light of the differentiated economic environment both within and between regions, industrial location theory can be interpreted as pointing out that countervailing forces in an economy are instrumental in determining its spatial structure. For instance, a concentration of economic activities is promoted by the extent that, *ceteris paribus,* significant benefits can be reaped from economies of scale and/or agglomeration economies, given insignificant increases in the cost of procurement and distribution. Where economies of scale and/or agglomeration economies are not important or are exceeded by the cost of procurement and distribution or where the price of immobile factors of production in agglomerated areas increases more than procurement and distribution costs decrease, a decentralization of economic activities is prompted.

As mentioned above, given supply and demand parameters entrepreneurs seek out the location where costs are minimized[48]. What cannot be assumed, however, is that all industries are affected by the economic environment parameters in the same manner, since the input and output structures as well as techniques differ. Thus in the case of those industries producing Ricardo goods[49], one would find that they would be located close to the natural resource base when large bulk causes high transportation costs. This is a prime example of supply-oriented production.

After initial processing, thereby reducing transportation costs, further refinement processing could then be shifted to locations where it can be most efficiently effected. In such cases the relative endowment with other factors of production is important[50]. Given the mobility of capital and the immobility of labour, investment will be made in those areas where, given output levels and prices and assuming other factors are not important, labour costs are minimized. If the price of labour correctly reflects its relative scarcity and human capital levels and *ceteris paribus* conditions prevail, production can be set up anywhere. Should distortions exist, such as measures aimed at maintaining equal income levels throughout an economy regardless of human capital differences, then investments will tend to flow into those areas where human capital levels (i.e. productivity levels) are the highest.

Given the spread and structure of population (i.e. markets) raw materials, transportation and labour costs as well as levels of human capital, an important additional factor can be seen as arising from spatial interactions within a given economic environment, i.e. agglomeration economies. But it is not the spatial interaction alone which engenders agglomeration economies; the existence of supraregional (or supranational) government, public or private institutions offering e.g. services (i.e. non-conventional inputs) can also be viewed in this direction.

Agglomeration economies are important in the context of this study because from them emanate the benefits (both of positive and negative nature) which a given entrepreneur can reap by merely locating in the area where they exist (this is in essence Weber's position)[51]. To the extent that they are positive, firms, *ceteris paribus*, will thus be able to lower their costs and either increase profits or decrease prices and thus improve their competitive position[52]. The cost reduction is not only seen as evolving from external economies by being able to establish large-scale production facilities (economies of scale).

Despite the importance attached to agglomeration economies – it is surely one of the most recurrent themes in the theory of industrial location[53] – empirical analysis has only brought forth a few convincing delineations of the impact of the immediate economic environment on production structures. Most recent and most thorough so far is the study by Townroe and Roberts (1980) which (based on special tabulations from census of production data) aims at examining whether variations in productivity and efficiency of specific industries are statistically associated with variations in the economic attributes of the respective locations of the industries. The results reveal that for specific industries the agglomeration economies do indeed seem to influence the performance of certain industries[54]. One basic problem of the Townroe and Roberts study is that it had to use aggregated (as opposed to micro) data, thereby making it difficult to filter out interfirm differences. Nevertheless two variables, crucial within the context of this study, were established as being generally significant in determining the performance of firms: the availability of services (i.e. non-conventional inputs) and the availability of skilled workers (level of human capital).

THE HYPOTHESES[55]

Given the preceding discussions on international trade, industrialization and regional economic development the central hypothesis of this study is that the growth of income and employment, be it in an international or intranational context, is best achieved via an exploitation of comparative advantages. Specified in an international context, this means that an industrialization path will be structured in accordance with economic efficiency criteria if those goods in line with the factor endowments of a country are produced (p. 21). The nature of the factor endowments, and hence the delineation of those goods in which comparative advantages exist, has been shown to depend on income levels (HOSS goods), on the availability of agricultural, mineral and environment resources (Ricardo goods), and on the innovative abilities (product-cycle goods). For a developing country *vis-à-vis* a developed country the posited comparative advantages exist in the production of and trade with a) labour-intensive goods with relatively low levels of human capital (p. 24), b) small-scale-industry-intensive products (under certain conditions, p. 23), and c) natural resource-intensive products, (i.e. to the extent that such are available, pp. 22-3).

While these same basic specifications apply in an intranational context, certain extensions are necessary to incorporate regional development considerations (pp. 26-7). These extensions account for regional differentials in transportation costs (pp. 27-8), in the endowment with non-conventional inputs (pp. 28-9), and the impact of agglomeration economies (pp. 28-9). By drawing on theories of industrial location behaviour in market-oriented economies it was shown, *ceteris paribus,* that entrepreneurs will opt for locations which will yield the highest profits (pp. 28-9). Given the posited distinguishing characteristics of less developed and more developed regions (p. 26) and their impact, in connection with factor endowments, on the locational behaviour of entrepreneurs, it was concluded that location preferences depended on the type of industry and the importance of the above-mentioned extensions (p. 28). Generally speaking, an improvement of income and employment levels in a less developed region *vis-à-vis* a more developed region via a more extensive exploitation of comparative advantages was seen as being hindered by the above distortions/differentials (p. 26). It should be noted, however, that even in the case of those ubiquitous industries considered to be producing only for local markets (in essence non-traded goods), thus distributed in accordance with the population and basically unaffected by such distortions/differentials, changes in transportation and/or production technologies can engender entirely different locational demands (pp. 26-7). Therefore, comparative advantages must be viewed as being dynamic and the competitive position considered to be potentially influenced by all factors.

Reformulating now the general hypothesis into a form applicable to the approach taken in this study, the following two hypotheses (the first aimed at the result of the industrialization process and the second aimed at measures promoting industrialization) constitute the basis upon which the quantitative analysis is structured:

1. A regional pattern of industrialization or changes therein will be in line with economic efficiency criteria if the factor intensity of production correctly corresponds with perceived regional factor endowments, given regional development characteristics. The factor intensity of production is represented, for example, by indicators of capital/labour intensity; factor endowments are measured, for example, by the availability of labour and natural resources; regional development characteristics are portrayed, for example, by agglomeration economies and transportation parameters.
2. Industrialization measures will promote a regional pattern of industrialization in line with economic efficiency if, aside from taking regional factor endowments into consideration, the impact of those factors posited as being responsible for hindering comparative advantages from being tapped, for example agglomeration economies or transportation parameters, is duly taken into account.

The main indicators used in connection with the hypotheses are as follows:

(a) capital intensity is represented (wherever possible) by fixed capital assets per full-time employee; analogously labour intensity is measured by the same indicator but interpreted in the opposite direction;

(b) establishment size is represented by the number of employees per establishment;

(c) resource intensity is deduced from information on manufacturing establishments and input-output tables;

(d) the existence of agglomeration economies is derived from population size and density as well as the availability of services (non-conventional inputs);

(e) transportation differentials are derived from distances, available means of transportation and information on specific industry demands;

(f) per capita income levels (in most cases) are used to delimit less developed regions from more developed regions.

CONCLUDING REMARKS

In concluding this chapter it should be remembered that since the analysis is based on partial equilibrium principles, statements made and conclusions drawn must be interpreted accordingly. Likewise it should be recalled that basically because of the partial equilibrium approach no attempt is made to deal with the problem of trade-offs in the growth of income and employment between reducing regional development disparities and overall economic growth. Aside from the fact that economists themselves are not certain as to what degree they occur, the desire to reduce regional development disparities is taken as given, that is, it is considered to be derived from the social welfare function of a country (see comments on pp. 3-4).

1 Throughout the book the argumentation is based on partial equilibrium principles. Granted such a partial equilibrium approach has its inherent weaknesses, but the state of the art of a dynamic and general equilibrium analysis, particularly as concerns regional aspects, does not necessarily allow more fundamental conclusions to be drawn. To be sure: 'Economics as a positive science is a body of tentatively accepted generalizations about economic phenomena that can be used to predict the consequences of changes in circumstances ... (but the) necessity of relying on uncontrolled experience rather than on controlled experiment makes it difficult to produce dramatic and clear-cut evidence to justify the acceptance of tentative hypotheses ... (nonetheless existing) relative price theory, which is designed to explain the allocation of resources among alternative ends and the division of the product among the co-operating resources ... seems to be both extremely fruitful and deserving of much confidence for (examining economic systems).' (Friedman, 1953, pp. 39-42.)

2 Kaldor notes, for instance, that although solving regional and country problems is not the same, it is 'illuminating to consider them as if they were, and apply the same analytical technique to both.' (Kaldor, 1970, p. 337.)

3 Such an approach is in general agreement with the foundations of mainstream theory, see e.g. Ohlin (1952, pp. vii-viii). It was namely his goal to consider the differences in the endowment with factors of production and analyse the domestic and international flow of the factors of production, particularly *vis-à-vis* commodity flows. On p. 581 he even notes that international trade theory is nothing but international location theory. See also Weber (1911) and Lösch (1954). Lösch, whose seminal writing stems from the 1930s first described in an abstract manner the economic interrelationships between all locations.

4 Isard (1956, p. 54). It can also be pointed out that Harry Johnson, in his succinct summary of international trade theory in the International Encyclopediae of the Social Sciences (1968, Vol. 8, pp. 84-5), comes to the same conclusions and notes that the 'separation of the two is unfortunate and their integration is a desirable objective of future development'.

5 Development economics is interpreted in this study in a neoclassical sense, incorporating the assumptions that economic development can be represented as a continuum, resulting from a harmonious and cumulative process of tending toward an equilibrium (here the philosophy of Adam Smith is evident), at which point everyone is better off or can be made better off by having the gainers compensate the losers (i.e. benefits of division of labour).

6 Thus the collapse of commodity prices in the aftermath of the Great Depression engendered the philosophy that development could only come about via rapid industrialization. Such approaches were often twisted into the capital-intensive direction by a Keynesian stress on the importance of investment and the rise in neoclassical growth theories. Further distorting the picture was an outgrowth of Leontief's input-output analysis and the seemingly successful implementation of planning methods in certain countries.

7 For a summary of some of these theories see Higgins (1968, pp. 55-160). It should perhaps be pointed out that one of the reasons for such a multiplicity of theories lies in the fact that a serious study of developing economies as such did not actually begin until after the second World War. Furthermore, development economics is not a discipline restricted to a specific area, but rather encompasses nearly the entire spectrum of economic theory. For a candid treatment of the problematic issues see Johnson (1975, pp. 282-302).

8 A brief but nonetheless relevant article, particularly as it deals with Malaysia, on the impact of inward versus outward development policies was written by Myint (1967, pp. 1-13). There the benefits already forthcoming from relatively open development strategies are pointed out, but also those which have been made from import substitution. However, the extension of domestic markets via regional customs unions (ASEAN) in order to increase the potential for import substitution policies is warned against and analogy drawn to the success of the Scandinavian countries – the solution rather was seen as lying in a stronger integration into world markets.

9 See Samuelson (1951, p. 49): 'The less developed nations cannot get their heads above water because their production is so low that they can spare nothing for capital formation by which their standard of living could be raised.' The scepticism was led, however, by Nurkse in his book, Problems of Capital Formation in Underdeveloped Countries (1953), and here in particular the formulations on 'the vicious circle of poverty'. Similar conclusions were also drawn by Myrdal, Singer and others. The fallacy in argumentation was simple to uncover since the mere existence of successful countries, that were poor before, sufficed.

10 Beginning with Viner (1950) the benefits resulting from a closer integration of economies received an explicit theoretical framework, later extended by Meade (1955), Lipsey (1970) and Vanek (1965). It was no doubt the discussions following the founding of the EEC (see Balassa, 1961) and the articles estimating the gains from freer trade and more efficient allocation of resources which acted as strong arguments in favour of outward-oriented strategies.

11 Smith's further succinct observations on trade of particular relevance for

developing countries include 'vent-for-surplus' argumentation (p. 372) and economies of scale as well as the advantages of large markets (pp. 446-7).

12 Ricardo treated commodities as being valued according to their labour inputs (wages are equal throughout a given economy) and productivity is constant over the relative range of the production function. Other factors of production (e.g. land, human and physical capital) are either insignificant, or considered to be combined with labour in a constant function or merely represent stored-up labour.

13 See Haberler (1936). For a recent treatment of the general applicability of the 'law of comparative advantage', see Deardorff (1980, pp. 941-57). He shows that among other things tariffs and transport costs can be taken into account in a general many-commodity model.

14 Heckscher originally published his contribution in 1919 (it was republished in 1949, pp. 272-300). Ohlin's work appeared in 1933. As opposed to Ricardo, Heckscher and Ohlin assumed that, independent of country location, the production functions for a given commodity were identical and the factors of production comparable. Thus the comparative advantage of a given country is considered to be determined by the relative supply of the factors of production.

15 Stolper and Samuelson (1941, pp. 58-73).

16 Samuelson (1948, pp. 165-84) and (1953, pp. 1-20). Due to these refinements the Heckscher-Ohlin Theory in its entirety is properly referred to as the Heckscher-Ohlin-Stolper-Samuelson Theory).

17 Leontief (1953, pp. 69-99). The article is abstracted from work done in connection with a larger study on the structure of the American economy also published in 1953.

18 In carrying out this analysis Leontief used data from the 1946 input-output table from which, for lack of comparable foreign statistics, estimates of the capital and labour intensities for import competing industries were derived. These estimates were then used as proxies for the imports, whereby those imported products not produced in the US, (e.g. coffee and tea), were excluded from the investigation. Despite the large number of statistical stumbling blocks embodied in this method, it is actually quite proper as it interfaces with the assumption of the HO theorem that production functions between countries are identical. In light of the literature to the contrary (see for instance Arrow *et al.*, 1961, pp. 225-50) this procedure came under strong criticism.

19 See Hirsch (1974, pp. 65-82). For a similar classification under different headings, see Giersch (1979).

20 While the discussion here rests basically on the manufacturing industry, that is on the processing of natural resources, in reality natural resource-intensive 'products' cover the entire economic spectrum. That is, comparative advantages in and hence the exportation of such products can exist in the form of optimal soil and weather conditions for certain agricultural products (e.g. rubber and palm oil), as well as in the form of sunshine and sandy beaches for the tourist industry (e.g. Penang or the East Coast of Malaysia). Likewise the existence of natural wonders (e.g. the Grand Canyon or the Alps), must also be considered as belonging to the set of Ricardo goods. Hence, an analysis of the factor intensity of exports should actually include such items as well. The failure to do so could lead to incorrectly specified policy conclusions. Every attempt will be made in this study to point out where such considerations are appropriate. However, as the secondary sector is the object under investigation, these hints are no more than caveats. It is otherwise understood that, as a partial equilibrium analysis, interpretation and conclusions drawn only for the secondary sector should not be interpreted as excluding activities in other sectors in accordance with the total comparative advantages of a region.

21 This problem was broached by Vanek (1959, pp. 146-54). Baldwin (1971, pp. 126-46) in noting that imports from LDCs were more capital/resource-intensive than US exports to the same, concludes that clearly the 'simple, single-factor (e.g. capital per worker), trade theories (must be discarded) in favor of multi-factor trade models', whereby it must be differentiated by, among other things, natural resource conditions.

22 The use of the term oil is in essence an example of an incorrectly specified natural resource. In the case of Malaysia, but even more so for the Arabic oil-producing countries, a correct specification would be energy, not only in the form of hydrocarbons but also in the form of sunlight which can be transformed into transportable energy.

23 In this refinement factor intensities, in compliance with Leontief's procedure, were also included and major resource-based as well as internationally non-mobile industries were removed.

24 See Moroney (1975, pp. 139-50).

25 In light of the distribution of the population and natural resources in a LDC like Malaysia, extensive labour-intensive downstream processing of natural resources would require a large migration of labour to the less developed regions. Since labour is considered to be relatively immobile, the alternatives would either be (a) transporting to areas of labour concentration, (b) small-scale processing, or (c) capital-intensive methods.

26 Investigations using physical capital as an explanatory independent variable have often been less than successful (Baldwin, 1971, 1979 and Wolter, 1977a) in finding the expected correlation. Baldwin (1970) in a study of the capital intensity of export vs. import competing production for some thirty countries finds that the Leontief paradox exists for any number of them. The reasons he provides are, among other things, the import-substituting and investment attraction policies in LDCs.

27 The term human capital as it is known and understood today did not come into being until the mid-1950s. While well-known passages from Smith (1776, chapter X), Fisher (1930, p. 9) and Marshall (1938, p. 564) can be cited, it was not really until the Leontief-Paradox debate that increased attention was given to the theoretical ramifications of human capital. Milton Friedman and Simon Kuznets (1945) are perhaps the earliest exceptions.

28 The concept of human capital as developed later by Schultz (1962) and Becker (1962 and 1964) had not been refined so as to allow its explicit incorporation into the theory. It was Kenen (1965) who quantified the investment in human capital and exhibited the conditions under which the Leontief-Paradox disappears. Any number of studies on this topic have appeared in the meantime. On the theoretical side, see particularly Bhagwati (1970), Kenen (1970) and Krueger (1970). Empirically the literature by Larry (1969), which dealt with developing countries in general (particularly as concerns the unskilled labour content) and Hufbauer (1970), in which two dozen countries are investigated, represent in-depth attempts to find reconciliation of the theory in the actual trade figures. See also Fels (1972), Heller (1976), Morrall (1972), Mansfield (1979) and Stern (1976). More recently Tuong and Yeats (1980) have shown that Larry's results can be duplicated or rather extended using 1976 production data.

29 Based on Leontief's (1956) initial attempts to introduce skill, Keesing (1966, 1968 and 1971) respecified skill levels. In a newer study, Weiss (1978), in examining the electrical engineering industry showed the content of unskilled workers and West Germany's competitiveness with LDCs to be negatively related.

30 One applies the term of non-homothetic production function in this respect. It should be added that such industries can be expected to be found particularly in those areas of production where (1) initial raw material processing significantly decreases further transportation/handling costs, (2) traditional products are produced with local labour-intensive methods and (3) production technology is internationally available and average costs do not decrease significantly over relevant ranges (Bruch, 1980, p. 430).

31 It might be noted that Hoffmann and Tan excluded such factors from their study.

32 Posner (1961) is generally attributed with having developed the theoretical underpinnings interfacing temporary innovative monopolies with trade performance.

33 At this point in time technology-induced monopolies have ceased to exist and competitors have entered the market.

34 A further obvious consequence of such a development is the establishment of overseas subsidiaries, particularly by MNCs. For a survey of the literature on this aspect, see Agarwal (1980, pp. 739-73). In attempting to better define the underlying determinants Grubel *et al.* (1971), Grubel, Vernon (1970), and Horn (1976) *inter alia* could show that R & D-intensive products belonged to the comparative advantage set of high-income industries. In connection with the introduction of new products, see for instance Finger (1975). Vernon (1979, p. 265) takes stock of the state of the art particularly in connection with the usefulness of this theory in explaining international trade ties both between the US and other high-income industrialized countries as well as between the latter and developing countries.

35 It cannot be overlooked, however, that the new microtechnology processes might well prompt a rethinking *vis-à-vis* which products can be produced under comparative advantage conditions in which country.

36 See for instance Grubel, Johnson (1977), Hiemenz, Rabenau (1973), Donges et al. (1973).

37 Disequilibrium exchange rates could also be mentioned. For NTBs see Baldwin (1970); for socio-economic/political aspects, see Pincus (1977), Glismann and Weiss (1980), Riedel (1977) and Hitiris (1979).

38 Obviously the goods produced should not be interpreted as encompassing only visible tradeable goods, as, for instance, business services (HOSS goods) or recreational activities (Ricardo goods) should also be included. Unfortunately such a misinterpretation occurs frequently and is in essence the outgrowth of the fixation on trade balances, that is, on balances of visible goods. Its impact on the formulation and implementation of regional development policies cannot be considered to be non-existent as evidenced, for instance, by British regional policies, where instead of allowing the unrestricted expansion of the business and financial service industries, an area where the British have obvious comparative advantages, exactly the opposite was done. First of all the manufacturing industries were subsidized and secondly the employment in the service sector was put at an additional disadvantage by introducing a tax on employment.

39 While here the term differential is used, in certain cases the word distortion might well be more fitting. Such might be the case with respect to transportation costs if these were higher in or between LDRs than in or between MDRs, if the reasons for such cost differentials can be traced back to intervention by government policies. Since a delineation between the differential and distortion is obviously difficult in many cases, these two terms are often considered to be synonyms.

40 Whatever policies are enacted it is not assumed that they are in existence for eternity's sake, but rather only over a period long enough to prompt investment and induce the necessary secondary expansion.

41 For a thorough treatment of such measures see Corden (1974).

42 As mentioned earlier, Deardorff's discourse (1980) shows how including transportation costs does not change the general validity of the law of comparative advantage.

43 Even today the potential for reductions in shipping costs is conceivably greater than for tariffs (see Yeats, 1977). Analysing 45 product groups which accounted for 85 per cent of Indian trade to the US he found that *ad valorem* transport costs amounted to 13.6 per cent (mean) but *ad valorem* nominal tariffs amounted to only 7.5 per cent.

44 There are other technological advances which might seem to reduce the volume of trade, e.g. the use of satellites to transmit newspapers to decentralized printing locations. This is not a reduction, however, as it is merely the shifting between visible trade and invisible trade on the one hand and the prompting of an increased demand for intermediate inputs (be these from domestic or foreign sources) on the other.

45 The indicator primarily used to determine the level of development, is per capita income; thus the terms development disparities and income disparities are assumed to mean the same thing. The author is, however, fully aware of the problems involved in making comparisons of income levels, not only on an international level, but also on a national level. Nonetheless it is as-

sumed that within countries the income data available reflect the ranking of the disparities even if the absolute magnitudes are distorted. It is further assumed that changes in such indicators are also reliable. Thus no attempt is made to adjust for intranational differences in purchasing power parities; such adjustments would no doubt be advisable for comparisons of international disparities. For the literature, see Beckerman (1966), but in particular, Kravis *et al.* (1978, pp. 215-42), and Sen (1979, pp. 1-45). For an in-depth survey of such international comparisons, see Marris (1979) and Kravis (1984).

46 It is perhaps worthwhile to recall the words of Lösch (1954, p. 4) who noted that it is necessary to differentiate between the actual location in the real world and a theoretically determined location – the two need not coincide, as the theory encompasses not all parameters envisaged in reality.

47 In principle this means that capital is considered to be relatively mobile; labour is considered to be relatively immobile.

48 This is in essence a Weber-oriented approach (1929) extended to include a variety of other factors, as Weber and those who extended his theory (Palander (1935), Hoover (1948), Smith (1971) and Isard (1956)) placed considerable stress on transportation costs, however, not neglecting thereby labour costs and agglomeration economies. The stress on transportation costs aptly reflects the era in which Weber developed his theory where, as alluded to above, transportation costs were high and often prohibitive. But technological breakthroughs in transportation methods as well as in the more efficient use of raw materials and the breaking down of the production process (made possible, for example, by becoming independent of primary energy sources – witness the shift of the textile industry in the United States from New England (water power) to the Southeast (electricity) reflected to some extent in the increase of intra-industry trade, have *(inter alia)* changed the situation considerably. To summarize, it can be stated that location theory as conceived by the Weberian school basically assumes that demand (markets) and raw materials (inputs) are given. Lösch (as well as Christaller) on the other hand deal with the problem of location and market areas from the point of view of firms competing with one another, given demand. Since the author does not intend to deal with all the fine points of the various location theories, the reader is referred to one of the standard texts, e.g. Böventer (1979).

49 Given Weber's stress on transportation costs, Giersch (1979) calls these goods Weber goods.

50 Giersch (ibid) refers to such goods as Thünen goods.

51 This is not to say, however, that all industries necessarily profit from them.

52 It should be noted that agglomeration economies are not restricted to business; there are also social and private agglomeration economies. In the case of the former, the interaction between population concentration and scale economies allows public services to be offered at lower prices. In this respect a study carried out by the Stanford Research Institute established that the unit cost of additional infrastructure investments in cities over 150,000 inhabitants declines very little. The study also suggests that, *ceteris paribus,* moving industry to cities larger than this size causes no significant economies of scale, but does cause increasing social costs. It consequently suggests that net social benefits will be increased if attention is paid to a decentralization to medium-size cities (see P. Rao, 1970). Other evidence, however, suggests that it is a myth to talk about an optimal city size; rather it is more important to pay attention to the rate of growth of cities (see Richardson (1977), pp. 12ff.). In the case of private agglomeration economies, one finds the ability to be able to enjoy the existence of public services which are hard to sensibly subdivide (operas, museums, certain types of sport facilities, etc.), as well as the possibility to be able to choose between many jobs offers and consumption options.

53 One of the more recent theoretical studies is by Kanemoto (1980), where primarily efficiency aspects of externalities are dealt with.

54 Other recent studies are those by Carlino (1978) and Normann (1979). For an overview of these and earlier studies see Reimers (1981). A special

treatment of problems relevant to developing countries is given in Linn (1982).

55 The page number(s) in parenthesis refer to the page(s) on which this aspect is mentioned.

3
The Policy Framework: Macro and Regional Aspects

INTRODUCTION

THE shift in the direction of industrialization strategies in Malaysia from generally macro-oriented goals in the first decade after independence to a pronounced regionally-oriented stance in years thereafter does not actually represent a change in basic philosophies. Granted that almost all economic policy measures have a regional impact to some degree and thus the various policy steps taken during the period of decolonization and after independence embodied regional aspects, such technicalities are nevertheless left aside for the time being. To be sure, the origins of Malaysian regional economic development plans can be traced back to the Draft Development Plan of 1950[1]. By this point in time, after having mended the worst scars of the Second World War as well as healing the wounds caused by the Depression (and despite the declaration of a state of emergency in 1948 to fight communist insurgents), Malaya was ready to turn to the development of its own economy. Since the political and economic future of Malaya towards the end of the 1940s was by no means certain, the specification of the development goals understandably did not extend beyond generalizations. Nonetheless, the ideas put forth therein set the stage for development planning henceforth, thus understanding them is essential to be able to appreciate correctly the policy shift beginning in 1968.

The Draft Development Plan (Malaysia Plan, 1950, p. 22) noted that over the long run the heavy reliance of Malaya in the past on mainly tin and rubber production had to give way to the primary or secondary production of other goods in which it also possessed comparative advantages (be it due to climate, soil, geographical location, level of human capital, etc.). Furthermore, a higher degree of self-sufficiency in food production should be aimed at and development in general should lead to an increase in the total natural wealth of the country. Of importance in the context of this paper was the stated goal that the development process should be shared evenly by all parts of the country.

Given the limited resources Malaysia possessed at that time, the thrust of the development was to concentrate on:

1 improving infrastructure, (i.e. services having a direct bearing on economic progress, whereby projects with shorter gestation periods were given a higher priority);

2 improving the competitiveness of traditional Malaysian products; and

3 widening the agricultural base.

A breakdown of the actual expenditures (Table 3.1) underlines these aims and reveals the initial importance given to improving the growth centres. In addition to the direct expenditure impact on regional development, other policies tended to work against the less developed regions: the distribution of

TABLE 3.1

Draft Development Plan, 1950-1955

	Initial Plan	*Revised (1953)*	*Actual*
Total public expenditure (M$ m.)	214.7	855.9	680.6
By sectors (per cent)			
Social development	27.2	9.2	7.1
Education	16.3	6.0	4.8
Health	7.9	2.2	2.2
Housing and other n.e.s.	3.0	1.0	–
Agricultural development[a]	21.7	22.1	22.9
Urban infrastructure[b]	51.2	67.5	58.0

Source: Rudner (1972, p. 67).

[a]Includes agriculture, resettlement, drainage and irrigation, land development, rubber replanting, RIDA and veterinary services.

[b]Includes public works plant and equipment, public utilities, transport and communications, and industry.

federal funds occurred in accordance with the assumed administrative capacities of the various state/settlement governments. Such capacities, however, were a function of the level of development already achieved (Rudner, 1972, p. 82).

While this policy was subjected to a change after 1955 (so as to effect a more proportional distribution of the funds), explicit regional industrialization poli-

TABLE 3.2

Regional Dispersion[a] of Manufacturing Industry in Malaysia, in Selected Years

Region/State[b]		Northern States					Southern States				Western States					Total[c]
		Σ	Kn.	T.	Ps.	Kd.	Σ	M.	J.	Pg.	Σ	NS.	Pk.	Pn.	S.	
Number of establishments	1959	16.11	3.88	1.02	.88	10.33	20.93	3.56	12.19	5.18	63.37	5.14	22.24	14.47	21.52	5,004
	1963	16.94	5.05	2.37	1.04	8.48	21.44	4.49	12.49	4.46	61.62	4.64	20.29	14.84	21.85	8,856
	1968	16.67	3.96	3.20	.92	8.59	21.52	4.57	12.48	4.47	61.81	4.54	18.78	14.99	23.50	9,013
	1973	14.77	3.83	2.95	.78	7.21	21.68	3.88	13.18	4.62	63.55	3.95	17.58	14.51	27.51	11,060
	1978	14.48	2.79	3.85	.70	7.14	22.48	3.81	13.90	4.77	63.05	4.39	17.94	13.24	27.48	13,217
Gross value of output (sales)[d]	1959	12.37	1.50	.30	.56	10.01	24.73	4.38	18.95	1.40	62.90	5.52	18.90	12.57	25.91	1,260,120
	1963	9.73	1.77	.45	.50	7.01	20.74	2.83	15.91	2.00	69.54	6.22	13.25	10.51	39.56	1,689,435
	1968	6.57	1.65	.36	.27	4.29	18.61	2.68	14.09	1.84	74.84	8.77	11.64	10.91	43.50	3,078,523
	1973	5.83	1.41	.78	.30	3.40	19.70	2.29	13.98	3.43	74.41	5.51	10.71	13.93	44.26	7,677,687
	1978	5.30	.92	1.46	.43	2.49	18.91	3.31	12.12	3.48	75.79	9.95	9.80	17.68	38.72	19,887,841
Number of paid employees[e]	1959	13.16	3.59	.90	.57	8.10	22.02	2.90	16.86	2.26	64.82	4.56	17.51	11.90	30.65	61,597
	1963	11.22	3.47	1.42	.46	5.87	21.44	3.36	15.23	2.85	67.34	4.36	14.49	11.71	36.78	87,450
	1968	8.39	2.87	1.15	.25	4.12	22.71	2.62	17.21	2.88	68.92	3.84	14.69	12.15	38.24	130,257
	1973	7.99	3.11	1.63	.45	2.80	22.37	3.43	14.71	4.23	69.63	2.77	13.90	17.07	35.89	278,935
	1978	8.02	2.44	1.65	.34	3.59	22.41	4.15	13.08	5.18	69.59	3.23	11.91	19.55	34.90	423,273
Salaries and wages paid	1959	11.27	2.32	.84	.52	7.59	22.73	2.79	17.58	2.36	66.00	4.85	15.78	11.23	34.14	89,549
	1963	8.86	2.22	1.26	.36	5.02	21.04	2.49	15.20	3.35	70.10	5.26	11.58	10.25	43.01	153,789
	1968	5.84	1.53	1.00	.19	3.12	20.50	2.06	14.83	3.61	73.64	4.88	11.63	10.24	46.89	266,957
	1973	5.17	1.43	1.14	.30	2.30	19.89	2.05	13.28	4.56	74.93	3.39	11.26	13.27	47.01	586,995
	1978	7.97	1.25	1.19	.33	2.60	20.12	3.16	12.23	4.73	74.50	3.58	9.66	16.93	44.33	1,456,133

Sources: Own calculations; 1959 and 1963 based on Hoffmann, Tan (1979, pp. 22 ff.); 1968 and 1973: Dept. of Statistics (CMI, 1968, Table 6a; 1973 Vol. 1, Table 4); 1978, own calculations based on 1978 Survey of Manufacturing Industry expanded to a census by using ratios between 1973 CMI and a fictitious 1973 survey.

[a] Percentage of total.

[b] Kn. = Kelantan, T. = Trengganu, Ps. = Perlis, Kd. = Kedah, M. = Melaka, J. = Johor, Pg. = Pahang; NS. = Negeri Sembilan, Pk. = Perak, Pn. = Penang, S. = Selangor.

[c] Either actual figures or in M$'000.

[d] Value added not used, as it has been in existence only since 1963; see Spinanger (1980, Table A4) for value added shares (and actual figures) up till 1973.

[e] Includes both full-time and part-time workers.

cies remained dormant for a long time to come.

1957-1967: A PERIOD OF MACRO-ORIENTED POLICIES

Objectives

Not long after the British protectorate became the independent Federation of Malaya on 31 August 1957 the government began to enact economic measures proposed by the 1955 World Bank Mission, many of which had been incorporated into the Report of the Industrial Development Working Party (1957)[2]. While general agreement on the necessity to industrialize prevailed, particularly in light of the desire to reduce dependency on tin and rubber (which then accounted for about 80 per cent of the exports and 30 per cent of GDP (Lee, 1978, p. 28), too large of a stress on industrialization was deemed undesirable because it would mean that:

(a) the urban/rural and thus the indigenous/non-indigenous population development differentials would be increased since, due to financial constraints, rural areas could not be adequately developed, so industries would settle in urban areas;

(b) the migration into the urban areas would rapidly increase and cause additional problems;

(c) the principles set down in the Draft Development Plan of 1950 that all parts of the country should profit from economic development would thereby be ignored.

The overall development policy followed by the Malayan Government proceeded along three major paths. First of all, the rural (agricultural) areas were given increased attention; this was accomplished by improving infrastructure (irrigation etc.) and introducing programmes specifically aimed at smallholders. Secondly, and of major interest in this study, a general programme to attract investors to widen the industrial base was instituted. The third path taken actually complemented the first two by aiming at improving the human capital base (in the widest sense).

Thus industrial diversification of Malaysia, namely the departure from an almost total dependency on tin and rubber, began without much regard towards regional aspects. As a matter of fact the initial steps taken, for example, the exploitation of agglomeration economies in growth centres, probably even widened the regional development differentials (as can be seen in Table

3.2). Particularly convincing in this connection was the growth in Selangor where from 1959 to 1968 the share of the gross value of output (as a percentage of total Malaysian output) increased by almost 70 per cent.

Pioneer Industries

The first major industrialization measure enacted (on 31 July 1958) was aimed at promoting and accelerating the overall industrialization process; that is, to encourage the establishment and development in the Federation of industrial and commercial enterprises by way of income tax relief (Government Gazette, 1958, p. 107). This measure, officially called the Pioneer Industries (Relief from Income Tax) Ordinance, 1958 (hereafter referred to as PIO) and patterned after similar schemes which already existed in a number of other countries ranging from Barbados and Jamaica, Nigeria and the Gold Coast (Ghana) to the Philippines and Singapore[3], assumed a central rôle in the industrial policy package[4].

It was felt that a tax exemption on profits of the pioneer industries would be more effective in attracting business, since, after all, the main reason to set up business (in market economies) is to make a profit[5]. Since it might also be assumed that the more successful companies make larger profits, a certain amount of positive selection would seem to take place. Finally, the cost of providing pioneer relief on 'tax holiday' lines was considered small since it was merely a matter of foregoing tax on profits which would not have arisen had not the new capital been attracted. An alternative method of encouraging investment by a general increase in capital allowances was deemed to be less efficacious than the 'tax holiday' method, since it was supposed that increased capital allowances would have far less of a psychological impact upon an investor that the feeling of confidence engendered in the knowledge that for a fixed period of years no tax will be payable (Report of the Industrial Development Working Party, 1957, pp. 37ff.)[6].

In light of what would seem to be (at first glance) attractive investment incentives, it can hardly be surprising that the number of pioneer certificates issued increased rapidly in the years following 1958. As a matter of fact, the structure of demand was such that the size groupings of the amount of investment needed to qualify for the various tax holidays proved to be too small; most applicants were easily able to qualify for the longest exemption period. Thus in 1965[7] the PIO was accordingly revised (see Appendix)[8].

With regard to an explicit regional component, the pioneer investment incentives by the end of 1967 were without one. Implicitly, however, the overt capital-intensive bias of the PIOs meant that the more developed (urban) areas (in particular the growing conurbation in the Klang Valley in Selangor) were put at an advantage, since only in such areas did an adequate amount of infrastructure and reserves of qualified human capital exist. This tilt towards such urban areas was even exacerbated by another major component of the Malaysian industrialization programme, namely the construction of industrial estates.

Industrial Estates

The establishment of industrial estates in Malaysia[9] was, *inter alia,* adopted as a main means of attempting to stem the wild growth of new industries, which would otherwise result in a hodge-podge landscape of housing and business/ manufacturing establishments. Industrial estates were also an integral element in the strategy to attract and encourage the founding of new industries (be it from domestic or foreign investors), within the framework of a general development policy. Given the constraints at the prevailing level of development such estates were established in areas where the necessary infrastructure was already (more or less) available and where external economies could be tapped; in other words these were set up in the major urban areas.

While the first attempt to offer 'packaged industrial sites' dates back to the establishment of Petaling Jaya in 1952[10] the actual starting point should probably not be dated before 1958 at which point the Federal Government, with its newly announced investment incentives, provided the needed impetus to the local development agency's (Petaling Jaya Authority[11], 1955) efforts to lease 300 acres of land cleared and developed from former rubber plantations and subdivided into lots (some of which had ready-to-use buildings on them). That their efforts to attract business were successful would seem to be documented by the fact that within two years (in other words by 1960) 80 factories had started up production activities and the initial 300 acres set aside for manufacturing were already proving to be too small. By 1965 these had been extended to cover 700 acres and within a short period of time even these were totally occupied, thereby employing about 10,000 persons (1966).

The success of the Petaling Jaya venture induced additional industrial estates to be set up in other major urban areas; first (1962 or earlier) in Penang (Mak Mandin), Perak (Tasek), Johor (Larkin and Tampoi) and then later (1966) in Selangor (Shah Alam - formerly called Batu Tiga) and Negeri Sembilan (Senawang). Thus, by the end of 1967, over 5 square miles[12] had been developed as industrial estates, all of which were concentrated around urban areas in regions with higher than average income levels (Table 3.3)[13].

The package that was offered in such industrial estates was virtually the same in every case: completely developed sites with utilities, good transportation connections and a long-term lease with a land title (of definite importance in the Asian land-tenure system)[14]. With respect to transportation connections, all estates were coupled to the highway system; most of the estates established earlier were also located on or near railway lines. While a premium (on a per acre basis) had to be paid for the developed site (aside from a yearly quitrent) the costs were often lower than what might otherwise have been the case. Nonetheless, the development of industrial estates was not intended as a measure with which private ventures would be subsidized just so they would settle in such estates, but was rather considered from the very beginning as a project from which development costs not only should be recovered but also should provide an adequate return on invested capital.

Institutions

In order to assist in financing and generally promoting the development of industrial estates, as well as supporting promising industries which might want to locate production facilities in such (or even other) areas, a number of organizations (institutions) were set up[15]. Among these and of direct importance to the individual investors was the Malaysian Industrial Development Finance Ltd. (MIDF, March 1960)[16]. Its specific purpose was to assist private enterprises by making medium to long-term loans (primarily, but not exclusively, on fixed capital), by helping to offer or even purchasing equity (which could later be sold to the public), by performing underwriting services and offering a variety of other services in connection with setting up production facilities. However, as Wheelwright (1965, p. 33) pointed out, MIDF, as initially set up, operated in an orthodox manner and granted loans to only totally solid ventures, since it too was interested in making profits. This not only meant that the largest companies were preferred, but also that foreign companies often crowded out domestic ventures. Such criticism (see also IBRD, 1963) finally led to a sizeable reorganization in 1963, and later on more attention was paid to supporting promising smaller and more labour-intensive ventures which might otherwise not have received the necessary financial support.

TABLE 3.3
Development of Industrial Estates in Malaysia

Region/Industrial Estate		1962	1964	1966	1968	1970	1971	1972	1973	1974	1975	1976	1977	1978	1979	1980	≥1981
Northern states																	
Trengganu	a	–	–	–	–	–	–	–	1	2	2	2	3	3	3	3	
	b	–	–	–	–	–	–	–	–	.11	.35	.35	.35	.46	.56	.58	.58
Kelantan	a	–	–	–	–	–	–	–	–	1	1	1	1	1	3	3	4
	b	–	–	–	–	–	–	–	–	.05	.05	.05	.05	.05	1.15	1.12	2.41
Perlis	a	–	–	–	–	–	–	–	–	–	–	–	–	–	–	–	–
	b	–	–	–	–	–	–	–	–	–	–	–	–	–	–	–	–
Kedah	a	–	–	–	–	–	–	1	4	4	4	4	5	5	6	6	6
	b	–	–	–	–	–	–	.15	.85	.85	.85	.85	1.35	1.36	1.30	1.30	1.30
Southern states																	
Pahang	a	–	–	–	–	–	–	–	2	4	4	4	5	6	6	7	9
	b	–	–	–	–	–	–	–	.82	1.01	1.01	1.01	1.12	1.76	2.76	2.96	3.50
Melaka	a	–	–	–	–	–	–	1	5	7	7	7	7	7	7	7	7
	b	–	–	–	–	–	–	.25	.58	.79	.79	.79	.79	.81	.85	.85	.85
Johor	a	2	2	2	2	2	2	4	5	5	5	5	6	6	8	9	10
	b	.41	.41	.41	.41	.41	.41	.69	2.99	2.99	2.99	2.99	3.09	3.09	3.28	3.64	3.94
Western states																	
Perak	a	1	1	1	2	2	2	3	5	5	5	5	6	6	6	6	7
	b	.37	.37	.37	1.18	1.18	1.18	1.27	1.59	1.59	1.59	1.59	1.69	1.69	1.69	1.69	3.21
Selangor	a	1	1	2	2	2	2	4	5	7	9	11	11	12	12	12	17
	b	.77	.77	2.13	2.13	2.13	2.13	2.45	2.50	2.69	2.79	4.57	4.84	5.20	5.20	5.20	6.03
Negeri Sembilan	a	–	–	1	1	1	1	1	1	2	2	2	2	2	3	6	6
	b	–	–	.33	.33	.33	.33	.33	.33	.39	.39	.39	.39	.39	.49	.67	.67
Penang	a	1	1	1	1	1	3	6	7	8	8	8	8	8	8	8	8
	b	.25	.25	.25	.25	.25	2.32	3.21	3.41	3.54	3.54	3.54	3.54	3.57	3.24	3.24	3.24
West Malaysia	a	5	5	7	8	8	10	20	34	44	47	49	53	56	62	67	77
Total[2]	b	1.80	1.80	3.49	4.30	4.30	6.37	8.35	13.06	14.00	14.34	16.12	16.93	18.01	20.51	21.25	25.73

Source: See Table 3.6, sources for cols. 1 and 2.

Key: a=number of industrial estates; b = total size of industrial estates (in '000s of planned acres): probably slightly overestimated in the first few years.

Notes : [1]For the odd-number years 1963-9 the values equal the respective preceding year.
[2]In '000s of acres.

A direct subsidiary of MIDF, the Malaysian Industrial Estate Ltd. (MIEL, founded at the same time as MIDF) was an organization established to reduce complications in setting up a new factory on an IE in Malaysia. MIEL offered standardized factory units or complete, made-to-order production facilities, which could either be leased or purchased at reasonable prices. These facilities were particularly attractive to foreign investors whose familiarity with Malaysian buildings codes and specific (perhaps regionally differentiated) construction requirements would be limited[17]. But MIEL also aimed at small-scale industries (handicrafts) and the trades, in other words at companies whose resources to invest in fixed assets were limited. While this particular organization did not explicitly embody a regional component, it is inherent in the provision of services to areas where they were lacking since they increase the economic attractiveness of such regions[18]. The regional impact was, however, minor compared with the locational advantages of industrial estates in the agglomerated areas.

The coordination of the various industrialization policies, essential to ensure that efficient and congruent steps are taken, was initially lacking and complaints about bureaucratic ineptitude were frequently raised. Accordingly, a coordinating body, the Federal Industrial Development Authority (FIDA, hereafter referred to as the Malaysian Industrial Development Authority or MIDA, the official name effective since 1978), was established in 1965[19]. Its specific task was to undertake industrial feasibility studies, carry out promotion activities (at home and abroad), facilitate an exchange of information and coordination of industrial development activities, recommend and, where necessary, carry out industrial site development, process pioneer status applications[20], and report and make recommendations to the Minister of Trade and Industry on industrial development issues. In essence MIDA was intended to be an all-purpose clearing-house; however, it did not begin to perform these functions until after 1967[21], the year in which it finally set up shop[22].

The regional impact of all these institutions created and measures taken to help industrialize the Malaysian economy during the period 1957-67 can be seen in the greater concentration of manufacturing activities around Kuala Lumpur, that is, in Selangor (Table 3.2) and in other higher-income areas. The major factors influencing this gravitating into such areas stemmed from the readily available labour supplies in the agglomerated area together with the industrial infrastructure (i.e. industrial estates) and the attractiveness of the investment incentives to foreigners who nearly always locate in agglomerated areas.

The government was not unaware of the consequences of its industrialization policies (note comment in the Rueff Report (IBRD, 1963, p. 31)). However, the measures instituted to date for the lower-income areas aimed at providing facilities and opportunities for the rural population to improve their levels of economic and social well-being (Malaya Plan, 1963, p. 6). This entailed on the one hand agricultural promotion policies to ensure that domestic supplies of agricultural products would be forthcoming and that the production of the country's main agricultural exports was based on the best methods possible. On the other hand, larger land development projects were being conceived either in the form of new villages or towns or within the framework of wide-scale, regional development plans (like Pahang Tenggara, Johor Tenggara and, later, Trengganu Tengah[23]) to provide completely new employment possibilities in connection with exploiting the local natural resource base[24].

These measures mainly outside the industrial sector along with a variety of other infrastructure investments were nonetheless paving the way for a more intensive and widespread industrial sector in the future. Thus the strategy incorporated in the First Malaysia Plan (1966-70), although outwardly placing more stress on regional inequality than in early five-year plans, still concentrated on achieving a stronger economic foundation[25], based primarily on a rapidly expanding manufacturing sector. These policies still did not differ in principle from those of the past; they were still basically formulated with the intention of maintaining a favourable investment climate by providing incentives, industrial estates and the necessary infrastructure (Malaysia Plan, 1965, pp. 130-6).

However, one aspect of government policies was beginning to change, namely that the development and integration of the indigenous Malaysian population, the *bumiputra*, was assuming an increasingly important role. While this aspect was not a real issue during the first decade of independence, its influence on the extent to which the government was able to follow the path it had set for itself with respect to the shift between industrialization wherever easiest to industrialization wherever deemed necessary would not be negligible. This path, which by the end of 1967 already seemed to be deviating from the projected direction, was in need of some repair.

1968-1980: INTENSIFYING AND REGIONALIZING INDUSTRIALIZATION POLICIES

As the first decade after independence was coming to a close the rapid growth rates of industrialization, e.g. the profile of investment in Diagram 1.2, had already given way to much more moderate ones. This was also expressed in the growth rate of output from PIs which had fallen below that of the total manufacturing industry[26]. The general weakening of the pace of economic growth (particularly with respect to the First Malaysia Plan) could thus hardly be overlooked and prompted government action, culminating in the Investment Incentives Act of 1968. This act, which still serves as the foundation for investment incentives in Malaysia, brought together, replaced and expanded all pieces of legislation or ordinances (then existing in West Malaysia, Sabah and Sarawak) concerning investment incentives.

With regard to PI incentives, although the basic concept had not been changed (the length of the tax holiday from income and payroll tax[27] remained a function of the amount of the capital investment (see Appendix)), the legislation had now been expanded beyond manufacturing companies to cover any kind of commercial undertaking. In a further extension it became possible to receive up to three additional years of tax holiday under certain conditions. One of these conditions represented the first explicit regional thrust the investment incentives received: an additional year of tax exemption was granted if the investment took place in a specific development area[28].

With the exception of certain extensions and revisions in the list of products (industries) designated as 'pioneer potential', the pioneer legislation has not undergone any wide-sweeping changes since 1968. One extension (the inclusion of hotels in the 1971 Investment Incentives (Amendment) Act (see Appendix)), however, is worthwhile noting since it provided a considerable degree of regionally differentiated tax abatements[29]. Given the fact that these incentives were granted under the stipulation that certain management and service standards (for luxury, first and medium class hotels) had to be maintained, it is obvious that the government was widening the development base (in line with comparative advantages such as natural beauty) to be exploited by foreign demand in particular. With this measure not only was an attempt made to decrease regional disparities, but also exports were being diversified and expanded (recall here the principles put forth in the Draft Development Plan, Malaysia Plan, 1950, p. 22).

In another extension of the PI legislation the government in one of the revisions of the list of industries/products likewise attempted to profit from foreign demand, this time the rapidly increasing demand for electronic components, and instituted special investment incentives (see Appendix). While the amendment did no more than extend the length of the tax holdings to a maximum of ten years (vs. eight under other conditions) for the specified industries, these industries were basically chosen for their high degree of labour intensity[30]. While the more extensive use of the factor labour interfaces with Malaysia's assumed comparative advantages, from which the country as a whole profits, the fact that the companies had to locate in special industrial estates (i.e. free trade zones) set up in areas like Penang and Selangor directly put the high-income areas at an advantage[31].

Realizing by now one weakness of the PI legislation (i.e. its capital intensive impact), the government introduced another type of investment incentive in 1971 - the labour utilization relief (LUR - see Appendix). This measure was specifically structured towards ensuring that the factor labour, rather than capital, would be more fully utilized; it stipulated that investment incentives would be granted according to the number of jobs created. Comparing this with the PIO, where the amount of capital investment alone determined the length of the tax holiday (thereby slanting the demand towards areas with sufficient skilled workers and adequate amounts of power), it was assumed that the LUR would lower the capital intensity of new investments and at the same time shift their location to the less developed areas.

In concert with this piece of legislation, which did seem to cause a shift away from the basic PI incentives (Table 3.4) as well as concurring with the

TABLE 3.4

Distribution of Approved Projects by Type of Incentive, West Malaysia, 1969-1981 (per cent)

	1969	*1970*	*1971*	*1972*	*1973*	*1974*	*1975*	*1976*	*1977*	*1978*	*1979*	*1980*	*1981*
Pioneer	82.5	49.0	42.3	43.1	37.7	31.1	20.7	24.7	24.5	25.7	21.9	20.3	17.0
Other incentives[1]	2.2	11.1	10.1	9.4	12.1	10.4	16.7	22.8	21.0	21.7	16.4	18.0	17.7
Without incentives	15.3	40.9	37.6	47.5	50.2	58.5	62.6	52.5	54.5	52.6	61.7	61.7	65.3
Total (actual number)	137	296	279	320	424	482	420	425	400	428	484	412	519

Source: MIDA (annual Report, 1973ff.).

[1]Includes investment tax credit; accelerated depreciation allowance, LUR, hotel incentives and locational incentives.

increased stress placed on a more even regional dispersion of industries in the Second Malaysia Plan, was the introduction of specific location incentives in 1973. This incentive, although it did not initially specify the areas in which location incentives could be received, represented the first major piece of legislation explicitly aiming at areas deemed to be in need of more development (see Appendix)[32]. By 1977 the following areas in West Malaysia had been officially designated by the Minister (without any limitations as of yet) as areas in which the location incentive was applicable (see Map 3.1).

1. Johor (only Tenggara area);
2. Kedah (excluding the Kuala Muda District);
3. Kelantan;
4. Pahang (excluding the Kuantan District);
5. Perlis;
6. Trengganu.

The 1973 amendment did not, however, invalidate the term 'development area' (contained in the 1968 Investment Incentives Act). As a matter of fact by 1977 the following areas in West Malaysia had been designated as being such an area, thereby permitting a year (or extra year) of tax exemption:

States	Industrial Estates[33]
Kedah	Bayan Lepas FTZ (2 April 1971)
Kelantan	Kamunting
Melaka	Senawang
Pahang	Sungei Way FTZ (31 March 1971)
Perlis	Tanjung Agas
Trengganu	Ulu Klang FTZ.

Although the delineation of a development area at such a low level as that of an industrial estate (particularly if it is located in a relatively high-income area such as Bayan Lepas FTZ in Penang) might seem to be going to unnecessary extremes, it probably reflects the result of having to fill industrial estates, rapidly planned and constructed during this period[34].

Although the establishment of such facilities had been recommended all along and was emphasized in the First Malaysia Plan (1966-70), the Mid-Term Review of the First Malaysia Plan (January 1969) was soon warning of the zea-

MAP 3.1
Areas of West Malaysia
in which Locational Incentives Granted

lousness with which the estates were established (i.e. to some extent without sufficient regard to probable demand for the facilities provided (Malaysia Plan, 1969, p. 82)). The government concluded that in the future it would provide assistance to the states for the establishment of additional industrial areas only after the project had been justified by thorough feasibility studies (ibid., p. 82). To what extent the industrial estates established since then were actually subjected to more stringent controls is not known; what can be observed, however, is that between 1970 and 1974 the number of industrial estates increased by over 400 per cent (from 8 to 44) and the area had been expanded by almost over 200 per cent (to 13,995 acres - Table 3.5). While it might be premature to conclude that this massive expansion of almost 30 square miles (from 1970 to 1980) was not adequately planned, the fact that a number of the newer IEs have less than complete utilities and communication infrastructure (see Tables A5 and A6) does not correlate with the stated policy of providing an industrial site with all the necessary facilities.

One major reason for the expansion at such a rapid pace was the above mentioned stronger thrust to promote the establishment of industrial activities in the less developed areas (Malaysia Plan, 1971, p. 156). As opposed to vague comments on policy measures in the Second Malaysia Plan, in the Third Malaysia Plan explicit measures to improve the relative position of the lowest income states were expounded upon[35]. These included the establishment of new growth centres and the location of a greater variety of government establishments in these areas. In order to encourage investment in the less developed states, a broad range of measures was to be adopted including fiscal incentives, the development of industrial estates and ready-built factories (Malaysia Plan, 1976, pp. 211ff.), as well as the improvement of electricity, interregional

TABLE 3.5

Regional Distribution[a] of Industrial Estates in West Malaysia

	1970	*1974*	*1980*	*≥1981*
Northern states				
Number of IEs[a]	-	13.6	17.9	16.9
Area of IEs[a]	-	7.2	14.1	16.7
Share of change[b]	-	10.4	27.4	28.8
Utilization rate[c]	-	48.0	62.2	-
Southern states				
Number of IEs[a]	25.0	36.4	34.3	33.8
Area of IEs[a]	9.6	34.2	35.1	32.2
Share of change[b]	-	45.1	36.8	18.8
Utilization rate[c]	-	45.0	61.0	-
Western states				
Number of IEs[a]	75.0	50.0	47.8	49.4
Area of IEs[a]	90.4	58.2	50.8	51.1
Share of change[b]	-	44.5	35.8	52.4
Utilization rate[c]	-	26.9	85.4	-
Total[d]				
Number of IEs[d]	8	44	67	77
Area of IEs[d]	4,301	13,995	21,253	25,728
Change in area[d]	-	9,694	7,258	4,475
Utilization area[d]	-	33.9	74.1	-

Source: See Table 3.6.

[a]Percentage share of region in total.

[b](Change in IE area in region since prior year/total change in IE area) · 100.

[c](Area sold in IEs/area saleable) · 100.

[d]Actual values.

[e]Average utilization of IEs in West Malaysia.

highways, marketing centres and ports. While this policy was to pay specific attention to creating agglomeration economies, excessive growth of the already existing urban areas was to be avoided. Furthermore, the policy was intended to place particular stress on the integration of the growth centres with their hinterlands.

It is obvious that the role of the industrial estates within the framework of the regional industrialization policies had changed considerably since first being set up (see pp. 59ff.). They were now an explicit part of the package to promote industrialization in the less developed regions where the infrastructure had yet to be fully developed or would be developed concurrently with the setting up of IEs. Thus, the expansion of the IEs was very rapid throughout the 1970s, particularly in the less developed regions (Tables 3.5 and 3.6). Likewise, within these regions, and within the more developed regions as well, the tendency can be observed of locating industrial estates closer to small towns (and further away from major airports or shipping facilities, Table 3.7) and equipped with less infrastructure. The same can also be said for the planned IEs[36].

Of course, as was pointed out earlier, the IE policies followed during the first fifteen years of independence were primarily based on the ability of IEs to serve as an integral part of the overall industrialization process by strengthening the industrial base. Just as this approach pre-empted the decision to place IEs in less developed regions, another policy measure, the decision to set up Free Trade Zones[37] (FTZs), enacted to help to accelerate growth via the export sector, further biased the establishment of IEs in areas where agglomeration economies existed. This piece of legislation[38], initially led to the designation of FTZs in three major areas, Penang, Melaka and the Klang Valley (Table 3.6). By 1977, ten FTZs had been established (all located in more developed areas) and accounted for about 10 per cent of the total developed IE area[39]. These IEs also played an important role with respect to the above-mentioned electronic industry incentives, as two of them (Bayan Lepas and Sungei Way), due to their close proximity to airport facilities, were almost exclusively reserved for such companies. In light of the success Malaysia has had in attracting investors into this industry – the exports of this industry (which includes electrical machinery and components as well as electronic products) increased from 1970-80 by 6,000 per cent (as opposed to only 960 per cent for total manufactured exports) and accounted for over one half of manufactured exports by 1980 – it would be justifiable to assume that the industrialization process (i.e. new employment opportunities and increased income), in the more developed areas was given an additional impetus. The extent to which backward (or forward) linkages developed (thus integrating the FTZ into the local economy and even into the less developed areas) must, however, be left open for the moment[40].

TABLE 3.6
Industrial Estates in Existence in West Malaysia as of 31.12.1980

Region/State/ Industrial Estate[a]	Year Estab-lished (1)	Size (acres)[b] Total Plan-ned (2)	Devel-oped to Date (3)	Still Unsold (*=100% full) (4)	Costs/sq.Ft. (M$) 1973[c] (5)	1980 (6)	Quitrent/Acre Years (M$)[b] 1973[c] (7)	1980 (8)	Length of Lease in Years (Option) (9)
Northern states									
Kelantan (462.9)									
Pengkalan Chepa I	1974	24	24	*	.60	.60	218	250	66
Pengkalan Chepa II	1979	800	243	213	-	1.00-1.50	-	250	66
Jeli	1979	89	89	*	-	.40	-	250	66
Tanah Merah	1979	209	170	*	-	.09	-	250	66
Trengganu (591.7)									
Jakar	1974	198	112	34	.70-1.00	.95	218	220	60
Gong Badak	1975	237	237	114	.40	.75	218	220	60
Kuala Ibai	1979	146	146	91	1.50	1.50	-	220	60
Perlis } (665.4) Kedah									
Mergong	1972	166	166	*	1.00	.50-2.20	260	217.8	60 (39)
Bakar Arang	1973	520	358	38	1.00	.80-1.00	260	217.8	60 (39)
Kuala Kedah	1973	46	46	10[d]	-	.40	-	217.8	60 (39)
Tikam Batu	1973	90	90	*	.48	.60-.70	260	217.8	60 (39)
Kulim	1977	430	29	*	-	.80-1.00	-	217.8	60 (39)
Mergong Barrage	1979	45	29	*	-	2.20	-	217.8	60 (39)
Southern states									
Melaka (798.3)									
Ayer Keroh	1972	253	253	13	.85	1.00	174	161	99
Alor Gajah	1973	100	40	3	.85	1.00	174	179	99
Batu Berendam FTZ	1973	52	33	2	.85	1.20	174	176	99
Tanjong Kling	1973	150	150	82	-	1.00	-	179	99
Tanjong Kling FTZ	1973	20	90	*	.85	.85	174	176	99
Bukit Rambai	1974	97	50	14	-	.85	-	179	99
Merlimau	1974	180	80	53	-	.85	-	179	99
Johor (900.4)									
Larkin and Tampoi	1962	413	413	*	.40	.40	196	196	60
Tangjong Agas	1972	241	112	24	.60-1.00	.80	200-400[e]	200-400[e]	60
Tongkang Pecah	1972	38	38	*	.60-1.00	.80	200-400[e]	200-400[e]	60
Pasir Gudang	1973	2,294	1,179	153	1.00-1.20	1.50	200-400[e]	200-400[e]	60
Senai FTZ	1977	100	90	54	-	1.00-1.50	-	200-400[e]	60
Segamat	1979	98	98	21	-	-	-	200-400	60
Parit Raja	1980	93	15	15	-	-	-	200-400	60
Bandar Tenggara	1980	287	179	75	-	-	-	200-400	60 (30)
Bandar Penawar	1980	75	6	6	-	-	-	200-400	60 (30)
Pahang (975.2)									
Peramu	1973	253	253	184	.60	.90	218	220	66
Semambu	1973	510	510	235	1.20	2.00	218	220	66
Songsang	1974	154	154	17	.60	1.20	218	220	66
Maran	1974	35	35	6	.40	1.20	218	220	66
Jerantut	1977	112	112	77	-	.60	-	880	66
Gebeng	1979	1,700	700	563	-	-	-	220	66
Mu'adzam	1980	200	65	28	-	-	-	224	99

(continued)

TABLE 3.6 (continued)

Region/State/ Industrial Estate[a]	Year Estab-lished (1)	Size (acres)[b] Total Plan-ned (2)	Devel-oped to Date (3)	Still Unsold (*=100% full) (4)	Costs/sq.Ft. (M$) 1973[c] (5)	1980 (6)	Quitrent/Acre Years (M$)[b] 1973[c] (7)	1980 (8)	Length of Lease in Years (Option) (9)
Western states									
Negeri Sembilan (979.4)									
Senawang	1966	330	330	*	.50	.50	800	500	99
Kampong Dioh	1974	57	57	*	.70	.70	800	500	90
Chengkau	1980	110	110	14	-	-	-	-	-
Gadut	1980	120	120	*	-	-	-	-	-
Simpang Pertang	1980	50	50	26	-	-	-	-	-
Perak (981.1)									
Tasek	1962	369	369	*	.50	.35-50[f]	120	120[f]	99
Kamunting	1968	808	586	208	.25	.001[f]	327	30[f]	99
Jelapang	1972	92	92	*	.65	.54-.60	849	940	60
Kuala Kangsar	1973	124	124	34	.30	1.00	372	329	60
Parit Buntar	1973	200	60	8	.30	1.00	90	300	60
Tupai	1977	98	98	*	-	.66-1.00	-	450	60
Penang (987.2)									
Mak Mandin	1962	285	185	1	.80	1.20	695	695	60
Bayan Lepas FTZ	1971	304	263	103	1.30	1.60-2.00	870	870	60
Prai	1971	1,659	623	144	.80	1.20-1.70	695	695	60
Prai FTZ	1972	416	303	90	1.00	1.40	870	870	60
Prai Wharves FTZ	1972	42	38	-	-	2.00[h]	-	-	60
Pulau Jerejak FTZ	1972	406	20	-[g]	-[h]	-	870	870	60
Seberang Jaya	1973	199	62	*[i]	1.00	1.40-1.60	695	-	-
Bayan Lepas	1974	128	30	2	-	1.40	-	895	60
Selangor (1616.5)									
Petaling Jaya	1958	770	770	*	1.60	2.00	2,091	3,136	99
Shah Alam	1968	1,362	1,362	*	1.00	2.00-2.50	1,307	785	99
Pandamaran	1972	172	172	*	1.50	1.50-2.00	1,960	2,345	99
Sungei Way/Subang FTZ	1972	141	141	*	1.50	2.00-3.00	1,960	2,681	99
Ampang/Ulu Klang FTZ	1974	50	50	*	1.50	1.50	1,960	2,010	99
Batu Caves FTZ	1974	142	142	*	-	1.50-2.00	-	2,681	99
Tolok Panglima Garang	1974	49	49	6	-	1.50	-	402	99
Ampang/Ulu Klang	1975	60	60	*	-	2.00	-	4,021	99
Telok Panglima Garang	1975	65	65	44	1.50	1.50	1,960	402	99
Selat Klang Utara	1976	1,654	545	202	-	2.50	-	785	99
Setapak	1976	170	145	*	-	2.00-2.50	-	4,021	99
Bangi	1979	387	70	38	-	-	-	3,351	99
Bukit Ragai	1979	351	149	*	-	-	-	804	99

Sources: Col. 1: FIDA (Annual Report, 1972 ff.); Wheelwright (1965); Courtenay (1972); Ooi (1976); and the SEDC publications. Cols. 2-4, 6, 8, 9: FIDA (Position of Existing IEs, 1978). Cols. 5, 7: FIDA (Annual Report, 1973 f.)

[a]Per capita income 1970 in brackets.

[b]Rounded off the nearest acre or M$.

[c]Most of the data from 1973 (even if estate established later); in some few cases, however, 1974 data used.

[d]Lots are unfilled land; investors must fill own land.

[e]200 for light industries, 300 for medium, and 400 for heavy.

[f]Undeveloped land.

[g]265 acres undeveloped land for sale.

[h]Negotiable.

[i]Land sales frozen.

TABLE 3.7
Locational Aspects of Malaysian Industrial Estates

Region/State/ Industrial Estate[a]	Distance[b] to			Population[c] in			Transportation Facilities[d]		
	Next Large Town (1)	State Capital (2)	Kuala Lumpur (3)	Town (4)	Next Large Town (5)	District (6)	Rail (7)	Major Air-port[e] (8)	Major Har-bour[f] (9)
Northern states									
Kelantan (686.3)									
Pengkalan Chepa I	6	6	414	-	55.1	208.1	20	408	433
Pengkalan Chepa II	6	6	414	-	55.1	208.1	20	408	433
Jeli	31	42	366	-	7.0	57.4	22	385	366
Tanah Merah	10	25	379	-	55.1	208.1	x	398	379
Trengganu (405.5)									
Jakar	-	90	205	-	12.5	44.9	75	205	230
Gong Badak	11	11	305	-	53.3	173.5	110	305	330
Kuala Ibai	5	5	311	-	53.3	173.5	40	311	330
Perlis (121.0)									
Kedah (954.7)									
Mergong	2	2	297	-	66.3	302.3	x	70	60
Bakar Arang	2	45	250	-	36.0	160.1	x	33	23
Kuala Kedah	6	6	301	4.6	66.3	302.3	6	75	65
Tikam Batu	8	50	245	.6	36.0	160.1	x	30	20
Kulim	4	65	232	-	18.5	88.1	12	26	16
Mergong Barrage	3	3	298	-	66.3	302.3	3	45	58
Southern states									
Melaka (404.1)									
Ayer Keroh	5	8	95	-	14.4	204.8	31	95	116
Alor Gajah	14	14	76	2.2	87.2	114.5	10	76	97
Batu Berendam FTZ	3	3	92	.9	87.2	204.8	26	92	112
Tanjong Kling	10	10	100	2.2	87.2	204.8	40	100	119
Tanjong Kling FTZ	10	8	98	2.2	87.2	204.8	40	98	118
Bukit Rambai	7	7	97	.5	87.2	204.8	32	97	117
Merlimau	14	14	104	.9	87.2	84.8	39	104	125
Johor (1277.0)									
Larkin and Tampoi	5	5	227	-	136.2	271.9	2	227	23
Tangjong Agas	1	109	119	-	61.2	279.2	43	119	127
Tongkang Pecah	3	80	147	2.3	53.3	249.7	10	147	98
Pasir Gudang	4	18	245	-[g]	2.2	271.9	14	245	35
Senai FTZ	3	18	210	-	6.6	271.9	2	210	36
Segamat	3	103	124	-	17.8	126.4	3	124	130
Parit Raja	3	77	150	-	53.1	249.9	19	150	74
Bandar Tenggara	14	40	187	-	11.8	271.4	14	187	40
Bandar Penawar	20	60	287	-	8.7	61.4	40	287	31
Pahang (504.9)									
Peramu	2	24	190	-	4.7	70.3	77	190	218
Semambu	3	3	167	-	43.4	96.9	84	167	191
Songsang	5	80	86	-	6.1	119.7	x	86	111
Maran	30	50	120	1.2	6.1	70.3	33	120	156
Jerantut	-	90	121	-	4.4	36.8	x	121	147
Gebeng	18	18	188	-	43.3	96.9	40	207	188
Mu'adzam	12	80	90	-	43.3	96.9	38	109	90

(continued)

TABLE 3.7 (continued)

Region/State/ Industrial Estate[a]	Distance[b] to: Next Large Town (1)	State Capital (2)	Kuala Lumpur (3)	Population[c] in: Town (4)	Next Large Town (5)	District (6)	Transportation Facilities[d]: Rail (7)	Major Airport[e] (8)	Major Harbour[f] (9)
Western states									
Negeri Sembilan (481.5)									
Senawang	4	4	44	-	80.9	168.9	x	44	66
Kampong Dioh	0	25	67	-	12.5	115.4	23	67	89
Chengkau	3	15	56	-	1.7	39.7	3	56	75
Gadut	7	7	48	-	79.9	167.9	x	48	67
Simpang Pertang	18	43	84	-	12.5	114.8	26	84	113
Perak (1569.2)									
Tasek	4	4	137	-	248.0	483.0	x	112	102
Kamunting	2	53	189	-	54.6	221.1	x	66	56
Jelapang	2	2	139	7.1	248.0	483.0	x	110	110
Kuala Kangsar	1	30	166	-	15.3	188.7	x	71	61
Parit Buntar	1	75	214	-	5.8	153.6	x	35	25
Tupai	1	50	189	-	54.6	221.1	x	66	56
Penang (775.4)									
Mak Mandin	2	2	237	-	61.2	161.3	x	16	x
Bayan Lepas FTZ	10	10	247	-[g]	269.2	60.6	10	x	10
Prai	3	3	237	-	61.2	117.7	x	14	x
Prai FTZ	3	3	237	-	61.2	117.7	x	13	x
Prai Wharves FTZ	3	3	237	-	61.2	111.7	x	12	x
Pulau Jerejak FTZ	3	3	246	-	1.0	60.6	8	5	8
Seberang Jaya	3	3	240	-	61.2	161.6	x	19	11
Bayan Lepas	9	9	246	.4	269.2	60.6	9	x	9
Selangor (1630.7)									
Petaling Jaya	-	8	8	93.4	451.8	876.4	x	8	20
Shah Alam	7	15	15	2.9	113.6	233.7	x	15	12
Pandamaran	5	25	25	-	113.6	233.7	5	25	5
Sungei Way/Subang FTZ	12	12	12	7.8	451.8	233.7	12	12	22
Ampang/Ulu Klang FTZ	5	5	5	11.1	451.8	876.4	5	6	31
Batu Caves FTZ	5	6	6	2.5	451.8	876.4	6	5	31
Telok Panglima Garang	10	34	34	.8	113.6	107.2	16	34	16
Ampang/Ulu Klang	5	5	5	11.1	451.8	876.4	5	6	31
Telok Panglima Garang	10	34	34	.8	113.6	107.2	16	34	16
Selat Klang Utara	6	25	25	-	113.6	233.7	x	25	x
Setapak	5	5	5	-	451.8	876.4	x	5	30
Bangi	3	18	18	2.0	22.5	96.3	x	22	29
Bukit Ragai	4	24	24	-	113.3	232.9	4	24	4

Sources: Cols. 1-3, 7-9: SEDC publications and own estimates. Cols. 4-6: Dept. of Statistics (A Preliminary Report, 1971).

[a] Numbers in brackets after states represent population in 1970 in '000s.

[b] Own estimates of highway distance in miles; Kuala Lumpur is taken as Selangor state capital.

[c] 1970 population.

[d] All estates located on highways; distances in miles; x means either directly in estate or close by.

[e] Penang airport for Kedah, Perak, and Penang; Kuala Lumpur for Trengganu, Kelantan, Pahang, Melaka, Selangor and Negeri Sembilan; Butterworth (Penang) for Kedah, Perak and Penang; Singapore for Johor.

[f] Pasir Gudang has a harbour recently put into use, but cannot be considered to be a major harbour.

[g] Located at airport.

Along with the more recent policy of establishing IEs in less developed areas, all the time there seems to have been a policy of differentiating prices between the various regions: both with respect to the development premium (cost/sq. ft) as well as the quitrent (cost/acre/year) sizeable differentials do exist. For example, the development premium in Ampang/Ulu Klang (Selangor) is 400 per cent higher and the quitrent almost 1,100 per cent higher than in Gong Badak (Trengganu, see Table 3.6). Granted, land prices differ considerably between the developed and the less developed regions and this might well account for most (or at least a sizeable share) of the difference in the quitrents, but it is difficult to explain the development premium differentials (assuming the input prices to be similar)[41] unless some attempt was being made to assist the less developed regions.

Analogous to the regionally differentiated cost structures in the IEs, the increase in such costs also seems to have followed a pattern whereby the increases both in the development costs as well as in the quitrent were the greatest in the more developed areas (Table 3.8). While it is not known to what extent these changes actually do reflect an attempt to steer the demand for lots in IEs (during this period of time) away from the more developed to the less developed regions (rather than reflecting differing regional price trends), there at least seems to have been a tendency within regions (e.g. Selangor) to direct demand away from those estates near capacity to those with lower occupancy rates. In other words, the price differentials between the IEs in the various states could very well reflect explicit policy measures, differences/changes in regional (land) costs and a reaction to the demand situation (as expressed by occupancy rates) within given states[42].

Aside from the rental and development costs, the expressed policies followed with respect to the other necessary parts of an industrial estate package appear to be unchanged from the initial period. In reality, however, the rapid growth in the number of IEs in the less developed regions has meant, as mentioned above, that the infrastructure differences have also become reflected to a greater degree in the facilities offered by the IEs. This applies in particular to the utilities[43], as not only are there certain supply constraints (amount of electricity available and/or number of telephone or telex lines) but also (to some extent as a result thereof) cost differences would seem to put the LDRs at a disadvantage. As can be seen in the summary of the electricity and water rates (Tables A5, A6), the East Coast rates for water and electric power (under certain conditions) are considerably higher than on

TABLE 3.8
Development and Occupancy Indicators and Changes in Development Costs and Quitrents for Industrial Estates, West Malaysia, 1973-1980[a]/percentages

Region/State Industrial Estate	Planned Acres already Developed	Developed Acres already Occupied (* = 100%)	Change[b] in Development Costs		Quitrents	
			1973-1977	1977-1980	1973-1977	1977-1980
Northern states						
Kelantan						
Pengkalan Chepa I	100.0	*	.0	.0	14.7	.0
Pengkalan Chepa II	30.4	12.3	-	.0	-	.0
Jeli	100.0	*	-	.0	-	.0
Tanah Merah	81.3	*	-	.0	-	.0
Trengganu						
Jakar	56.6	69.6	5.3	87.5	.0	.0
Gong Badak	100.0	51.9	.0	6.1	.9	.9
Kuala Ibai	100.0	37.7	-	114.3	-	.0
Perlis	-	-	-	-	-	-
Kedah						
Mergong	100.0	*	-25.0	86.7	-16.2	-.1
Bakar Arang	68.8	89.4	63.6	20.0	-16.2	-.1
Kuala Kedah	100.0	78.3	-	.0	-	-.1
Tikam Batu	100.0	*	35.4	.0	-16.2	-.1
Kulim	6.7	*	-	.0	-	-.1
Mergong Barrage	64.4	*	-	.0	-	.0
Southern states						
Melaka						
Ayer Keroh	100.0	94.9	.0	17.6	1.1	-8.5
Alor Gajah	40.0	92.5	.0	17.6	1.1	1.7
Batu Berendam FTZ	63.5	93.9	.0	41.2	1.1	.0
Tanjong Kling	100.0	46.1	-	17.6	-	1.7
Tanjong Kling FTZ	100.0	*	.0	.0	1.1	.0
Bukit Rambai	51.5	98.0	-	.0	-	1.7
Merlimau	44.4	33.8	-	.0	-	1.7
Johor						
Larkin and Tampoi	100.0	*	.0	.0	.0	.0
Tangjong Agas	46.5	78.6	.0	137.5	.0	.0
Tongkang Pecah	100.0	*	.0	68.8	.0	.0
Pasir Gudang	51.4	87.0	36.4	200.0	.0	.0
Senai FTZ	90.0	40.0	-	40.0	-	.0
Segamat	100.0	78.6	-	87.5	-	.0
Parit Raja	16.1	0.0	-	-	-	-
Bandar Tenggara	62.4	58.1	-	-	-	-
Bandar Penawar	8.0	0.0	-	-	-	-
Pahang						
Peramu	100.0	75.9	25.0	20.0	.9	.0
Semambu	100.0	79.4	16.7	42.9	.9	.0
Songsang	100.0	89.0	50.0	33.3	.9	.0
Maran	100.0	82.9	50.0	100.0	.9	.0
Jerantut	100.0	31.3	-	66.7	-	300.0
Gebeng	41.2	19.6	-	14.3	-	.0
Mu'adzam	32.5	56.9	-	-	-	-

Western states						
Negeri Sembilan						
Senawang	100.0	*	.0	-28.6	.0	-37.5
Kampong Dioh	100.0	*	.0	.0	.0	-37.5
Chengkau	100.0	87.3	-	-	-	-
Gadut	100.0	*	-	-	-	-
Simpang Pertang	100.0	-48.0	-	-	-	-
Perak						
Tasek	100.0	*	-5.0	-10.5	.0	.0
Kamunting	72.5	35.5	-56.0	-99.1	-90.8	.0
Jelapang	100.0	*	12.3	.0	10.7	.0
Kuala Kangsar	100.0	27.4	233.3	.0	5.4	.0
Parit Buntar	30.0	13.3	233.3	.0	233.3	.0
Tupai	100.0	*	-	.0	-	.0
Penang						
Mak Mandin	64.9	99.5	50.0	25.0	.0	.0
Bayan Lepas FTZ	86.5	60.8	38.5	25.0	.0	.0
Prai	37.6	76.9	81.3	3.4	.0	.0
Prai FTZ	72.8	70.3	40.0	1.3	.0	.0
Prai Wharves FTZ	90.5	*	-	-	-	-
Pulau Jerejak FTZ	-	*	-	-	.0	.0
Seberang Jaya	-	*	50.0	-	.0	-
Bayan Lepas	23.4	99.3	-	57.1	-	.0
Selangor						
Petaling Jaya	100.0	*	25.0	20.0	25.2	19.8
Shah Alam	100.0	*	125.0	.0	-40.0	.0
Pandamaran	100.0	*	6.7	.0	16.8	2.4
Sungei Way/Subang FTZ	100.0	*	66.7	-20.0	66.8	-28.9
Ampang/Ulu Klang FTZ	100.0	*	.0	.0	.0	2.6
Batu Caves	100.0	*	-	14.3	-	17.1
Telok Panglima Garang FTZ	100.0	87.8	-	.0	-	-79.5
Ampang/Ulu Klang	100.0	*	-	50.0	-	53.6
Telok Panglima Garang	100.0	32.3	.0	16.7	.0	-79.5
Selat Klang Utara	33.0	62.9	-	.0	-	.0
Setapak	85.3	*	-	33.3	-	36.7
Bangi	18.1	45.7	-	.0	-	.0
Bukit Ragai	42.5	*	-	.0	-	.0

Source: Own calculations based on sources in Table 3.6.

[a]Most of the data from 1973 (even if estate established later); in some few cases, however, 1974 data used.

[b]Increase calculated on average of range; - means that no data available for base year.

the West Coast[44]. While it is understandable that the utility-pricing policies might be conceived so as to induce a structuring of new investments in such a way that their production activities are in accordance with the factor intensity of a given region, the above-mentioned pricing policies could very well induce unwanted negative effects in certain cases[45]. This would be the case, for instance, if natural resource intensive industries, which correspond to the comparative advantage of the LDR, were energy intensive[46].

NEW ECONOMIC POLICIES AND THE BUMIPUTRA

The above overview of measures influencing the regional spread of industrialization in Malaysia would be incomplete if it did not include the intensified efforts to achieve a more even ethnic balance. That is, the economic position of the indigenous population, although continuously improving throughout the 1960s, was, relative to the other ethnic groups (Chinese and Indians), still poor and served to kindle the racial riots in 1969. The problem, expressed for instance by income or wealth differentials, was considerably aggravated by a growing mass of urban unemployment, being fed by a flow of workers from the rural areas where a lack of (suitable) job opportunities prevailed. While the government was not unaware of the problem up to this point, in the period prior to 1969 the formulation of a programme to increase Malay participation in commerce and industry was conceptually weak and its implementation half-hearted. The racial riots of May 1969 were no doubt an ugly reminder of what could happen if the consequences were ignored, and since then there has been much rethinking (Lim, 1973, pp. 210f.).

This process of rethinking culminated in the wide-sweeping New Economic Policy (NEP) put forth in 1971 in the Second Malaysia Plan. This policy incorporated 'the two-pronged objective of eradicating poverty, irrespective of race, and restructuring Malaysian society to reduce and eventually eliminate the identification of race with economic function' (Malaysia Plan, 1971, p. v.). One of the important targets set in the Second Malaysia Plan was that at least 30 per cent of the total commercial and industrial activities should have participation of Malays and other indigenous people in terms of ownership within two decades (ibid., p. 158). In order to effect the rapid development of a Malay entrepreneurial class necessary to achieve this goal, the following (interrelated) steps, along with increased envolvement of the public sector, were to be taken:

1. measures to promote the development of the necessary skills and attitudes among the indigenous population;

2. measures to promote Malay entrepreneurship and to assist in procuring financing and suitable locations;

3. the formulation and implementation of measures to nurture balanced development between existing urban areas and new growth centers;

4. the formulation and vigorous implementation of rural industrialization policies;

5. the enlistment of non-Malay and foreign assistance in all facets of promoting the economic well-being of the indigenous population.

These policies were followed with a great deal of determination throughout the Second Malaysia Plan, and in the Third (1976) and Fourth (1981) Malaysia Plans they have been expanded to form the foundation for an enlarged effort to ensure that the poor obtain increasing opportunities to improve their income and quality of life and that the current economic imbalances between racial groups and regions in the country are reduced as a result of the growth of the economy. To achieve this goal, an increasing share of total development expenditure was to be directed to the task of redressing poverty in both the rural and urban areas of the country irrespective of race as well as for narrowing current economic differentials among the major racial groups in the population. Specific poverty redressal projects were also to aim at increasing the participation of the Malays and other indigenous people in the modern sectors of the economy (Malaysia Plan, 1976, p. 39). In implementing the necessary measures, agricultural development was to stress the opening up and settling of new lands and concomitantly industrial and urban development was to provide opportunities for the indigenous population to diversify its economic structure[47].

In light of these *bumiputra* policies[48], the rapid pace with which IEs were set up can be better understood. Even the establishment of industries in the less developed regions (particularly small-scale industries) was fostered and backed up by technical and financial support from institutions specifically established for such purposes. The MIDF, for instance, whose initial policies had been criticized for favouring those ventures which actually needed no support (see p. 64), acted not only more in accordance with its principles, but also seems to have incorporated a regional accent into its policies. However, possibly of greater importance in this respect was the Perkadanan Nasional Berhad (PERNAS)[49] explicitly set up in 1969 (after the riots) as a public corporation to advance the economic status of the *bumiputra*; a goal which is expressly stated as not running counter to the profit-making objectives of the organization[50]. Complementing the more macro-oriented goals of PERNAS, the Urban Development Authority (UDA, 1971) aimed at smoothing the difficulties for *bumiputra* wanting to establish businesses (mainly) in urban areas by providing housing, services, real estate and business structures via sale, leasing and/or financial assistance. The UDA also participates in ventures with *bumiputra* and non-*bumiputra*. Another institution mainly active in rural areas, the Council of Trust for the Indigenous People (Majlis Amanah Ra'ayat-MARA)[51] has been involved in a wide range of projects, many of which concentrate on upgrading the level of human capital of the *bumiputra* (e.g. training programmes, technical schools, universities), while others provide services (similar to those offered by UDA)[52].

Furthermore, the introduction of the NEP and the measures therein was followed by the enactment of a 5 per cent excess profit tax (in 1974)[53] and the Industrial Coordination Act (ICA, 1975, effective on 1 May 1976)[54]. These taken together began to create the impression that Malaysia's relatively basic adherence to the principle of a free and open market economy was in the process of being abandoned. While every effort was made to soothe both foreign and domestic investors, investment was nonetheless negatively influenced, as evidenced for instance by the drop in the number of approved projects since 1974. Despite the fact that part of this drop can be attributed to the worldwide slowdown in economic growth rates since 1974, the negative impact of these policy measures is generally agreed upon[55]. The government which had obviously underestimated the degree of disgruntlement, subsequently saw the need to amend some provisions of the act (Malaysian Industrial Digest, Vol. 10, 1977, No. 3, pp. 6 ff. and 11). Further changes to satisfy the business community[56] have been made since[57].

While it might surely be worthwhile within the context of this study to distil the specific regional implications out of these (and other) organizations (primarily set up to encourage and support *bumiputra* activities) and then analyse their regional impact, – it could well reveal how deep government policies have permeated all strata of the economy and unearth thereby inefficiencies in the allocation of scarce resources – unfortunately the unavailability of data prevent this from being done in an adequate quantitative manner. The ramifications of this aspect will thus be dealt with at best in a qualitative manner, leaving a more empirical analysis to other authors.

CONCLUDING REMARKS

In rounding out this policy overview the coordination between the various organizations mentioned above and their goals, as well as the difficulties emanating from rivalries between them, should be mentioned as a factor influencing regional industrialization. While the initial organizational structure seemed to be on the right track with the establishment of MIDA and particularly after its ensuing reorganization in 1969, when the Capital Investment Committee (CIC)[58] was created to simplify the administrative processing of investment requests, many of the organizations born out of the New Economic Policy paralleled MIDA. As Esman points out, this could lead to complications, as, for instance, between MIDA and MARA, where there were no agreed principles or procedures to delineate MARA's activities on behalf of the Malays from MIDA's on behalf of the entire economy, yet MARA was in a position to veto pioneer certificates for non-Malay investors[59] even when it did not intend to enter the field. Furthermore, MARA had ambitious plans to participate in joint ventures with foreign firms and even to operate industries at a time when it was without doubt lacking sufficient trained and qualified personnel (Esman, 1972, pp. 234 ff.). Obviously, the failure to agree properly on priorities and delineate between fiefs weakened the national industrial development effort.

A further stratification of the bureaucratic process was reflected in the gradual founding of State Economic Development Corporations (SEDC)[60] in the late 1960s and early 1970s. During the latter period, regional offices of MIDA[61] were also established in a number of mainly less developed regions as the authority became more actively involved in selling its services and propagating investment opportunities. Whereas all these organizations were interlinked through numerous committees and information channels, the various vested interests nonetheless led to bureaucratic dis-economies[62] and red-tape entanglements. Thus it is not surprising that after investment activity slowed down in recent years, the government increased its efforts to accelerate the approval process and implemented in 1978 a further streamlining of the 'Package Deal' for investors, including the formation of the Central Unit in MIDA, comprising representatives from various government departments at one central location (Jan, 1978, p. 11). Whether the arrangement can solve the problem is still an open question[63]. An answer to this question is all the more crucial with respect to the dispersal of industries, since, for instance the formation of a Central Unit in MIDA in Kuala Lumpur obviously is of limited direct help to an investor in Kota Bahru (Kelantan). Only if the regional offices of MIDA are imparted with the same authority would such an arrangement not turn out to counter the goal of spreading the industrialization process more equally among all regions.

One final point should be made with regard to all the industrialization policies in West Malaysia, namely that the policies as defined by their legal framework were often extended in their implementation by the respective authorities. Legally such an extension was entirely within the jurisdiction of the authority in question (usually the Ministry of Trade and Industry), as all pieces of legislation contained clauses which endowed the authorities with a considerable degree of latitude. A case in point would be where an industry were granted pioneer status under the condition, *inter alia,* that it was considered expedient with respect to the public interest. In recent years there has been reason to believe that the authorities have been giving this clause a regional interpretation[64]. That is, a company might not be granted pioneer status in Penang, but would obtain pioneer status if it were to be located in Kelantan. This might tend to be more relevant to companies producing primarily for the domestic market than for foreign companies. Thus the various comments made earlier with respect to the interpretation of the possible regional impact of certain policies must also be viewed as embodying such implicit, and hard to define, aspects[65].

In summarizing the above overview and interpretation of industrialization policies in Malaysia and their regional impact it perhaps suffices to note that the policies have exhibited a noticeable shift during the last decade towards an intensified effort (and intensification of efforts) to decrease regional development differentials. Furthermore, it can be stated that, although not without some erraticism and incongruencies, they can be construed as generally thrusting on two (not entirely independent) levels (see Table 3.9 for a summary of the important policies), whereby permeating the entire policy spectrum since the 1960s has been the attempt to improve the economic well-being of the *bumiputra.* First of all, there was the attempt to depolarize the growth of economic activity from the parameters (growth centres) given upon becoming an independent nation in 1957, as well as after the break with Singapore in 1965, by setting up new growth centres. This initially encompassed a basic improvement in the social infrastructure of the less developed regions, but later was

TABLE 3.9
Regional, General[a] and Export Investment Incentives for Manufacturing in Malaysia as of 1981 - A Summary of Selected Measures

Incentive Name	Type of Incentive	Length and Conditions of Incentive	Impact of Other Incentives: Devel.Area	Impact of Other Incentives: Prior.Prod.	Impact of Other Incentives: Malay.Content	Special Treatment of: Dividends	Special Treatment of: Depreciation	Special Treatment of: Losses	Other Features Comments/Conditions
<u>Regional</u> <u>Locational</u> Incentive		Exemption based either on amount of capital investment or number of employees as follows: <u>Capital:</u> <$250,000 5 years $250,000-$499,999 6 years $500,000-$999,999 7 years >$999,999 8 years <u>Employees:</u> < 100 employees 5 years 101-200 employees 6 years 201-350 employees 7 years > 350 employees 8 years		One additional year exemption		Direct share-holders and shareholders of holding companies exempted	Depreciation of capital assets com-mences upon termination of incentives	Losses dur-ing exemption period can be offset in post-incentive period	Areas for which incen-tive applies: Kedah (except Kuala Muda District) Pahang (except Kuantan (District) Kelantan Trengganu Perlis Sabah Sarawak Johor Tenggara area. Have right to deduct qua-lified overseas promotion expenditures in post-in-centive period
Development Area	Tax exemption[b]	For investments located in de-signated areas, one year tax exemption	-	-	-				Areas for which incentive applies: <u>State</u> / <u>IEs</u> Kedah / Bayan Lepas[c] Kelantan / Kamunting Melaka / Senawang Pahang / Sungai Way[c] Perlis / Tanjung Ayas Sabah / Ulu Klang[c] Sarawak Trengganu
<u>General</u> <u>Pioneer</u> Industry		Exemption based on amount of capital investment as follows: <$250,000 2 years $250,000-499,999 3 years $500,000-999,999 4 years >$999,999 5 years		One additional year exemption					Have right to deduct qua-lified overseas promotion expenditures in post-in-centive period
Labour Utilization Relief		Exemption based on number of employees as follows: 51-100 employees 2 years 101-200 employees 3 years 201-350 employees 4 years >350 employees 5 years							

(continued)

TABLE 3.9 (continued)

Incentive Name	Type of Incentive	Length and Conditions of Incentive	Impact of Other Incentives: Devel.Area	Prior.Prod.	Malay.Content	Special Treatment of: Dividends	Depreciation	Losses	Other Features Comments/Conditions
Increased Capital Allowances	Accelerated depreciation	For existing companies not qualifying for other incentives an accelerated first year depreciation of 40% on plant capital expenditure allowed (3% on newly constructed buildings and 1 1/2 times normal rate on purchased buildings) for modernization	One year exemption			-	-	-	
Investment Tax Credit	Tax credit	Tax credit based on 25% of capital investment up to a period of maximum 5 years	5% additional credit			Direct shareholders exempted to extent that dividends paid out of tax credit	-	If tax credit exceeds actual taxes, credit can be carried over until fully utilized	-
Priority Product	Tax exemption[b]	For products/industries designated as 'priority' one year tax exemption	-	-	-	Direct shareholders and shareholders of holding companies exempted	Depreciation of capital assets commences upon termination of incentives	Losses during exemption period can be offset in post-incentive period	-
Malaysian Content		For products incorporating at least 50% raw materials and/or parts made in Malaysia (excluding wages, etc.)							
<u>Export</u> Export Allowance	Export allowance	The amount of the allowance is 2% of ex-factory value of export sales plus 10% of difference between ex-factory export sales in given and base year. New exporters receive full 12%.	One year exemption		If 50% allowance=8%	-	-	-	Does not apply to primary commodities (i.e. only manufactured products) and non-resident companies
Accelerated Depreciation Allowance	Accelerated depreciation	For companies, whose exports amount to at least 20% of sales (in value terms) an accelerated depreciation allowance of 40% for modernizing production facilities (or setting up new plant) is available.	One year exemption			-	-	-	Pesident companies only. Normal first year depreciation = 20%.
Deduction for Promotions of Exports	Tax bill reduction	For expenses incurred overseas for promoting exports (e.g. advertising, market research, public relations, expenses for exhibits ... etc.)	-	-	-	-	-	-	PI, LI and LUR recipients can deduct such expenses after tax relief period.

[a]Some of these (and other measures) are considered as having an implicit regional impact.

[b]Tax exempted: Income Tax (40 per cent) and Development Tax (5 per cent).

[c]FTZ.

expanded to include the establishment of industrial estates and new towns, in addition to the massive development of wide-ranging regional development areas (e.g. Pahang Tenggara)[66]. Secondly, explicit investment incentives were granted to investments made in selected development areas. While these were minor to begin with, they have been noticeably widened during the last decade.

1 With regards to earlier economic growth and policies (i.e. before the Second World War) in Malaya, Rudner (1972, p. 63) points out that it would be a mistake to attribute it solely to the initiative and enterprise of private individuals and firms acting independently of government. On the other hand, colonial government policy was compartmentalized and uncoordinated, and macro-level policies were non-existent, so that whatever economic growth did occur involved unplanned and largely uneven development.

2 The Working Party (appointed in May 1956) was given the task of aiding the government in formulating an industrial development policy. The Working Party did not conceive of its task as including specific and detailed recommendations, but rather felt it should lay down the broad lines on which incentives to promote the establishment of industries should be granted.

3 For a brief review of the schemes, see Report (1957, Appendix X).

4 IBRD (1955, pp. 436ff.). The Mission was of a different opinion and put a much larger stress on protective measures (pp. 428-30) than the Working Party did.

5 The Mission felt that new industries should grow mostly out of the wide range of existing enterprises. Special tax concessions to new industries would only complicate the situation since they involved invidious comparisons of a very difficult and unnecessary kind. Generous depreciation allowances were seen as the appropriate way to favour industries and enterprises that were developing most rapidly in terms of the acquisition of capital assets. Losses over a six-year period in the past could be used to offset current profits in figuring out taxable income. Initial depreciation allowances were 10 per cent on buildings and 20 per cent on other capital expenditure; thereafter 2 per cent for buildings and 5 to 20 per cent for other capital equipment.

6 In the PIO, as enacted in 1958, pioneer status (PSD) was granted (pioneer certificate) to companies fulfilling certain conditions with respect to the given or future production/market of a given product (see Appendix), thereby allowing such companies to be exempted from paying (income) tax on profits once production began. The length of time for which a company would receive the tax holiday depended on the amount of the initial fixed capital expenditure; it ranged from 2 to 5 years. Although expenditures for capital equipment could not be treated in accordance with the rules governing capital consumption allowances (sections 16-22 of the 1947 Income Tax Law) during the tax holiday, they could be fully depreciated (at an accelerated rate) beginning immediately after the tax holiday expired.

7 Since the Federation of Malaya (consisting of those states in the Malay Peninsula) had been united in the meantime (1963) with Singapore, Sabah and Sarawak to form the Federation of Malaysia, the Pioneer Ordinance of all four political entities had to be amended. Singapore withdrew from the Federation in 1965, after which the Federation comprised West Malaysia, Sabah and Sarawak.

8 The 1965 revision also contained a correction of the provision which granted tax exemption on dividends only to the shareholders directly receiving such payments from a pioneer company. Such a limitation obviously put holding companies at a disadvantage, since the dividends they received from pioneer companies (during the tax holiday) could not be passed on without having them subjected to taxation.

9 See Draft Development Plan (Malaysia Plan, 1950, p. 154) and IBRD (1955, p. 437). The World Bank Mission pointed out that such policies had already been successfuly practised in Singapore since the end of the Second World War.

10 In that year, in the mushrooming Klang Valley between Kuala Lumpur and Port Klang (Swettenham, as it was then called), the new town of Petaling Jaya, with specific residential, commercial and industrial areas, was inaugurated. Although Petaling Jaya was originally planned to house 70,000 persons, the population in 1970 was 93,000 and since then it has passed considerably beyond the 100,000 mark.

11 The Petaling Jaya Authority was incorporated into the Selangor Development Council in 1964.

12 The various sources used in compiling Table 3.3 were by no means in agreement. While every attempt was made to apply the same criteria to figures so as to allow complete comparability, conflicting figures on year of opening, size of estate and number of employees were often impossible to reconcile. Thus, should the figures differ from reality, the author would appreciate knowing where he erred. This comment applies to similar tables in the text and Appendix.

13 Although the state of Johor as a whole is not a higher-income state as such, the area immediately adjacent to Singapore (to which it is linked via a road/rail causeway) is definitely one of the higher-income areas in Malaysia, since it has greatly profited from the spill over effects from Singapore.

14 Wheelwright (1965, p. 30) notes that the state of Perak offered a concession for settling at the Tasek IE, namely a reduction in the property tax from 21 to 6 per cent.

15 Complementary to these and beginning with the Development Fund Ordinance (1 January 1958) which specified that all appropriated money and all sums representing the proceeds of any loan raised by the Federation for the purpose of the Development Fund be paid into the Fund (Government Gazette, 1958, p. 61), the government began to attempt to make the flow of development funds more transparent. The purpose to which these funds could be applied included all forms of infrastructure as well as industrial development and the purchase of land therefor. In the period 1956-60 the government spent M$11 million on industrial site development, most of which was spent in Petaling Jaya. For the period 1961-65 (Second Malaya Plan) M$7.5 million were allocated (partly in the form of loans) to all levels of government for the same purpose (IBRD, 1963, pp. 29ff.).

16 MIDF's capital (M$25 million; raised to M$50 million in August 1962) was subscribed by both the Federal Government as well as semi-public and private domestic and foreign investors.

17 It was often mentioned that when it came down to extra demands on standardized factories or special exceptions from building codes, the authorities were almost always flexible enough.

18 Although no attempt will be made at this point to further delve into the economic ramifications of such measures, it might be added that any conclusions drawn from a comparison of the regional welfare in the case where local inputs are used for MIEL units as opposed to design and construction being carried out entirely on a local basis would be incorrect, *ceteris paribus,* if it was primarily the existence of MIEL units which prompted the decision to move into a given region. That is, without MIEL the region would not have been considered; ergo, such a comparison misses a key point.

19 To be sure, it was frankly noted in the Rueff Report (IBRD, 1963) that if the desired rate of expansion in the manufacturing sector was to be achieved, the private investor (both domestic and foreign) must be provided with more substantial and vigorous assistance and encouragement than was then available in Malaya (several agencies and government institutions were carrying out various forms of promotional activities). Thus an autonomous public industrial development agency, in which officials from all responsible institutions, and also from various regions, would be represented in order to facilitate coordination and cooperation, was suggested (IBRD, 1963, pp. 34-7).

20 MIDA was responsible for the PI processing up to the time of production, at which point the company had to report to the responsible ministry.

21 Considerable criticism was directed at the government for allegedly dragging its heels on setting up MIDA, which did not actually come into being until 4 April 1967.

22 The background to getting MIDA established, the initial difficulties encountered and the adaptation of the organization to the specific needs of the Malaysian economy is well described by its first Director, Heinz Rudolph (1970). Of particular interest are the comments made in respect to the above-mentioned ethnic differences and level of human capital. Rudolph notes that the level of qualification of the Malaysian nationals was quite high so that there was no problem in filling positions with them as opposed to foreign experts. The only difficulty in this respect was that the number of adequately trained Malays was limited, thus creating a problem in trying to fit the employment structure to the structure of the Malaysian population. An area in which Rudolph had to tread very softly was in respecting the mores and folkways of the three major ethnic groups, the integration of which was just beginning.

23 Trengganu Tengah covers an area of 1.1 million acres of which almost 300,000 acres are to be developed for agricultural purposes by 1990; 86,000 immigrants are being forecasted for an area that is to have a population of 134,000 in 1990 (Malaysia Industrial Digest, 1976, No. 2, p. 6).

24 For a detailed treatment of land development schemes see S.C. Lim (1976).

25 'The Government will continue to make every effort to alleviate poverty by providing improved facilities and opportunities for regionally disadvantaged groups. The resources needed for this effort, if they are not to be extracted at great sacrifice from the rest of the population, can only come from economic growth' (Malaysia Plan, 1965, p. 6).

26 See, for instance, Nachrichten für Außenhandel, Frankfurt a.M., 12 May 1967: 'Malaysia wartet auf ausländische Hilfe'.

27 While some sources (see, for instance, Hoffmann, 1980) state that the 5 per cent development tax (introduced in 1967) was also exempted in the Act, there is actually no explicit statement of this effect. As a matter of fact Part II of the Act is entitled 'Relief from Income Tax and Payroll Tax'. Although exemption from the Development Tax is now granted and has been for a number of years, the exact date of its inclusion remains somewhat vague; most likely it was rescinded on 1 January 1971, when the Payroll Tax was removed.

28 It was left to the prerogative of the Minister of Trade and Industry to declare a specific area in Malaysia to be a development area in which companies (but only pioneer companies) would then be able to receive one (extra) year of income tax exemption.

29 The tax reductions amounted to 15 per cent of chargeable income in Kuala Lumpur vs. 30 per cent on islands, in hill resorts and other designated areas.

30 The reason for limiting these incentives to projects approved by 31 January 1973 was not explicitly stated, but it can be assumed that this restriction was intended to force foreign investors to decide quickly to invest in Malaysia as opposed to other South-East or East Asian countries.

31 Regardless of this point, these industries were to a large extent integral parts of international companies requiring quick ties to the outside world (e.g. air transportation and telecommunications), and they would have probably settled in the agglomerated (high-income) areas anyhow.

32 The term 'development area' in the 1968 Act was not a major piece of legislation, although it was important in the sense that it for the first time explicitly recognized regional aspects. Despite its introduction in 1973, LI was not granted until 1975. Of particular interest in this amendment was the degree of prerogatory powers (flexibility) with which the Minister of Trade and Industry was equipped. It allowed him not only to specify areas, but also industries within areas, as well as the length of the tax holidays and the deadline for application thereof.

33 The dates in parentheses represent the dates on which development area incentive became effective. Other areas, such as Pulau Penang (2 April 1971) and Muar (24 May 1972) have been taken off the development area list since.

34 It would seem that the Minister of Trade and Industry uses his prerogative powers in declaring an industrial estate to be a development area in much the same way that a travel agency offers unfilled seats (on a charter flight) at a reduced price.

35 Malaysia Plan (1976, p. 205). It might be noted that whereas only a few paragraphs were dedicated to the regional issue as such in the Second Malaysia Plan, an entire chapter on it was contained in the Third Malaysia Plan.

36 In this context it is worthwhile noting that the attempt to integrate better the IEs with the hinterland is well illustrated by the types of industry to be represented in these IEs. That is, a more explicit attempt is being made to utilize the natural resource base than was the case with the IEs established earlier. See Table A7 and Spinanger (1980) Table 12.

37 Government Gazette, 30 April 1971. Act 24, Free Trade Zones Act: Goods of any nature (except those legally prohibited) can be moved into a free trade zone without payment of any customs or excise duties. Goods (excepting those otherwise so declared) brought in from Malaysia are eligible for drawback.
Any such goods moved into a FTZ must be dealt with as follows: be removed from FTZ for export or shipment to another FTZ; be stored, sold, manipulated etc. in accordance with regulations; be destroyed; be sent to other parts of Malaysia after authorization; not be consumed without permission. In 1972 exemption was extended to sales tax as well (Government Gazette, 30 September 1972, Act 146).

38 It empowered the Minister of Finance (after consultation with the state government) to declare and delineate any area to be an FTZ.

39 About 10 per cent of the employment in the manufacturing sector was also accounted for by the FTZs.

40 Zehender *et al.* (1978, pp. 204f.) note, for example, that in certain respects the IE policies in Malaysia did actually promote such linkages. For a dissenting view, see Fröbel *et al.* (1977).

41 Wage differentials, for instance, can hardly account for the differences as can be shown by the coefficient of variation for average annual earnings, in the manufacturing industry: in 1973 it amounted to only 20.75 per cent.

42 This stratified and perhaps somewhat contradictory approach to the seemingly simple problem of inducing a regionally more even level of industrialization was the result of the competency of the various authorities; that is, while the supraregional MIDA and the government could direct demand to the less developed regions, the state development corporations were responsible to a large extent for the thrust of development within a given state.

43 Notwithstanding these (and other) deficiencies, it has been pointed out that the unbureaucratic manner in which it has been attempted to master them in Malaysia has been an important, although not necessarily crucial, advantage *vis-à-vis* other Asian countries (Kapoor, 1973, pp. 91-115).

44 Whereas the West Coast basically relies on hydroelectric power, the East Coast is mainly supplied by diesel power generators, the reliability of which was to some extent a problem.

45 It is interesting to note that in Melaka an explicit attempt is made to differentiate between water usage inside and outside of industrial estates, thereby obviously aiming at directing industries to the IEs.

46 One of the probable reasons for the failure to ensure that utilities were available in the same quantity and with the same quality in all areas (or at least to an extent which did not run counter to regional industrialization policies) was the lack of coordination between the authorities responsible for

such facilities and the agencies in charge of industrialization policies (MIDA, SEDCs, Ministry of Trade and Industry, etc.).

47 The specific goal of the New Economic Policy, which had in the meantime been set for 1990, was a 30 per cent ownership of equity capital by Malays. Starting at about 2.4 per cent in 1970, the share had been increased to 7.8 per cent by 1975. Assuming that this rate of change were to be maintained up till 1990, a share of only about 25 per cent would be reached by that year. With respect to restructuring employment, greater strides seem to have been made (see Malaysia Plan, 1976, pp. 32ff.).

48 No attempt will be made in this paper to explain all of the various organizations set up to deal primarily with the promotion of *bumiputra* activities.

49 PERNAS is entirely government owned, i.e. its capital is subscribed to by the Minister of Finance, the Bank Negara Malaysia, Bank Bumiputra Malaysia Berhad and, *inter alia,* the State Economic Development Corporations. The company acts as a holding company and (at last count) was involved in 66 ventures including 8 wholly-owned subsidiaries; see 'The Intentions of Pernas' (Asian Finance, 15 August 1978). While the shares PERNAS holds in the various ventures are to be passed on to *bumiputra,* this has yet to be done, i.e. more stress has been placed on increasing the share of *bumiputra* in employment, particularly in higher positions.

50 The wide-spread activities of PERNAS have not explicitly been directed at regional diversification, but the regional aspects have not been ignored either.

51 Government Gazette (1966, Act 20). MARA replaced herewith the Rural and Industrial Development Authority (RIDA) set up in 1953.

52 Of particular interest is the participation in companies, which, after becoming going concerns, are then turned over to the respective entrepreneurs. The companies totalled ten in 1974 (employing about 3,000 people) and ranged from suppliers of raw materials for batik, to the manufacture of leather goods, starch powder, timber and plywood products, agricultural machinery and batik cloth, to name just a few.

53 Pioneer companies and those receiving other exemptions (as well as petroleum companies) were not affected by this tax. The tax was applied to chargeable income exceeding 25 per cent of shareholders' funds or M$ 200,000, whichever was greater.

54 For a summary of the ICA, see Appendix.

55 The ICA stated that all companies covered by the law have to apply for a licence, which would then be virtually automatically issued. The concern aroused about its effect, however, was not based on this but rather on what was further stated in the law, which provided the respective authority with sweeping powers, for instance, to enter and search manufacturing establishments suspected of wrongdoing. Such provisions were played down and the ICA was presented in essence as the only sensible way to avoid a haphazard development which would be of detriment not only to existing industries but also the country (Jan, 1975). Also, unhealthy competition and excess capacities would be avoided and comprehensive information for future development policies would become available for the first time.

56 See, for instance, 'ICA will be diluted further' (Asian Finance, 15 August 1978, p. 58).

57 See Ministry of Finance, Economic Report 1980/81, pp. 190-1. In the case of export-oriented industries exceptions could be made and 100 per cent foreign participation allowed. Thus it was no doubt the Chinese who were the most worried, particularly in light of the Investment Guarantee Agreements signed with a number of countries. Malaysia has investment guarantee agreements with eight countries, with seven other agreements pending.

58 The functions of the Tariff Advisory Board, which dealt with matters concerning tariff reduction, were also integrated into MIDA later on.

59 It has also been reported that industrial sites and financial assistance were often given to Malays, despite economic considerations to the contrary.It

should be noted, however, that in the meantime MARA has been thoroughly reorganized and inter-institutional cooperation improved.

60 The SEDCs are publicly-owned institutions which assist in formulating and carrying out economic development programmes within each state, and are often the sole agency under which the IEs and FTZs operate. They perform in essence many of the functions at a state level that MIDA does at a national level.

61 The regional offices of MIDA were set up concomitant with the increased stress on a regional dispersal of policies, so as to assure that the same services are available everywhere to reduce information cost differentials. In West Malaysia they are located in Kedah, Pahang, Perak and Kelantan.

62 Despite these bureaucratic obstacles, the industrial development programme seemed to be well off as compared with rural development programmes, where land applications were directed through a multi-levelled bureaucracy and took anywhere from 270 to 564 days on the average to be processed (Esman, 1972, p. 212).

63 This is particularly the case in light of the realization that FIDA's fief is not the one-stop service centre which Singapore's Development Board offers. See Asian Finance, 15 July 1980, pp. 47-51.

64 To what extent such interpretations were also applied in order to differentiate between non-Malay Malaysians and Malays, or foreigners and Malaysians, is not known, but the probability of such behaviour can be considered to be rather high.

65 It is obvious that the interpretation of the regional industrialization policies becomes all the more complicated or even approaches the realm of speculation, the greater the tendency of the authorities to revert to implicit measures and apply them without any degree of regional consistency. However, as long as the application of implicit policies was consistently edged in the direction explicitly expressed, then, *ceteris paribus,* the results can be interpreted as reflecting the stated goals.

66 This aspect of creating new towns and agricultural areas has been briefly mentioned several times in this chapter, but no attempt will be made to go into detail on the ramifications of this measure. To do so would increase the study beyond the author's initial aims, particularly because of the importance placed in these areas on the agricultural sector. Without denying the fact that they will be playing an increasingly important role in the future, interested readers are referred to the various Malaysia Plans and to Krüger (1982).

4
A Quantitative Assessment of the Regional Impact of Investment Incentives

INTRODUCTION

IN accordance with the central hypothesis of this study (see Chapter 2) the major industrialization measures outlined above are analysed in this chapter with respect to their impact on factor intensities and regional allocation of resources. It is thereby kept in mind that if the policies instituted in Malaysia are to achieve efficiently the prescribed goals they should be promoting a more extensive use of the factors of production with which it is relatively well endowed, namely labour, small-scale industries and natural resources. In a regional context this means that since the less developed regions in Malaysia are assumed to possess comparative advantages in the production of labour, small-scale industry and natural resource intensive products, industrialization measures need be structured accordingly. The analysis first addresses itself to the following question:

Did the major industrialization measures (investment incentives) aim at influencing production structures in such a way so as to ensure that Malaysia's comparative advantages, in a macro but particularly in a regional context, were exploited in an economically efficient manner?

Secondly, realizing that, regardless of the impact of the policies on the factor intensity of production, the success of the industrialization policies themselves induces economic development with regional implications, the following question is addressed:

Did the success of industrialization policies, as expressed by the rapid expansion of non-traditional exports, particularly from the electronics industry in connection with FTZs, exert an influence in such a way so as to influence negatively regional development disparities?

STRUCTURE AND IMPACT OF MAJOR INVESTMENT INCENTIVES

As expounded in Chapter 3, the major investment incentives in Malaysia, be they macro or regionally orientated, have been basically centred around tax exemptions, the length of which was initially determined by the amount of capital invested. This approach was expanded later to cover the amount of employment created. While the domination of the PIs, which accounted for almost 50 per cent of approved projects in the initial period, has been reduced considerably, it can be seen that the increase in the share of projects without incentives outweighs the shift between the various groups of projects with incentives (see Table 4.1).

Of the specific industrialization measures introduced by the Malaysian government only the location incentives (LIs) and development area incentives (DAIs) can be seen as explicitly aiming at overcoming disparities between more developed regions (MDRs) and less developed regions (LDRs)[1]. And of these two, the LI would seem to be the one which could compensate for locational disadvantages, as the length of the tax holiday would help allow companies to overcome barriers to entry (infant-industry arguments). The DAI on the other hand (for which data unfortunately do not exist) can hardly be considered a measure that would crucially influence investment decisions since it is only applicable for one year. At the most it might be considered as having an impact if everything else were to equal, particularly if first year profits are expected to be quite sizeable, a case which doesn't seem very likely[2].

The extent to which LIs have been granted to approved projects can be seen as being relatively small in terms of the absolute number in the total economy (Table 4.1) but increasing somewhat over time. In terms of employment, as well as in terms of capital, its share was proportionally larger, thereby giving the first indication as to the impact of this measure. It should, however, be noted that both of these have been decreasing in recent times, a sign that employment size and capital intensity of projects have become smaller.

In a regional context, a differentiated trend can be observed. Whereas the share of projects without incentives in the LDRs has tended to decrease somewhat after the initial period, the share in MDRs has increased continuously over time and now accounts for over two-thirds of approved projects in the western states. These developments, but in particular the differences in the WI levels between the LDRs and the MDRs, would seem to indicate the extent to which locational disadvantages exist. That is, if the entrepreneurs went to the LDRs under the condition that they receive incentives, then the incentives

TABLE 4.1

Structure and Development of Various Investment Incentives[a] in Malaysia (in per cent)

Incentive/ Period[b]	Approved Projects	Potential Employment	Approved Capital	Intraregional Distribution			Interregional Distribution		
				North	South	West	North	South	West
LI									
70-72	--	--	--	--	--	--	--	--	--
73-75	0.7	4.5	9.0	3.2	1.9	--	41.7	58.3	--
76-78	2.7	8.2	12.8	17.7	2.0	--	73.6	26.4	--
79-81	1.8	4.2	2.5	15.1	0.6	--	93.9	6.1	--
LUR									
70-72	0.8	1.4	0.7	--	1.0	1.0	--	22.2	77.8
73-75	3.1	4.5	1.7	7.2	2.2	3.1	21.9	18.2	60.0
76-78	1.9	3.8	2.6	3.2	2.0	1.9	15.6	27.3	57.1
79-81	0.6	1.3	0.3	3.7	--	0.4	66.7	—	33.3
PI									
70-72	48.5	68.4	68.4	66.7	45.7	47.9	5.7	20.4	73.9
73-75	30.0	46.1	49.5	38.1	28.6	27.6	11.7	25.6	62.7
76-78	25.0	39.8	40.6	23.6	24.4	24.1	10.7	28.0	61.3
79-81	19.7	45.7	28.8	22.5	21.0	20.1	13.1	26.5	60.4
ITC									
70-72	6.4	10.7	10.1	15.3	10.1	5.5	12.0	32.9	55.0
73-75	6.8	11.7	13.8	8.3	20.6	5.6	8.3	51.0	40.7
76-78	16.2	14.0	20.9	22.9	26.2	11.8	17.0	38.4	44.5
79-81	14.7	11.9	19.0	19.9	16.7	12.4	15.7	31.2	53.1
WI									
70-72	41.1	17.1	15.0	14.1	40.4	46.5	1.3	19.7	79.0
73-75	56.8	30.3	24.5	40.1	44.1	61.8	6.1	20.9	72.9
76-78	53.2	33.5	21.9	28.4	46.7	61.6	5.7	23.5	70.8
79-81	63.2	36.8	48.6	38.3	61.4	67.2	7.2	26.0	66.8

Source: Own calculations based on MIDA (Annual Report, 1972 ff.)

[a] Figures do not always add to 100% since minor incentives excluded.
[b] Period average - for meaning of abbreviations, see listing.

can be interpreted as compensating (or maybe overcompensating) for possible locational disadvantages. Furthermore, if an even larger group of companies rejects incentives for LDRs and remains in MDRs, then the locational disadvantages are also revealed; this time they are greater than the perceived benefits from the incentives.

It is of course one thing to compensate for locational disadvantages, but it is another thing to structure measures so as to induce development in line with the comparative advantages of the regions. This would mean, for instance, to ensure that small-scale establishments and/or labour-intensive industries are encouraged or at least not put at a disadvantage. In the case of the small-scale establishments the employment size classification, which determined the length of the tax exemption for LIs, offered an extension of the tax holiday period only above 100 employees. To receive the longest exemption (8 years) at least 351 new jobs had to be created. Knowing that about 90 per cent of the population in the LDRs lives in districts with towns with less than 15,000 inhabitants (see Table 1.3) and that only 2 per cent of the companies existing in 1973 in the LDRs had more than 99 employees (see Table 4.2), it becomes obvious that the LI can hardly be considered as being correctly specified. Regardless of such aspects the entrepreneurs investing in the LDRs would no doubt attempt to become eligible for the longest exemption possible based on employment criteria, or on the invested capital criteria, depending upon which criteria yielded the longest exemption. Such behaviour can indeed be deduced from Table 4.3 where it can be seen that the average establishment size was often the largest of all incentive categories[3], and, in the initial phase, the capital intensity was also the highest[4]. The development of capital intensities of LI projects in recent years with values actually below the national average, is at least an encouraging sign that more labour-intensive production techniques seem to be prevailing.

Although LIs were the major incentive aimed at dispersing industries, entrepreneurs in LDRs actually received more PIs and ITCs (see Table 4.1). These measures also distorted the factor intensity of production as is clearly revealed in Table 4.3. In the case of the PIs, the employment size has been influenced throughout time; for the ITCs it is the capital intensity. As concerns LUR, it is for sure quite labour intensive, but likewise of very large establishment size. *Vis-à-vis* LIs it was even less ideally structured as the initial tax exemption group began at 50 employees and not at 1. In other words none of the fiscal policy measures instituted by the federal government exerted an influence on entrepreneurs in such a way so as to allow the comparative advantages of the LDRs to be exploited in an economically efficient manner. It might be added that the group without incentives exhibits the smallest capital intensity and employment size, thereby underlining the distorting impact of existing investment incentives on the factor intensity of production.

REGIONAL POLICIES, INTERNATIONAL TRADE AND THE FREE TRADE ZONES

If the major locational and macro-oriented fiscal incentives turned out encouraging a more intensive use of the factor of production not in agreement with assumed comparative advantages, thereby upping private at the cost of public welfare, then a closer look should be taken at another major incentive and its regional impact, namely the establishment of the IEs/FTZs (together with the electronics industry incentives), and in this connection analysing the potential impact of international trade on regional development.

Although the theoretical considerations about the impact of IEs/FTZs are vague, it is assumed here that, in the case of foreign firms, their decision to invest in IEs/FTZs does not reflect investment diversion and hence trade diversion, but rather generally reflects an effort to profit from the specific comparative advantages of the Malaysian economy. Particularly in the case of FTZs

TABLE 4.2

Structure of Employment Size of Manufacturing Establishments in Malaysia by States, 1968 and 1973

Region/State	*Total Number of Establishments*	*Number of Full-time Employees per Establishment (percentage)*				
		0	*1-9*	*10-49*	*50-99*	*≥100*
			1968			
Northern states	1,502	44.21	42.94	10.32	1.66	.87
Trengganu	288	58.33	32.99	5.21	2.78	.69
Kelantan	357	44.82	39.50	12.61	1.40	1.68
Perlis	83	27.71	67.47	4.82	-	-
Kedah	774	40.44	45.61	11.76	1.55	.65
Southern states	1,940	41.44	38.61	14.07	2.78	3.09
Pahang	403	51.86	30.27	13.15	3.23	1.49
Melaka	412	40.53	45.12	12.14	.97	1.21
Johor	1,125	38.04	39.20	15.11	3.29	4.36
Western states	5,571	33.73	41.30	18.63	3.52	2.82
Perak	1,693	38.04	41.17	16.48	2,78	1.54
Selangor	2,118	25.68	39.90	24.08	5,71	4.63
Negeri Sembilan	409	39.12	39.85	17.11	1.71	2.20
Penang	1,351	39.30	44.12	13.25	1.55	1.78
Total/average	9,013	37.14	41.00	16.27	3.05	2.55
			1973			
Northern states	1,633	36.19	45.01	14.08	2.63	2.08
Trengganu	326	54.91	29.75	8.28	4.29	2.76
Kelantan	424	26.65	46.70	20.05	3.77	2.83
Perlis	86	27.12	68.60	10.47	1.16	1.16
Kedah	797	35.51	47.80	13.68	1.51	1.51
Southern states	2,398	32.11	39.57	17.64	4.84	5.84
Pahang	511	39.14	34.25	14.48	6.07	6.07
Melaka	429	33.57	46.62	13.99	2.10	3.73
Johor	1,458	29.22	39.37	19.82	5.20	6.38
Western states	7,029	25.42	41.78	22.51	4.89	5.41
Perak	1,944	27.93	44.80	20.32	3.50	3.45
Selangor	3,043	19.22	39.40	27.74	6.51	7.13
Negeri Sembilan	437	35.93	39.82	15.56	5.26	3.43
Penang	1,605	31.28	43.12	17.13	3.43	5.05
Total/average	11,060	28.46	41.77	20.21	4.55	5.01

Sources: Own calculations based on Dept. of Statistics (CMI, 1968, Table 12; 1973, Tables 74ff.)

Note: The underlined figures are above national average.

TABLE 4.3

Size and Capital Intensity of New Investments[a] in Malaysia[b] by Incentives

Incentive	*1970-72*	*1973-75*	*1976-78*	*1979-81*
	Average number of employees/project			
LI	--	491.9	226.6	251.3
LUR	255.9	191.9	155.6	255.8
PI	217.4	199.3	125.0	238.5
ITC	271.3	243.3	68.2	81.9
WI	62.2	128.9	50.2	60.5
Total	153.4	128.9	78.7	104.1
	Average capital[c] intensity (M$'000/employee)			
LI	--	75.4	43.4	15.0
LUR	7.2	10.3	13.7	6.4
PI	21.7	26.2	26.6	15.4
ITC	22.4	34.7	37.7	36.3
WI	18.8	21.5	17.4	34.4
Total	21.7	26.6	26.0	24.3

Source: See Table 4.1.

[a]Only major incentives included.
[b]Includes Sahah and Sarawak.
[c]Approved capital.

(freed of many distortions otherwise affecting domestic industries) should production be able to be efficiently structured. The fact that Malaysia is but one of many countries offering such enticements means that the probability of efficiently interfacing production needs with given factor endowments is all the greater[5]. In the case of local investors, it is a moot question as to whether these investments can be seen as diverting local capital, where the social return might have been higher. It might just as well be the case that, even if local capital is diverted, the long-run social returns in the form of better trained personnel, international contacts and bandwagon effects will be greater than what otherwise would have been the case. Of equal importance in this connection is to ensure that the benefits so derived do not remain concentrated in one region, but rather induce other regions to attempt to profit from the shift in the production structure of the regions with the IEs/FTZs.

Without neglecting the above caveats, a central aspect in this analysis is the direct impact of IEs/FTZs on the factor intensity of production methods. While obviously a review of overall data on investments in states, inside and outside industrial estates, must be viewed with the necessary scepticism, information has been culled from a number of sources so as to avoid major distortions and is presented in Table 4.4 (for data from another source see Table A10). The following conclusions are cautiously drawn from this Table[6]:

1. The capital intensity in IE/FTZs in most of the more developed (western) states tends to be lower than outside of such areas; in most of the other states the reverse is true.

2. The capital intensity in IEs in the less developed states tends to be higher than in the more developed states; outside of IEs the reverse tends to be true.

3. Land is used more extensively in the LDRs than in the MDRs; this can be construed as occurring roughly in a manner negatively corresponding to IE rents and premiums or expected land rents (Table 3.6)[7].

4. Assuming regional wage differentials did not change substantially (and the data seem to bear this out), it can be noted that, *ceteris paribus,* land prices increased on the average faster in the more developed areas than in the less developed.

It might also be noted that the rough correlation between capital intensity and employment density, which becomes evident in Table 4.4, can also be established when analysing FTZs by relatively homogeneous industry groups (Table 4.5).

According to these figures[8], it would be seem that IEs and FTZs generally exerted an influence in the direction of greater capital intensity, whereby the FTZs seemed to have induced less of a thrust toward greater capital intensity. On a regional basis, the greater capital intensity in IEs in LDRs tends to substantiate the above described impact of the incentive measures, namely that their misspecification prompted the use of the factor of production not in agreement with the assumed comparative advantages of the regions. However, the evidence is weak and needs substantiation by data disaggregated by industries and incentives as well.

This breakdown, which, due to data limitations, could neither be performed for all industries nor for the regional disaggregation[9] used otherwise in this study, was carried out not only for capital intensity but for employment size and year as well. The figures (Table 4.6) reveal that although IEs do

TABLE 4.4

Indicators of Factor Intensities in Regions and States and in IEs or FTZs, 1968, 1977 and 1978

	Capital Intensity[a]					Employees per Acre in IEs or FTZs	Employees per M$'000 Land Valuation[b]		
	in IEs or FTZs	not in IEs or FTZs	in State (average)[b]						
Region/State	1977[c]		1968	1978	1968-78	1977[d]	1968	1973	1968-73
Northern states	32,130	30,366	2,427	9,280	14,357	5.15	3.19	2.39	2.00
Trengganu	13,671	14,553	1,728	9,894	15,288	5.15	8.78	3.52	1.18
Kelantan	-	17,284	1,773	3,854	6,132	-	4.30	3.13	2.64
Perlis	-	170,343	4,206	60,219	85,526	-	4.01	5.01	5.45
Kedah	35,044	18,154	2,969	7,418	10,838	-	2.31	1.60	1.11
Southern states	39,867	35,511	3,671	12,316	16,702	10.25	2.35	1.88	1.30
Pahang	33,424	23,198	2,383	11,770	14,068	5.25	3.05	1.72	1.45
Melaka	20,807	11,244	2,766	9,202	10,940	29.62	1.08	1.92	3.07
Johor	46,558	40,588	4,023	13,546	20,786	7.51	2.73	1.93	1.47
Western states	30,377	25,671	8,414	13,583	16,284	23.92	1.50	1.25	1.11
Perak	20,099	25,705	6,395	12,070	16,533	16.06	2.60	1.85	1.50
Selangor	35,156	24,715	8,275	14,041	17,288	17.00	1.41	1.01	.80
Negeri Sembilan	19,417	32,243	23,003	29,813	35,187	14.97	.56	1.25	-1.62
Penang	27,523	29,947	6,683	10,963	12,229	50.66	1.90	1.65	1.56
Average	33,153	28,365	6,835	12,958	16,242		1.72	1.42	1.25

Sources: Own calculations based on unpublished MIDA data and Dept. of Statistics (CMI, 1968, Tables 3, 25; 1973, Vol. 1, Tables 4,42; 1978, unpublished data).

The underlined figures are above national average.

[a] In M$.

[b] Based on CMI data.

[c] Based on a sample of 513 registered companies (using total expected capital and potential employment) of which 219 were in IEs and 294 not in IEs.

[d] Based on unpublished MIDA data.

have an impact on capital intensities and employment size, it is the incentives which have the greatest impact, an impact which was in many cases increasing over time. The bottom lines in both breakdowns show the coefficient of variation for the various categories. This statistic substantiates prior hypothesized influences of incentives, namely that they cause factor intensities to exhibit lower variation, regardless of changes in economic parameters. In other words, regional differences in factor intensities are ignored in favour of standardized capital and employment size-intensive production methods.

Despite the fact that the FTZs catering to the electronics industry measure up well against the other FTZs and IEs with respect to capital intensity[10], the question is still open as to whether these institutions actually serve the domestic economy (via linkages, purchasing power, demonstration effects, etc.) or whether multinational corporations use such arrangements to exploit the low-priced labour in LDCs (i.e. pay lower wages than would otherwise have been the case) and crowd out potential domestic investors. Some aspects of this problem have been mentioned above but as far as the FTZs in Malaysia are concerned, they do not seem to contain industries of the type which would have been set up by domestic entrepreneurs – that is, the assembly of electronic parts is not an industry for which domestic producers would be competing. While possible demonstration effects are not known, the dovetailing of the in-

TABLE 4.5

Capital Intensity and Employment Density in FTZs by Industry

Code[a]	Industry[b]	MIDA Employees/Acre 1977	MIDA Assets (M$)/Employee 1977	CMI[c] Assets (M$)/Employee 1973	CMI[c] Assets (M$)/Employee 1978
32200	Clothing factories	172.1	5,404	1,698	3,115
38530	Watches and clocks	345.3	8,294	8,346	15,724
38520	Photographic/optical goods	220.0	10,364	5,461	10,265
38320	Radio, TV equipment etc.	240.5	13,719	3,121	5,047
38510	Professional/scientific goods etc.	159.5	14,107	6,597	12,648
35599	Rubber products n.e.c.	167.2	16,746	4,230	11,008
35593	Rubber footwear	46.5	17,008	4,473	6,365
38191	Tins cans and metal boxes	43.1	18,000	6,624	13,364
32111	Natural fibre spinning/weaving mills	270.8	27,734	12,443	25,059
32115	Synthetic textile mills	52.5	50,111	17,549	23,237
32112	Dyeing/bleaching etc. yarns/fabrics	15.2	89,612	12,397	18,377

[a]Based on 1973 Malaysian industrial classification.
[b]n.e.c. = not elsewhere classified.
[c]For the economy as a whole.

dustries into the domestic economy and the promotion of employment (purchasing power) seem to have been rather successful[11]. First of all, value added rapidly increased in the course of the years (Table 4.7)[12]. Secondly, the trade balance has turned positive. Thirdly, and the share of domestically supplied inputs expanded considerably over time, from about 3 per cent (1974) to over 15 per cent (1979) of total inputs. As for capital goods their erratic movements do not allow conclusions to be drawn. Fourthly, employment increased at a rate which exceeded other areas (more than doubling in the 1974-9 period), thereby, via multipliers, causing the purchasing power to increase. The share of manufacturing employment in IEs increased from only 12 per cent in 1968 to 65 per cent in 1977, whereby over half (60 per cent) of this is located in the two FTZs[13]. Wages, as a matter of fact, were higher than the Malaysian average and were even above industry averages after the initial adjustment period (till 1973).

While on the one hand, the level of income (i.e. wages) and the expansion of the income base, are important for consumption levels (i.e. standard of living and investment), on the other hand they represent costs to entrepreneurs and thus affect locational decisions. Within Malaysia no major policies existed which aimed at explicitly levelling regional wage disparities or maintaining specific socially (or politically) determined income levels, thereby causing the labour cost differentials to be below productivity differentials. Under these circumstances, the locational decision within Malaysia was one determined to a

TABLE 4.6

Impact of IEs and Incentive Status on Factor Intensity by Selected Industries and Location

Major Industry Group	Year	National Average	Rural				Urban			
			NIE		IE		NIE		IE	
			WI	I	WI	I	WI	I	WI	I
			Capital Intensity (M$ /employee)							
311+	1970	28,742	11,963	43,850	8,608[b]	8,527[a]	22,628	36,769	33,484	36,979
312	1978	33,951	11,012	43,971	24,209	45,066	18,911	33,407	34,911	39,958
321	1970	16,594	19,216	21,730	3,872[b]	-	5,556[a]	16,182	-	14,975
	1978	18,685	10,808	27,209	9,463	38,705	7,252	26,759	11,022	16,538
331	1970	21,595	10,712	9,435	-	17,713	46,596	14,866	-	53,298
	1978	21,351	8,555	30,113	11,628	30,934	23,742	10,453	-	24,820
352	1970	26,710	-	-	8,467[b]	6,101[a]	-	-	15,310[b]	28,304
	1978	25,624	14,552	26,810[a]	19,747	26,299[b]	18,535	46,680[b]	33,800	24,560
355	1970	14,463	7,558[a]	-	-	-	14,154	3,906[a]	10,556	29,911
	1978	18,717	6,667[a]	39,745	-	12,894	14,778	12,339	5,000[a]	25,747
369	1970	24,551	51,732	8,449[b]	40,000[a]	-	30,204	10,267[a]	17,678	21,994
	1978	35,618	47,647	54,477	24,535	-	18,857	20,553[b]	36,933	22,338[b]
381	1970	16,676	17,970	5,430	3,099[a]	-	17,405	3,448[a]	26,671	14,391
	1978	23,211	13,789	36,566[a]	25,114	28,181	10,273	31,767	23,765	35,483
383	1970	16,784	-	5,435[a]	36,207[a]	11,460	8,961[b]	14,731[b]	14,260	21,134
	1978	15,636	-	12,655	16,091	11,658	16,150	16,781	21,116	18,957
Total	1970	22,531	14,960	23,131	13,082	16,079	20,247	28,669	20,938	26,626
$\frac{s}{\bar{x}} \cdot 100$		103.6	98.4	129.3	97.6	70.5	137.0	92.5	102.0	80.5
	1978	23,657	18,833	37,964	26,938	26,330	14,098	24,415	23,389	27,647
$\frac{s}{\bar{x}} \cdot 100$		110.4	153.4	89.1	97.4	103.3	113.0	92.1	109.5	97.1
			Employment Size[c]							
311 +	1970	221	133	184	515[b]	563[a]	255	190	204	251
312	1978	137	328	203	39	124	58	107	98	129
321	1970	435	139	828	117[b]	-	315	384	-	166
	1978	308	83	659	57	791	73	24[b]	90	354
331	1970	277	127	487	-	338	132	500	-	56
	1978	203	152	299	86[a]	276	92	239	-	281
352	1970	141	23[a]	263[a]	95[b]	287[a]	-	65[b]	257[b]	134
	1978	46	25	21[a]	65	134[b]	18	63	51	47
355	1970	534	86[a]	-	-	-	876	32[a]	168	1,134
	1978	247	60[a]	190	-	468	946	204	200[a]	255
369	1970	279	519[b]	336[b]	25[a]	-	373	487[a]	79	274
	1978	67	43	125	30	-	30	142[b]	51	218[b]
381	1970.	144	69	166	102[a]		146	58[a]	94	193
	1978	75	69[b]	106[b]	98	205	41	104	42	97
383	1970	209		184[a]	87[a]	360	86[b]	78[b]	93	312
	1978	369		730	57	467	52	489	71	374
Total	1970	230	137	389	170	616	184	246	177	226
$\frac{s}{\bar{x}} \cdot 100$		138.2	127.8	92.1	158.8	83.7	213.3	87.9	139.1	129.2
	1978	168	106	297	68	349	70	164	92	196
$\frac{s}{\bar{x}} \cdot 100$		168.7	121.7	138.0	82.5	126.5	210.1	118.8	140.1	149.4

Source: Own calculations based on data provided by MIDA.

The underlined figures are above average in the respective industry.

[a]Only one observation.

[b]Only two observations.

[c]Employees/establishment.

large extent by other factors such as market or supply orientation, agglomeration economies, etc. and to the degree to which these could be overcome by the investment incentives.

Between Malaysia and other countries, however, the story was (and still is) different, because attractive (efficiency) wage levels in addition to investment incentives, infrastructure facilities, political stability, etc. were all offered so as to produce a package of features aimed at profit motives. The more interesting the package, the greater the extent to which this country can successfully compete for new investments. While in many respects the package offered by Malaysia was not substantially different from those offered by its rivals (e.g. Singapore, Taiwan, Hong Kong and South Korea), it had the advantage of being able to profit from the experience made in other FTZs. Although the figures in Table 4.7 have been interpreted above as pointing to a successful operation of the FTZs with respect to the domestic economy, another important question is whether Malaysia was successful in the international market[14].

To verify whether this actually did occur it would suffice for the moment to determine if Malaysia's share of those particular goods produced in FTZs increased or decreased. The type of goods involved here are (mainly) electronic components and these can be narrowed down to a select number of SITC groups (see Table 4.8 for description of groups). The market shares of Malaysia and other selected developing countries in the imports of OECD countries from all non-OECD countries for the time period 1970-9 were examined. As revealed by Table 4.8, Malaysia's share increased rapidly once the FTZs (with the electronics industry incentives) had been set up. The result – from almost nothing in 1970 to over 10 per cent in 1980, a growth path matched by none of the other competitors in this time period. Furthermore, there are even indications that the slowing down of world economic growth in recent years has not severely affected Malaysia's FTZs. At least, as far as the important US market is concerned they have been able to increase their share in the rapidly growing electronics sector.

CONCLUDING REMARKS

While the success with which Malaysia was able to compete in world markets with its package of measures to promote the establishment of labour-intensive (electronics) industries is quite evident, generally speaking it was shown that the fiscal incentive package induced production structures to be distorted away

TABLE 4.7

Performance of FTZs in Penang, 1972-1979

	Unit	*1972*	*1974*	*1976*	*1978*	*1979*
Imports	Mill. M$	4.08	311.22	572.38	844.18	936.41
Domestic inputs	"	.54	10.10	47.79	124.09	171.41
Wages	"	2.63	38.57	52.88	96.36	114.65
Value of manufacturing	"	13.67	170.85	714.66	1391.68	1775.15
Value added	"	9.05	-150.46	94.49	423.41	667.33
Exports	"	12.06	164.01	639.70	1268.01	1564.00
Trade balance	"	7.98	-147.21	67.32	423.84	627.59
Local sales	"	1.60	6.32	74.96	21.77	55.85
Capital goods						
Imports	"	-	131.55	24.19	27.73	117.96
Domestic	"	-	46.70	59.90	6.21	47.56
Trade Balance	"	-	-84.85	35.71	-21.51	-70.40
Employees	'000s	4.11	17.41	25.98	30.55	35.83
Value added/employee	M$'000	2.20	-8.64	3.64	13.86	18.63
Aver. annual earnings/ employee	"	0.64	2.22	2.04	3.15	3.20

Sources: Own calculations based on SEDC (Annual Report and Financial Statements, various years) and unpublished data from Statistics Office.

TABLE 4.8

Imports of Electronics Industry Products[a] into OECD Countries from Selected Developing Countries, 1970-1979

	1970	*1972*	*1974*	*1976*	*1978*	*1979*
OECD electronics imports (US$ m.):						
Total	8,430	12,216	20,687	26,580	36,952	44,585
From non-OECD countries	805	1,450	3,695	4,528	6,950	6,097
Percentage of total	9.55	11.87	17.87	17.04	18.81	13.61
Percentage share by country in OECD electronic imports from non-OECD sources:						
Malaysia	.11	.16	5.04	6.92	9.12	9.8
Singapore	5.31	12.07	11.60	12.61	11.94	14.0
South Korea	4.23	6.77	11.92	15.21	15.33	15.2
Taiwan	17.59	25.97	22.19	21.09	21.76	20.6
Hong Kong	19.67	17.70	12.70	14.12	11.87	11.1

Source: Calculations based on data from OECD (various years).

[a]The electronics industry is considered to be made up of the following nine SITC classifications (Rev. I):

714.2	calculating and accounting machines, including electronic computers
714.3	statistical machines, including electronic machines
714.9(2)	parts of office machinery
724.1	television broadcast receivers
724.2	radio broadcast receivers
724.9	telecommunications equipment, n.e.s.
729.3	thermionic, etc. valves and tubes, transistors, semiconductors, etc.
729.9(5)	electrical condensers and parts
891.1	phonographs, tape and other sound recorders, etc.

from Malaysia's comparative advantages, be it in a macro or a regional context. Although in recent times it could be established that an improvement has been registered (at least with regard to capital intensities), the degree to which the FTZs could tap a large and rapidly expanding world market put MDRs relatively better off. This would particularly be the case if other policies were not instituted to make the LDRs more attractive for investments corresponding to their comparative advantages. The relative improvement in the welfare of the MDRs due to the success of the FTZs was all the more probable given the fact that the industrial structure of the LDRs did not interface very well with the input demands of the respective industries in the FTZs. The only basic way the LDRs could thus profit would be through the process of trickle-down via

TABLE 4.9

Correlation[a] between Structure of Manufactured Exports and Structure of Manufacturing Industry by State

Region/State	*Coefficient of Correlation* 1968	1973	1977
Northern states			
Trengganu	0.237	0.391	0.446
Kelantan	0.298	0.476	0.631
Perlis	-	-	-
Kedah	0.614	0.754	0.909
Southern states			
Pahang	0.294	0.423	0.407
Melaka	0.744	0.839	0.899
Johor	0.798	0.863	0.825
Western states			
Perak	0.623	0.752	0.864
Selangor	0.575	0.651	0.760
Negeri Sembilan	0.785	0.873	0.791
Penang	0.466	0.594	0.866

Source: Own calculations based on UN commodity trade statistics rebased from SITC to ISIC and Department of Statistics (CMI, 1973).

[a]Coefficient of correlation.

the increased purchasing power in the MDRs[15]. Of potential benefit to the LDRs, however, is the fact that the correlation between the structure of the manufacturing industry in the LDRs and the structure of manufactured exports has increased considerably over time and was actually quite high in 1978 (see

Table 4.9)[16]. In other words, if fiscal investment incentives were structured more in line with factor endowments in the LDRs, then by ensuring that an appropriate economic environment was created, for instance by initially compensating for differences in the availability of non-conventional factors of production and industrial infrastructure, a greater integration of the LDRs into world markets could be achieved.

1 While IEs can also be considered as a measure to promote development in LDRs, they are not explicitly used for such purposes, aside from the fact that SEDCs were responsible for them. They will thus be treated in detail in the ensuing chapter.

2 As the extra year can also be granted in connection with other incentives it also can hardly be considered to be a sufficient measure to compensate for regional development disparities.

3 Large firms are an efficient way to spread industrialization in rural areas; for instance as Bruch (1978) points out they are often less efficient in utilizing the factors of production than small firms.

4 A word of caution is due with respect to the figures used here and in other Tables. First of all, these figures are for approved projects, not for those which were actually carried out. This means that a sizeable share will never be realized. Of all projects approved for the period 1971-9, 56.6 per cent were implemented and 22.1 per cent not implemented. The position of the remaining 21.3 per cent of the projects was indefinite. Secondly, the figures on employment and capital are potential figures, and thus blown up beyond what is realized later. While this could well distort the employees/ project figure, the capital intensity figure is probably less distorted (since both numerator and denominator are affected). Thirdly, the extent to which other items aside from equipment and buildings are included is not known, but since they are stated as being quite small, the possible distortion can be ignored, particularly as the relative figures are interpreted.

5 This does not, however, exclude the possibility that the capital intensity of the investment is far above what would constitute optimal conditions. The reasons for this lie elsewhere and are not seen in the institution of the FTZ.

6 The author is fully aware of possible distortions due to different industry mixes but ignores this for the moment.

7 Penang and Melaka, with their relatively high employment/land utilization indicators, are two states in which investments in the electronics industry (highly labour-intensive and of a large employment size) played an important role. These labour-intensive industries thus caused the above average values.

8 A word of caution is in order with regard to the data on IEs. First of all, to the extent to which the industries have just recently been set up, and this would generally be the case in IEs, it is probable that the number of employees lies below the 'normal' level; i.e. start-up distortions, which could cause the capital intensity to be higher. Secondly, and working in the other direction, is the fact that the employment figures are proposed employment, and are usually distorted upwards; i.e. capital intensity would tend to be decreased. While it is difficult to state which factor prevails, the author tends to believe that the upward bias on capital intensity is probably greater. Nonetheless, it is not likely that the distortions are large enough to negate the above contention. The fact that capital intensities generally tend to decrease in the last years can be shown by data from Penang (Table A11).

9 The regional breakdown was limited to a rural/urban classification, whereby urban covered basically Georgetown, Kuala Lumpur and the Johor Bahru.

This is in essence a clear breakdown, since if agglomeration economies can be expected anywhere it is in one of these three areas.

10 In Bayan Lepas FTZ the employment/acre is almost 140 (Table A10) and the capital intensity is less than half the Penang average. For individual companies the employment/acre even approaches 1,000.

11 These comments refer to the FTZs in Penang. For a more detailed analysis of the performance of FTZs in Malaysia and in other Asian countries, see Spinanger (1984).

12 The initial negative value-added figures can be attributed to start-up difficulties.

13 In Penang manufacturing employment developed as follows:

	1968	*1970*	*1973*	*1975*	*1978*
CMI	15,828	.	50,463	.	68,968
PEDC	.	18,600	46,900	58,200	.
per cent in IE/FTZs:					
CMI	12.3	.	49.0	.	61.1
PEDC	.	20.7	52.7	56.1	.

Sources: Own calculations based on data from the Penang Economic Development Corporation and Department of Statistics.

14 The success noted in Table 4.7 could have been prompted by a generally strong demand for the electronic products, whereby Malaysia's share in world markets for all other products could have remained unchanged or even decreased.

15 The possibility cannot be excluded that the (alleged) attempt by the Malaysian government to grant incentives only if the location was considered to be in line with what they thought to be suitable (i.e. generally speaking in LDRs) was a possible countermeasure. To what extent it was involved, however, is not known.

16 It is interesting to note that the increases in the coefficient of correlation are often higher in the LDRs than in the MDRs – perhaps a sign that they are indeed profiting more than before.

5
Compensating for Regional Economic Environment Differentials: The Case of Industrial Estates

INTRODUCTION

HAVING established the direction of the impact of the main fiscal investment incentives on the factor intensity of production and regional economic development trends, the question now raised is about how those policies which were aimed at providing or creating an economic environment conducive for the growth of the new investments were structured. After all, the incentives themselves were basically meant to attract investments and to compensate for difficulties emanating over a certain initial period of time. Following such a period, that is after the incentives have expired, investments were supposed to be economically viable. Their viability, however, depends, *ceteris paribus,* on the quality of the economic environment. In Malaysia one key measure instituted in this respect was the industrial estate (IE) or free trade zone (FTZ)[1]. After briefly examining the essence of such policies in compensating for regional differentials in economic environment, the discussion turns to the question of whether IE-policies in Malaysia were appropriately structured in line with the posited comparative advantages in a given region. Deviations from such a path are considered to reflect a misallocation of resources. Furthermore the stated policy goals are compared with the actual measures to determine whether both goals and policies were consistent with one another.

THE ESSENCE OF INDUSTRIAL ESTATES[2]

The rationale behind employing industrial estates in industrialization strategies is backed up by well-founded experience in a wide range of countries[3], founded upon theoretical argumentation derived from, *inter alia,* the theory of the firm, urban economics and customs union theory (see, for instance Grubel (1982, 1983)). Four main, but not necessarily independent reasons can be given for the establishment of an industrial estate:

1. The IE represents a seemingly simple solution to the problem of zoning, i.e. it can achieve a straight-forward delineation between various (perhaps non-compatible) types of economic activities. Assuming that, *ceteris paribus,* within a given area locational preferences for a manufacturing company do not exist, then the possible infringement of industrial activities on the quality of (residential) life, for instance, is reduced[4].

2. Such industrial areas can assist in reducing infrastructure costs by allowing development economies of scale to be taken advantage of. Furthermore, by bunching industries into certain areas, forecasts of future demand for utilities, transportation services, etc. can be more easily made, thereby allowing capital to be more efficiently used.

3. The existence of prepared industrial areas can act as an investment enticement, since the difficulties in setting up new production facilities (particularly for foreigners) are reduced considerably. Furthermore, complementary industries and services can help simulate agglomeration economies and, should complementary services such as marketing or exporting assistance or training facilities be offered, then smaller scale establishments, which often are hindered by deficiences in such areas, will also be promoted. Knowing that in some cases smaller scale establishments produce more with less capital but at higher employment levels than larger scale establishments, underemployment can be reduced. Strong impulses for the overall rate of industrialization could well result.

4. Industrial estates, when coupled with other necessary measures, can provide the means of regionally distributing the industrialization process within a given country, in accordance with the agreed-upon economic and political welfare function, by attracting new industries into designated areas (or keeping other industries from migrating out of such areas) and thus provide new job opportunities. Assuming that in most cases the expected income level in the former inward migration areas is now matched by the perceived income from the new job opportunity in the former outward migration area, then an unwanted depopulation of given areas can at least be hindered.

All of these aspects played a role in Malaysia's involvement with IEs. Of importance within the context of this study, however, are the last three points, as the first point deals basically with intra-regional or intra-urban economics. In analysing IEs, it should be noted that they are basically nothing else than a microcosm of (usually but not necessarily exclusively) manufacturing activities within a specifically delineated area in a given region. The extent to which an IE is incorporated into the region and the extent to which the factor intensity of production therein reflects the factor endowment of the region determines the degree to which an efficient allocation of resources has occurred. Two general areas of investigation can be distilled therefrom: first of all the manner with which IEs have been structured according to the economic environment they have been placed in, and secondly the pricing policies directly influencing the behaviour of companies within IEs. In other words, the process by which IEs are established thus begins with a feasibility study that includes all relevant regional and national parameters, thereby taking into consideration not only the specific regional factors, but also with respect to the size of the city, town or village in (or near) which it is to be located. Furthermore, the particular function an IE is seen as serving, i.e. whether aimed at local, national and/or international markets, also influences the structure of IEs. Obviously, conclusions resulting from such considerations for an agro-based, rurally situated IE will be of a different nature than those drawn from an analysis of an IE, where basically export-oriented companies are to be located. The degree to which the above-mentioned points actually received the necessary amount of attention in the course of the IE-policies followed in Malaysia should be briefly reviewed before trying to determine the overall affectiveness of this policy measure.

FITTING INDUSTRIAL ESTATES INTO THEIR ECONOMIC ENVIRONMENT - THE MALAYSIAN EXPERIENCE

Under the term economic environment, such aspects such as transportation and communication facilities, access to raw materials and intermediate inputs, availability of non-conventional inputs (e.g. financial, marketing and export services) and nearness to an adequate number of (potentially) qualified workers are included.

As far as the transportation and communications infrastructure is concerned, all of the estates are located on or are directly hooked up to major roads. However, access to other parts of the country or to international markets differs widely (as can be seen in Table 3.7 and the maps in the Appendix). Whereas the majority of the IEs are located near railway lines, major harbour facilities or for that matter airports, are basically limited to the regions with higher incomes.

Despite the fact that harbour facilities have been or are being expanded only two major ports have been in existence for a longer period of time and offer a full range of facilities: (Port Klang)[5] in Selangor and in Penang[6] (Butterworth)[7]. The direct incorporation of harbour facilities into IEs has only been really instituted in one case – Prai Wharves FTZ[8]. Similar disparities exist with respect to the airports: here the only long-standing international airport is located in Selangor (near Kuala Lumpur), although the Penang airport (in Bayan Lepas) has been expanded rapidly in recent years[9]. The specific advantages of an airport location, i.e. quick connections with plants in other countries for receiving/shipping of inputs/finished products[10], were used only in the case of Bayan Lepas FTZ, although Sungei Way FTZ is located quite close to the Kuala Lumpur airport.

Likewise the interregional (and the intraregional) highways are better between (within) the more developed regions than between (within) the less developed regions or rather between the less and more developed regions. While a number of connecting highways have been built over the years or are in the process of being built, (the all-important East-West Highway between Penang and Kelantan should be mentioned here[11]), the lack of roads in the east-west direction has been a definite problem which has put the East Coast regions, and accordingly their IEs, at a certain disadvantage; that is, of course, to the extent that the industries settling there intended to supply more than local markets.

While the telephone and telex communication facilities belong to those features which definitely must be included in an IE-package, and generally were by Malaysian authorities, there have been indications of certain deficiencies. First of all, communication facilities in some of the well-established IEs became overcrowded, thereby making new entries and expansion difficult. Secondly, the facilities offered by IEs in the outlying areas in recent years were often incomplete or inadequate, with mere promises that complete facilities were due to be completed within a short period of time[12]. This applies particularly to the international communications to and from the less developed ares.

To sum up the Malaysian experience in ensuring that an IE was adequately and effectively integrated into the transportation and communications system, it would seem that at least with respect to transporting goods beyond local markets, many of the IEs located in less developed areas were put at a disadvantage. That is to say, to the extent that these LDRs had comparative advantages (domestically as well as internationally) for certain products, the inefficiencies in the transportation system might well have kept the IEs from exploiting them. A similar conclusion could be drawn in connection with the impact of less than adequate communications, whereby this factor is all the more crucial the greater the ties with other parts of the country or with other countries are.

As concerns the availability of raw materials or intermediate inputs, generally speaking, the industrial structure of IEs was not planned to the extent that a certain core of industries was deemed to be appropriate and the rest selected on the basis of the backward and forward linkages of this core group. This can, for instance, be deduced from Table A7 (as well as from information in the various SEDC publications), where the type of industry in existence (or desired) is often merely described as 'general'. Exceptions, however, are also noticeable and, as a matter of fact, these exceptions are apparently becoming more the rule. In particular the IEs still in the planning and development stage (Spinanger, 1980, Table 12) reveal the attempt to aim at developing backward linkages to the natural resource base (Ricardo-type goods): the same holds true for those IEs recently established in the less developed areas. Although the linkages do not appear to have been explicitly planned within the industrial estates in MDRs, it can no doubt be assumed that small-scale industries moving into MIEL-constructed workshops fulfil this function to some extent.

It would probably be correct to state that until recently no real attempt was made to structure carefully the IEs in accordance with the desired industries. That is, the industrial structure which developed was, with some exceptions[13], the result of decisions of entrepreneurs, made either with or without regard to the given or potential industrial structure of the IEs. While this market-economy approach has a definite advantage over a regulated settlement, as distortions are kept to a minimum, it does implicitly favour those IEs located close to growth centres (where agglomeration economies can be tapped) and transportation facilities (where easy access to world markets is possible) if nothing is done to attract industries to the development regions. This not being the case means that the less developed areas were put at a disadvantage, since they would basically harbour those industries producing for smaller and less dynamic domestic markets. It would thus seem quite congruent that a promotion of the tapping of the natural resource base (comparative advantages) in the less developed regions be instituted and facilitated by the establishment of IEs for downstream processing. It should be noted, however, that the effectiveness of such policies might well have been hindered by possible inadequate transportation facilities and by the regional utility rate differentials mentioned above.

The policies pursued in Malaysia, with respect to ensuring that an industrial establishment in an IE had easy access to the necessary inputs and ancillary services so as to facilitate the flow of information and assistance from outside commercial and government institutions, were concentrated until recently on the larger urban areas, i.e. in the more developed states. MIDA, for instance, opened its first regional office in West Malaysia in Kuantan in 1972 (followed by Alor Setar in 1973, Kota Bahru in 1974, Ipoh in 1975 and Johor Bahru in 1978); a similar pattern of dispersal can be observed for MIDF (which is now located in Penang, Ipoh, Johor Bahru, Kuantan and Kota Bahru). Complementing this regional dispersal of offices have been the current attempts to inform the (potential) business community via investment seminars at state or regional level. Furthermore, manpower training institutes are being set up in Kuala Trengganu and Johor Bahru. However, as opposed to the various organizations supporting agricultural establishments[14], there are no organizations set up specifically to promote the marketing or exporting of products produed in IEs[15]. As a matter of fact, not in a single IE are there consulting facilities. It is thus a matter of relying on local assistance, a considerable problem if an IE is not located in an urbanized area or in a state capital and this is the case in many of the newly established IEs (Diagram 5.1.).

With respect to ensuring that IEs were located near adequate supplies of labour, the authorities in Malaysia initially did so by establishing them essentially in the largest (in terms of population) urban areas (Tables 3.7 and 5.1). Thus, by 1970 all eight IEs in existence had been established in districts with towns of more than 50,000 inhabitants. By 1978 and particularly in the case of the planned IEs, however, the industrial dispersal policies had led to an increased establishment of IEs in districts with towns of less than 15,000 inhabitants (Table 5.2 contains an overview of regional and state population by town size, density and growth rates).

While, once the political decision has been made to decentralize, there might seem to be no serious doubt about using IEs as an integral part of an industrial decentralization policy also aiming at, *inter alia,* 'catching' migrants leaving the rural agricultural sector who would otherwise have flocked to the urban areas (thereby encountering or inducing the well-known problems[16]), two basic questions must still be raised. First of all, were those districts (towns) selected potentially large enough to support an IE? That is, placing them in communities too small could quite possibly handicap enterprises and easily result in a wasteful use of investment funds (Bredo, 1970, p. 22). Although the population in 1970 should not be taken as a potential indicator of a long-run labour supply, it does seem to be less than prudent to locate IEs in districts where (in some cases) up to 75 per cent of the (relatively small) number of inhabitants population are living in towns either with less than 5,000 inhabitants, or in non-incorporated areas[17]. As has been pointed out before (see, for instance, Davies, 1967), the fact that the degree of utilization of the labour supply in less developed areas is generally lower than in developed areas must not be misinterpreted. The problem is, namely, that the labour supply is scattered over such a wide area that it is much more difficult to round labourers up for work in a given location than in areas of high population density. Furthermore, when it comes to looking for a particular type of skilled labor, the local supply might either be extremely small or even nonexistent. Such difficulties are reduced considerably in large urban areas where agglomeration economies (in the form of better communication and transportation facilities) exist. Thus, the type of industries which lend themselves to being established in rural areas, aside from the (capital-intensive) extractive industries (i.e. those of the Ricardo type), are in such cases obviously small scale (see, e.g., Staley, Morse, 1965, pp. 242ff., 313).

This brings the discussion to the second question, namely, what attention was paid to trying to ensure that IEs catered to industries suited for location in such areas? One aspect has been given increased attention in recent years – the raw material advantages (Ricardo goods) of a given region. Despite the fact that the exploitation of the resource base might be both technically feasible and economically profitable (in terms of opportunity costs), the question of downstream resource processing in remote areas must be carefully examined, particularly with respect to the employment possibilities. To be specific, while the initial exploitation of Ricardo goods often demands capital-intensive techniques, thereby pre-empting an aiming at employment goals, it was pointed out earlier (Donges, Riedel, 1977) that in downstream-processing activities labour-intensive methods are available. To the extent that the economic environment allows these methods to be instituted, then IEs with such processing facilities (and towns into which they are incorporated) can serve employment goals. Likewise, the IEs in the less developed areas can be structured so as to allow small-scale industries to prosper. Such, however, does not seem to

DIAGRAM 5.1
Development of Industrial Estates and Distance from Major Urban Centres in West Malaysia

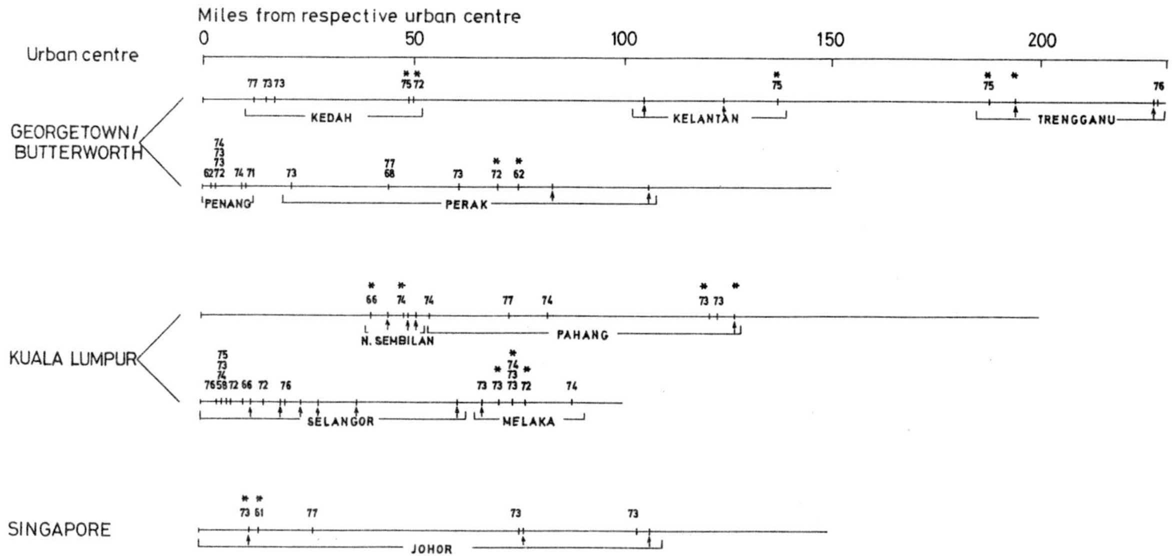

Key: The numbers above the distance line represent year in which IE established.
* means that IE located in or near (10 miles) state capital.
↑ means that IE is planned.

TABLE 5.1
Development of Industrial Estates *vis-à-vis* Town Populations, 1970–1978

	Number of IEs in Districts with Towns of ... Inhabitants											
	1970			*1974*			*1978*			*Planned*		
Region/State	*<15,000*	*15,000 -50,000*	*>50,000*	*<15,000*	*15,000 -50,000*	*>50,000*	*<15,000*	*15,000 -50,000*	*>50,000*	*<15,000*	*15,000 -50,000*	*>50,000*
Northern states	–	–	–	1	2	3	1	3	4	3	–	1
Trengganu	–	–	–	1	–	–	1	–	1	1	–	1
Kelantan	–	–	–	–	–	1	–	–	1	2	–	–
Perlis	–	–	–	–	–	–	–	–	–			
Kedah	–	–	–	–	2	2	–	3	2	–	–	–
Southern states	–	–	2	4	2	10	5	2	11	2	2	1
Pahang	–	–	–	3	1	–	4	1	–	–	1	–
Melaka	–	–	–	1	1	5	1	1	5	1	–	–
Johor	–	–	2	–	–	5	–	–	6	1	1	1
Western states	–	–	6	1	6	15	1	6	20	5	6	–
Perak	–	–	2	1	1	3	1	1	4	–	2	–
Selangor	–	–	2	–	–	7	–	–	11	3	3	–
Negeri Sembilan	–	–	1	–	1	1	–	1	1	2	1	–
Penang	–	–	1	–	4	4	–	4	4	–	–	–
Total	–	–	8	6	10	28	7	11	35	10	8	2

<u>Sources</u>: See Tables 3.6 and 3.7.

have been the case: that is, small workshops and ready-made facilities were offered by MIEL basically in the better developed areas. Furthermore, and perhaps more important, consulting and marketing services integrated into such IEs were not offered at all.

One other factor of crucial importance in this context is the quality of the labour supply. As has been the case in many industrialized countries, policies which have been instituted to help ensure equal pay for equal jobs in all parts of the country have caused, *ceteris paribus*, production techniques to be more capital-intensive in less developed areas[18]. The reason for this economically undesirable behaviour[19] lies in the (generally) lower level of the quality of human capital in less developed regions, which induces entrepreneurs to shift to a more capital-intensive production structure so as to maintain a given level of productivity (unit labour costs). In the case of Malaysia, it was al-

TABLE 5.2
Degree of Urbanization and Population in West Malaysia by Regions and States

	Population							
	Percentage Distribution by Town Size							
		Number of Inhabitants						
Region/State	*Not in Town*	*<5,000*	*5,000-15,000*	*15,000-50,000*	*>50,000*	*'000*	*Density per sq.Mile*	*Annual Growth Rate(%)*
				1970				*1957/70*
Northern states	74.15	8.62	6.55	3.32	8.07	2,166.12		
Trengganu	60.23	10.94	11.37	4.32	13.15	405.37	81.0	2.6
Kelantan	75.10	6.57	10.25	-	8.09	684.74	118.7	2.3
Perlis	85.02	7.74	7.24	-	-	121.06	394.1	2.8
Kedah	76.38	9.22	1.78	5.68	6.92	954.95	261.7	2.3
Southern states	60.06	11.40	6.43	6.68	15.43	2,186.26		
Pahang	63.87	12.93	6.41	16.79	-	504.95	36.2	3.6
Melaka	67.40	6.14	5.06	-	21.39	404.13	632.7	2.5
Johor	56.23	12.46	6.88	4.80	19.64	1,277.18	173.5	2.4
Western states	46.85	8.30	9.29	4.73	30.83	4,457.19		
Perak	50.76	11.71	11.28	6.90	19.36	1,569.14	192.5	1.9
Selangor	42.51	5.77	8.30	3.07	40.36	1,630.37	513.5	3.6
Negeri Sembilan	61.86	10.73	10.74	-	16.67	481.56	187.2	2.1
Penang	38.85	5.28	6.48	6.74	42.65	776.12	1,938.2	2.3
Total	56.67	9.15	7.91	4.86	21.48	8,809.56	172.8	2.6
				1980				*1970/80*
Northern states	63.93	6.21	5.22	5.78	16.00	2,681.13	177.0	1.9
Trengganu	48.53	7.57	1.07	8.41	34.41	542.28	108.4	3.0
Kelantan	64.74	3.64	8.34	4.09	19.19	888.83	154.2	2.6
Perlis	83.83	7.38	8.79	-	-	147.38	480.1	2.0
Kedah	68.18	7.45	4.25	6.62	6.50	1,102.64	281.8	1.5
Southern states	57.91	6.90	6.98	5.07	23.14	2,844.65	130.2	2.7
Pahang	63.71	5.08	8.03	5.91	17.28	790.54	56.9	4.6
Melaka	67.79	5.81	3.09	3.87	19.44	453.16	711.4	1.2
Johor	52.24	8.11	7.57	5.00	27.07	1,600.95	218.4	2.3
Western states	42.72	7.28	5.85	4.14	40.01	5,662.33	397.6	2.4
Perak	48.52	12.69	7.87	5.56	25.35	1,773.64	218.7	1.2
Selangor	34.80	3.55	3.68	1.93	56.04	2,413.22	762.2	4.0
Negeri Sembilan	54.98	9.64	6.95	4.26	24.15	563.80	219.8	1.6
Penang	44.80	5.17	7.02	7.12	35.89	911.67	2,284.9	1.6
Total	51.66	6.93	5.98	4.77	29.96	11,188.10	281.7	2.4

Sources: Own calculations based on Dept. of Statistics (Field Count Summary, 1971; General Report 1970; Local Authority Areas: Population, Households and Living Quarters, 1982, Tables 1-12).

The underlined figures are above national average.

ready noted that the average level of general education was relatively high, but regional differences were nonetheless quite sizeable and specific educational programmes for industrial jobs were lacking[20]. Malaysian authorities were well aware at an early stage of how essential programmes were to increase the levels of both general and, particularly, specific education[21]. However, the regional dispersion of such programmes, although intensified in recent years (see above), has probably favoured the large urban areas, thereby increasing regional human capital differentials; industrial training institutes, for instance, exist only in Prai (Penang) and Kuala Lumpur[22]. While the reasoning behind such a concentration would seem obvious (greatest impact and effectiveness, economies of scale, etc.), of immediate importance to firms in the IEs would be facilities located nearby or even on the IEs' grounds where general training programmes could be carried out. Such facilities could offer production and marketing advice to entrepreneurs or even function as a trading house between small-scale businesses and distant markets.

The interfacing of IEs into the given (and expected) supplies of labour would seem to have functioned better in the more developed areas of Malaysia. The resulting increase in regional human capital disparities, although no doubt alleviated by counterpolicy effects in recent years, can be viewed as a shortcoming which bears with it the seeds of increased development disparities in the future. To avoid such a tendency more attention should be given to the differentiated labour demands between the less and the more developed areas (or in the small and large towns), e.g. by providing all relevant facilities for small-scale companies and ensuring that the quality of entrepreneurs and labour does not prove to be a limiting development factor in the less developed areas. While it is the entrepreneurs (incorporating the Schumpeterian spirit) whose function it is in a market economy, which Malaysia is, to act as the driving force of development, it is the labour force upon which increasing human capital demands are placed in a growing economy. It is thus of crucial importance to institute human-capital building measures, particularly in the less developed regions, whereby general and specific (vocational/technical) educational facilities (as opposed to academic institutions) need be given more stress[23]. After all, Malaysia's position in the world economy is one of an emerging industrialized country and a reliance on past human-capital structures would make it increasingly less competitive.

PRICING POLICIES FOR INDUSTRIAL ESTATES AND THEIR SERVICES

As mentioned earlier, the policies practised in supplying the necessary utilities[24] would seem to have run counter to the proposed goal of promoting a dispersal of industries, as electricity and water rates tended to be higher in the less developed than in the developed areas (Tables A5 and A6). If such a policy was based on the assumption that utility-intensive industries were also capital-intensive and as such were to be discouraged from settling in less developed regions because, *ceteris paribus,* factor endowments dictated labour-intensive industries in such regions, then regionally differentiated utility prices could be understood, although they were not necessarily economically efficient. First of all, if all other parameters were equal, the the lower utility prices in developed areas would give them an advantage. As a matter of fact utility costs are actually not an insignificant part of total input costs or value added of certain industries and can thus affect location decisions. While on the average they amount to 3.15 (7.25) per cent[25], they amount to only 1.63 (1.60) per cent for the manufacturing of radio, television and communications equipment (industry code 38320) but 20.04 (14.87) per cent for the manufacturing of pottery, china and earthenware (industry code 36100) and 71.72 (50.00) per cent for ice factories (industry code 31211). Secondly, by deflecting the utility-intensive industries into the developed areas (IEs) the demand for utilities increased at faster rates than anticipated, thereby causing overloading and power shortages. Thirdly, to the extent that utility-intensive industries are necessary to exploit the comparative advantages of a given less developed region, the utility price differentiation in effect in Malaysia tends to increase their prices as well as all prices in downstream industries *(ceteris paribus)*. In light of such considerations it would be difficult to contend that general regional policy aims, in particular with respect to IEs, were decisively supported by accommodating utility rate structures.

With respect to renting out the developed lots in IEs at competitiveprices (perhaps with the possibility of renting flexibly designed factory buildings or workshops for small-scale industries), it is unfortunately quite impossible with the given data constraints to determine the extent to which such policies were explicitly followed. What can be attempted, however, is an implicit approach in which the capital invested in each IE is determined, premiums and rents are analysed and the degrees to which the IEs were utilized are examined. By comparing these figures it should be possible to determine the direction and force of the pricing policies, particularly with respect to helping overcome locational disadvantages caused by factor and product market distortions.

As was seen in Table 3.6, there is already quite a regional premium (cost) and rental differential which can be interpreted as reflecting either an explicit attempt on the part of the authorities to compensate for (create) locational disadvantages (advantages) or rather merely reflecting actual relative land prices and agglomeration economies. Although the former would correspond with the expressed intent of the Malaysian government's dispersal of industries policy, it cannot be excluded that the latter also influenced the scope of the differentials. One reason for expecting the latter is simply that most of the IEs were set up by the individual State Economic Development Corporations (SEDCs).

Without delving any deeper into this aspect at the moment, but not forgetting the ramifications, it should be possible, if the various costs and receipts are known, to calculate

1. a potential return on investment if the entire IE was occupied,
2. the actual return on investment based on occupancy data (available through the end of 1977) and
3. the critical level of utilization (CLOU) of an IE necessary to achieve a full return on investment.

Knowing these figures and the speed with which occupancy occurred as well as regional differences therein, conclusions about whether *de facto* policies jibe with intended or economic efficient ones can be drawn.

Despite the lack of specific and detailed information on the development costs of each IE, enough data are available on a number of IEs so as to allow average per acre development costs to be estimated and then applied to all IEs[26]. Granted, such an estimate does not account for the idiosyncrasies of constructing each IE, but the assumed average cost/acre of M$15,000 does not exceed (or fall below) actual figures by more than 25 per cent; major distortions are thus assumed not to exist.

An examination of these calculations[27] (Table 5.3) reveals that

1. in almost all cases the IEs provided a sizeable, positive potential return on (estimated) investment capital (col.3). Even those IEs in the less developed regions exhibited sizeable positive returns, although these were considerably higher for the IEs in the more developed regions.
2. the critical level of utilization (CLOU) seems to be at a level which allows the investment to be recouped rather quickly.

3. the speed with which this level was reached (col. 8) was, surprisingly enough, not any slower in LDRs than in MDRs.

What can be concluded from these observations is that, in accordance with the stated policy intentions, the IEs seemed to be (real) money-making ventures – at least, in an accounting fashion (where revenues are in excess over expenses). The question which must still be answered is to what extent the premiums and rents actually reflected prevailing market prices. In light of the fact that, given the zoning restrictions, there were hardly any *de jure* restrictions on setting up plants outside IEs (and ignoring possibly *de facto* barriers), it would seem quite obvious, keeping in mind the speed with which the IEs filled up, that industrial sites were priced well under market rates.

This contention can indeed be substantiated, as in many cases prices for properties outside industrial estates were up to ten times higher than prices paid for land inside industrial estates[28]. Knowing this to be the case it is possible to calculate the amount of income which would accrue if all the parcels of land in the IEs were to be sold at market prices – the difference between potential actual prices and potential market prices is considered to be a subsidy[29]. It can clearly be seen from Table 5.4 that in all of but two states, IEs are implicitly subsidized, whereby the amount in the MDRs is not always the lowest. In other words, although the IEs seemed to be profitable ventures, they were actually priced in a way which implicitly worked as a subsidy, and not structured so as to necessarily promote a better exploitation of the regional comparative advantages in the LDRs. How companies would have reacted without the subsidies is a mute question, but given the (usually) easy access to infrastructure and the secure lease most of them would probably have located in the IEs at market rates anyhow. This being the case, the SEDCs would now be operating extremely lucrative ventures.

As has already been pointed out, merely the creation of regionally dispersed, developed industrial sites is not a sufficient condition to attract investments into LDRs; i.e. it is but one ingredient in the policy package. Since it has already been established that an enticement via regionally differentiated IE infrastructure was not offered (at least, not in the direction of the LDRs), then at least some similarly oriented measures might be expected with respect to the pricing of land or buildings, if the regional aims of IEs are to be fulfilled. But even if this were done, for instance, in the case of quitrents for land, it can hardly be expected to have a noticeable impact since quitrents represent merely a minute fraction of value added[30]. Buildings would seem to be a more promising area (after all they represent about 27 per cent of assets), but such policies were not instituted[31].

In light of the information revealed on invested capital in the MDRs (Table 5.4, col. 5), and knowing that the responsibility for the development of IEs was primarily in the hand of the SEDCs, it can be deduced, that the locational advantages of the MDRs were further positively influenced (thus running counter to stated goals), since the receipts could be used by the SEDC for a further betterment of the competitive position of the state[32]. This situation is the result of a financial set-up in Malaysia which (at the moment) does not allow a full coordination and management of both policy and financial matters at the federal level (see, e.g. Holzhausen, 1974). That is to say, although the position of the federal government is theoretically strong enough to carry out a strict policy of regional equalization, there were indications that it was felt that such a policy would be economically unwise and financially too costly (Holzhausen, 1974, pp. 175ff.). Generally speaking, the problem of equity in the context of federal finance arises from the fact that states exhibit differing gaps between their fiscal capacities and financial needs. In Malaysia very substantial differences in the fiscal capacities of the states can be observed[33].

In other words the more productive revenue sources are in the hands of the federal government. The fiscal gap between the states' own domestic revenues and their expenditures amounts from 15 to 75 per cent. While Holzhausen points to the possibility of higher taxes in the richer states, he rejects this possibility on the grounds of inefficiency and cost. Of crucial importance is also the possible conflict between the regional equity goal and the goal of more growth on a macro-level[34]. In light of the Malaysian free market oriented approach it seems likely that such an aspect was given considerable attention; i.e. the federal government merely set up the foundations upon which the economy could be allowed to expand. Furthermore, given the financial constraints, it seemed to be in the best interest of the country to direct infrastructure investments into areas where the highest returns could be expected, and this was precisely the policy which initially dominated the establishment of IEs in Malaysia. In switching to more regionally-oriented policies in Malaysia it is likely that the policy mix was not shifted accordingly. Ergo, despite the success of achieving relatively high IE occupancy levels in LDRs, the LDRs' success was overshadowed by that of the MDRs and they were put to a further disadvantage in the absence of an effective burden (revenue) sharing between the various states. Such a policy, should it be desired, could be efficiently

TABLE 5.3
Development Costs and Return on Investment in Industrial Estates in Malaysia

Region/State/ Industrial Estate	Potential Premium[a]	Estimated Development Costs[b]	Potential Return on Investment (1:2)·100	Actual Premiums Received[c]	Actual Return on Investment (4:2)·100	Critical Level of Utilization[d] (CLOU)	Years Since Establishment	Years Needed to Reach CLOU[e]
	M$m		per cent	M$m.	per cent			
	1	2	3	4	5	6	7	8
Northern states								
Trengganu								
Gong Badak	3.51	3.56	98.6	.40	11.2	101.4	3	-
Jakar	.75	.37	202.7	.75	202.7	49.3	4	1
Kelantan								
Pengkalan Chepa	.52	.36	144.4	.29	80.6	69.3	4	-
Perlis								
Kedah								
Bakar Arang	8.31	3.98	208.8	6.08	152.8	47.9	5	2
Kuala Kedah	.61	.71	85.9	.37	52.1	116.4	4	-
Kulim	5.41	2.51	215.5	2.91	115.9	46.3	1	-
Mergong	5.13	2.25	228.0	5.13	228.0	43.9	6	2
Tikam Batu	2.08	1.50	138.7	1.95	130.0	72.1	5	1
Southern states								
Pahang								
Jerantut	2.40	1.68	142.9	.28	16.7	70.0	1	-
Maran	.62	.53	117.0	.52	98.1	85.5	4	-
Peramu	8.00	3.79	211.1	1.54	40.6	47.4	5	-
Semambu	19.69	7.65	257.4	10.17	132.9	38.9	5	2
Songsang	3.85	2.31	166.7	3.43	148.5	60.0	4	2
Melaka								
Alor Gajah	1.26	.60	210.0	.66	110.0	47.6	5	2
Ayer Keroh	7.89	3.80	207.6	5.67	149.2	48.2	6	1
Batu Berandam FTZ	1.11	.50	222.0	.96	192.0	45.0	5	1
Bukit Rambai	1.05	.48	218.8	.64	133.3	45.7	4	1
Merlimau	2.81	1.20	234.2	.22	18.3	42.7	4	-
Tanjong Kling	5.00	2.25	222.2	.74	32.9	45.0	5	-
Tanjong Kling FTZ	.68	.30	226.7	.68	226.7	44.1	5	2
Johor								
Larkin and Tampoi	6.85	6.20	110.5	6.85	110.5	90.5	17	?
Pasir Gudang	54.56	19.74	276.4	50.05	253.5	36.3	5	2
Senai FTZ	1.09	.30	363.3	.0	.0	27.5	1	-
Tanjung Agas	3.19	1.16	275.0	2.71	233.6	36.4	6	1
Tongkang Pecah	.93	.42	221.4	.73	173.8	45.2	6	3

(continued)

TABLE 5.3 (continued)

Region/State/ Industrial Estate	Potential Premium[a]	Estimated Development Costs[b]	Potential Return on Investment (1:2)·100	Actual Premiums Received[c]	Actual Return on Investment (4:2)·100	Critical Level of Utilization[d] (CLOU)	Years Since Establishment	Years Needed to Reach CLOU[e]
	M$m		per cent	M$m.	per cent			
	1	2	3	4	5	6	7	8
Western states								
Perak								
Jelapang	1.21	1.38	87.7	1.21	87.7	114.0	6	-
Kamunting	.23	8.79	2.6	.12	1.4	3,816.8	10	?
Kuala Kangsar	4.09	1.86	219.9	2,19	117.7	45.5	5	2
Parit Buntar	2.35	.90	261.1	1.16	128.9	38.3	5	2
Tasek	6.04	5.54	109.9	6.04	109.0	91.7	16	?
Tupai	2.64	1.46	180.8	2.64	180.8	55.3	1	1
Selangor								
Ampang/Ulu Klang	6.66	.90	740.0	6.66	740.0	13.5	3	1
Ampang/Ulu Klang FTZ	2.83	.75	377.3	2.83	377.3	26.5	5	1
Batu Caves	9.71	2.13	455.9	9.71	455.9	21.9	4	1
Pandamaran	11.46	2.58	444.2	11.46	444.2	22.5	6	2
Petaling Jaya	60.06	11.55	520.0	60.06	520.0	19.2	20	?
Selat Klang Utara	83.09	5.70	1,457.7	15.75	276.3	6.9	2	2
Setapak	7.14	2.18	327.5	4.94	226.6	30.1	2	2
Shah Alam	92.17	20.43	451.2	92.17	451.2	22.2	6	1
Sungei Way/Subang FTZ	8.17	2.11	387.2	7.61	360.7	25.8	6	2
Telok Panglima Garang	2.03	.72	281.9	1.17	162.5	35.5	3	3
Telok Panglima Garang FTZ	3.14	.79	397.5	3.08	389.9	25.2	4	1
Negeri Sembilan								
Kampong Dioh	1.37	.86	159.3	.81	94.2	62.8	4	-
Senawang	5.44	4.95	109.9	5.44	109.9	91.0	6	3
Penang								
Bagan Serai	2.80	2.09	134.0	2.80	134.0	74.6	5	3
Bayan Lepas	.93	1.50	62.0	.24	16.0	161.3	4	-
Bayan Lepas FTZ	20.21	4.10	492.9	9.17	223.7	20.3	7	2
Mak Mandin	9.71	2.98	325.8	8.21	275.5	30.7	16	?
Prai	37.76	18.82	200.6	1.29	6.9	49.9	7	-
Prai FTZ	20.03	5.62	356.4	1.74	31.0	28.1	6	4
Prai Wharves FTZ	3.31	.57	580.1	1.02	178.9	17.2	6	2
Pulau Jerejak FTZ	n.a.	.29	n.a.	n.a.	n.a.	n.a.	5	?

Source: See Table 3.6.

[a]Based on saleable acreage as of 31.12.77 as shown in Table 10.

[b]Based on an average development cost per acre of $15,000. See Table A8 for known development costs for certain IEs. Acreage is equal to developed acreage as of 31.12.77 and includes streets, docks, etc., so it differs from saleable acreage which includes only the lots.

[c] As of 31.12.77. Calculating by multiplying acres occupied by premium/acre.

[d]Represents the occupancy rate in IEs necessary to ensure a 100% return on investment.

[e]? = Year in which CLOU reached unknown; - = CLOU not yet reached.

carried out (in a second best manner) by charging near market prices for IE land in the MDRs, and, in addition to the implicit subsidization in the LDRs, redistribute the additional revenues from the MDRs to improve the competitive position of the LDRs.

To summarize, the IE pricing policies do not seem to have been structured in such a way so as to support forcefully a more equal regional dispersion of industries in accordance with the given comparative advantages. Nonetheless, the IEs did fill up quickly to a level at which a return on investment was achieved (without taking opportunity costs into account); the question as to whether the IEs attracted the investment or whether the investment would have occurred anyhow, however, has yet to be answered.

TABLE 5.4

Degree of Subsidization of Industrial Estates in Malaysia, 1978 (M$'000)

	Premium				*Quitrent*		
Region/State	*Potential Actual Prices (1)*	*Premium Market Prices (2)*	*Subsidy (-) (3)*	*Degree of Subsidization (%) (4)*	*Potential Actual Prices (5)*	*Rent Market Prices (6)*	*Subsidy (-) (7)*
Northern states	29,572.3	134,397.9	-104,825.8	454.5	225.1	1,392,0	-1,167.0
Trengganu	4,261.9	13,309.8	-9,047.8	312.3	44.8	142.6	-97.8
Kelantan	3,776.7	21,941.2	-18,164.5	580.9	54.8	675.5	-620.8
Perlis	-	-	-	-	-	-	-
Kedah	21,533.7	99,146.9	-77,613.2	460.4	125.5	573.9	-448.4
Southern states	157,292.2	237,727.7	-80,436.5	151.1	832.4	5,654.5	-4,901.0
Pahang	37,033.2	43,836.5	-6,804.3	118.4	236.8	239.8	-3.0
Melaka	19,808.9	11,652.3	+8,156.6	58.8	94.2	54.7	+39.4
Johor	100,450.1	182,238.9	-81,788.8	181.4	501.4	5,360.0	-4,858.6
Western states	511,862.5	1,247,004.9	-735,142.4	243.6	5,312.7	37,906.3	-32,593.6
Perak	167,112.8	300,725.2	-133,612.4	180.0	179.8	8,269.9	-8,090.1
Selangor	243,171.5	550,916.4	-307,744.9	226.6	3,765.6	24,829.4	-21,063.7
Negeri Sembilan	6,819.5	5,785.5	+1,034.0	84.8	236.1	203.1	+33.0
Penang	94,758.7	389,577.8	-294,819.1	411.1	1,131.2	4,603.9	-3,472.8
Total	698,727.0	1,619,130.5	-920,404.7	231.7	6,370.2	44,952.8	-38,661.6

Sources: Own calculations based on data from industrial estates in 1978 and information on market prices for industrial property near industrial estates (Ministry of Finance, 1978).

[a]100% in column (4) or a + in columns (4)/(7) = no subsidization.

CONCLUDING REMARKS

In this chapter, the purpose of which was to determine whether the Malaysian IE policies were adequately structural so as to interface with the respective locational comparative advantages and in line with pronounced policy aims (i.e. reducing regional development disparities), it has become evident that the whole of the IE policy package was not so formulated. While it is true that the total impact of the IE policies can only be fully interpreted within the context of all macro and regional industrialization measures, knowing thereby the extent to which IEs actually influence investors in their investment behaviour and, given the necessary information, prompt entrepreneurial activities to be forthcoming, it is true that the failure to ensure the fulfilment of basic preconditions (also essential for industrialization in general) was not compensated for by other measures. Particularly as far as the trend towards setting up IEs outside agglomerated areas is concerned it is necessary to pay attention to the ingredients missing in the economic environment that have hindered and/or would hinder economic growth[35]. The ingredients lacking, in particular, are those which provide information so crucial to the functioning of a market economy – in essence institutions offering non-convential inputs. This not being the case in Malaysia, where the IEs seemed to be better equipped in MDRs, aside from being able to profit from agglomeration economies, IE policies tended to counter the stated policy aims.

1 The author neglects the more broader based policies of the government to promote regional growth centres. Growth centres were defined as towns with populations from inhabitants where certain conditions were fulfilled (see Krüger, 1982, pp. 143-7). While it is realised that these growth centres represent an important part of the overall local economic environment and as such are essential for the functioning of firms in industrial estates, a more detailed explicit analysis of the wide variety of measures applied in this connection would, as in the case of the new development areas, have expanded the research beyond the initial aims. That agglomeration economies do make a difference is shown by Townroe, Nigel (1980) and by Wang, Wong (1980) for Malaysia.

2 A description of what is understood to be an IE can be found on pp. 62-3. FTZs are also covered by this definition, the only difference being that they have been delineated out of the country in some respects (e.g. no trade barriers). In a case where no trade barriers existed in a country the term FTZ becomes superfluous. Hong Kong or even Singapore (to a large extent) would be examples of such.

3 Industrial estates as they are understood today date back to the Trafford Park Estates Ltd. in Manchester, England (1896) and the Clearing Industrial District in Chicago, Illinois (for more details, see Bredo, 1960). Their use has spread rapidly, particularly since the Second World War, throughout the industrialized and the industrializing countries. Considerable success, especially in interfacing industrialization developments with increased productivity in the agricultural sector, has been achieved in Taiwan. By the end of 1978 there were 40 industrial estates in existence in Taiwan, with 6 more being developed and 47 planned (Industrial Development Bureau, 1978). India on the other hand, with over 600 industrial estates, has not been able to copy this success (for a description of India's programme, see Sanghvi, 1979).
Free trade zones, albeit in a somewhat different form, date back to the roots of organized trade (e.g. at Tyre, Carthage, Utica and other places in the Mediterranean). Hamburg, for instance, was explicitly given a charter by Frederick I of the Holy Roman Empire to exempt it from the payment of customs duties (see Thoman, 1956; for an overview of existing FTZs in the world, see Currie, 1979, 1983; for FTZs in Asia see Spinanger, 1984).

4 To be specific, since it is assumed that the investment decision is not affected by the existence of an IE, and since there are not extra costs which must be borne by the companies or the government, there remains the individual citizen who, assuming he prefers more purely residential areas, profits from not having to live among or next to factories. Of course, should residential areas be far removed from IEs, then additional problems occur, as can be evidenced by the dying out of the city centres in the United States. There, industries migrated out of the city, beyond the suburban ring and sprouted up around the circle freeways, outer belts and inter-state highways which not only twisted commuter traffic flows, but also meant that those without private cars (often the blacks) – since public transportation often did not exist – were cut off from job opportunities. Furthermore, as the tax base of the cities was reduced, the ensuing structural problems could not be dealt with adequately.

5 Draft up to 40 ft.

6 In recent years a medium-sized port has been developed in Johor (Pasir Gudang – draft: 36 ft.) and smaller facilities exist or are being developed in Pahang (Kuantan), Trengganu (Kuala Trengganu) and Melaka (Melaka). The lack of major port facilities in the southern part of Malaysia is due to the existence of the excellent facilities in Singapore, the second largest port in the world (1983, based on tonnage in international trade).

7 Draft up to 32 ft.

8 In the case of Pasir Gudang the plan also calls for such an integration.

9 Other domestically-oriented airports are located in Perak (Ipoh), Melaka, Johor (Senai) and Kelantan (Kota Bahru).

10 This proves to be of particular importance in the case of the electronics industry.

11 This highway reduces by more than half the distance by road between the two coasts.

12 See, for instance, SEDC (Investment Prospects, 1976, Suppl., p. 61): 'Telecommunication services like telephone and telex are readily available ... Automatic dialing for Tikom Batu and Bakar Arang throughout the country can be made available with the completion of the new telephone exchange in Sungai Petani soon. As for Kulim, automatic dialing can be possible by September 1978'.

13 Aside from the raw material based industries, export industries (e.g. Bayan Lepas with the electronics industries), whose demand for services is quite large, were also an exception.

14 These include, for instance, the Food Industries of Malaysia Sdn. Bhd. (FIMA) which assists in setting up and expanding agricultural production as well as helping to market the products; the Federal Agricultural Marketing Authority (FAMA), which not only helps in marketing agricultural products but also seeks to discover new markets and marketing possibilities; basic and applied agricultural research and development is carried out in the Malaysian Agricultural Research and Development Institute (MARDI).

15 In 1982 the Malaysian government decided to consider sitting up trading houses along the lines of the Japanese organizations. Although these are not to be specically coupled to IEs, they could well be used to help market products produced in IEs.

16 For a survey of the literature on this area, see the various articles in Sabot (1978).

17 Mersing, for instance, in Johor has over 78 per cent of its total population of roughly 35,000 located in towns under 5,000 inhabitants or in unincorporated areas.

18 This was, for instance, the case in Great Britain (Impact, 1969).

19 It is considered to be undesirable because it is assumed that, *ceteris paribus,* the comparative advantage of the less developed regions lies in their supply of less expensive human capital.

20 The terms general and specific education are adopted from Becker's reference to general and specific training (Becker, 1975) and are considered to be more all-encompassing.

21 These included, in addition to certain services offered by FIDA and the Ministry of Labour, in particular the National Training Service (NTS) which provided comprehensive training for industry and the trades - the National Productivity Centre (NPC, 1962), vocational and technical training courses in the lower level of schools (1964), the MARA Institute of Technology (1965), aimed at the indigenous population, and the National Apprentice Scheme (1967).

22 It should be mentioned that a number of others are in the planning stage. It might be noted that the aims of the New Economic Policy (NEP) to, *inter alia,* have employment in companies reflect the national racial composition have led (at least in one case) to a situation where a sufficient number of skilled Malays (to meet implicit quota – 40 per cent – requirements) were difficult to find (see von der Mehden, 1973, p. 29). Another interesting observation in this study was that it was mainly the females who profited from the large-size, labour-intensive industries set up in two IEs in Penang. That is, lower pay and higher manual dexterity (i.e. lower unit wage costs) and shorter on-the-job-training periods gave them a competitive edge.

23 Such vocational education may not only be essential and economically rewarding in the economy as a whole, but as Mazumdar points out (1981, p. 358) it also provides persons with attractive returns to investment in education by ensuring them a disproportionately higher share of employment.

24 Sewage facilities were not provided in the IEs – each company had to ensure that its expended water was in line with national pollution regulations.

25 The figure in parenthesis is for value added.

26 The development costs were collated from various issues of the Annual Report of the Penang Development Corporation and other information kindly provided by this SEDC. See Table A8 for a breakdown of costs by IEs within Penang.

27 For data on saleable and sold acreage as well as occupancy rates of the IEs (1970-7) see Spinanger (1980), Tables A9-A11.

28 The differences between the actual costs to the state for a given piece of land inside an IE and the market price for a similar piece outside an IE, *ceteris paribus,* would be the potential opportunity costs at a given point in time. The difference between the actual cost and the price received for land within an IE can be considered to be the realized opportunity costs. The difference between the potential and realized opportunity costs, although not an explicit monetary transfer as such to an entrepreneur, (i.e. the non-realized opportunity costs) can nonetheless still be considered a subsidy since exactly the same impact would have resulted if the land had been sold at market prices and then direct subsidies (amounting to this foregone amount) paid to the entrepreneur. To the extent that economies of scale are achieved in setting up large areas of fully developed industrial sites, and this can be expected to be the case in reality, welfare would increase additionally.

29 A similar technique was applied to the rent. Here the percentage of actual quitrent was calculated from the 1978 data and this same percentage rate applied to market value of the land in the IE.

30 On the average quitrents represent only 0.21 per cent of value added in the years 1969-73. On a 4-digit industry basis not one single industry averaged more than 1 per cent over this 5 year period. On a regional basis, the quitrents (as percentage of value added) were neither consistently higher or lower in LDRs than in MDRs.

31 Transportation subsidies, which might possibly help promote an efficient regional impact, were not included in the policy mix either.

32 The question about the source of the price differences is not examined in this respect and is actually not relevant. That is, whether the SEDCs are collecting monopoly rents for agglomeration economies and excess demand for

industrial sites in the high income states or not, does not influence the interpretation of the exceptional returns on investment in IEs with respect to bettering the position of the state.

33 This difference stems from the fact that the revenue of the states is mainly derived from forestry as well as licences and royalties on land and mines and thus accrues chiefly to the richer states.

34 Assuming that regional policies actually do cause a better allocation of the factors of production and a better exploitation of Malaysia's comparative advantages, then the conflict would tend to be more of a short-run nature.

35 Of course, if the non-existence of developed land in LDRs was the basic reason why the industrialization process was not forthcoming, and establishment of IEs now relieved this problem, then their mere existence would indeed attract new investments.

6
The Malaysian Industrialization Policy Package: Its Impact on the Regional Flows and Factor Intensity of Investments

INTRODUCTION

IN the following, Malaysian industrialization policies in their entirety are dealt with, combining thereby the main aspects of the last two chapters and extending the analysis of the regional thrust over time as well as trying to provide a more solid substantiation of their impact on factor intensities through rigorous econometric techniques. The purpose of this exercise is to attempt[1] to offer a more definite answer to the basic question of whether Malaysian industrialization policies as a whole influenced the spread, structure and factor intensities of manufacturing activities in line with the posited comparative advantages of the various regions.

After a brief overview of the regional spread of industrialization in Malaysia during the 1968-73 period (based on data from the Census of Manufacturing Industries – CMI), a detailed investigation (based on firm-level data from the Directory of Approved Companies – DAC) of the regional flow (overtime) and structure (by various criteria) of investments is presented[2]. The impact of the policies on the factor intensities of manufacturing activities is then analysed by applying OLS regression methods to firm-level data[3], given *inter alia* their location and incentive status.

AN OVERVIEW OF THE INITIAL SPREAD OF INDUSTRIALIZATION IN MALAYSIA, 1968 - 1973

It has been pointed out in Chapter 1 that the size of regional development disparities (based on per capita income) in Malaysia can be considered to be relatively small (see Table 1.3) and even decreasing. From the same table, however, it can be deduced that regional industrialization disparities (based on the manufacturing sector) are not nearly so small, although they too have been decreasing over time. Since an examination of such aspects using the state or regional breakdowns tends to minimize disparities, by presenting averages for large, rather heterogeneous areas, it would seem advisable to attempt examine the spread of industrialization on a lower, internally more homogeneous level of disaggregation. Ideally such would best be performed on a level where physical geographical differences are at a minimum, where the impact of gerrymandering or other political factors is small and where a delineation conforms largely to economic criteria. For Malaysia the district level comes closest to meeting these conditions. It might also be added that an analysis on the district level would also be of importance, e.g. in correctly structuring specific infrastructure facilities and policy measures.

The regional industrialization disparities which become evident from an analysis of district-level data (see Table 6.1) fit quite well into the picture developed so far of an economy, where disparities have began to decrease since the early 1970s. At the same time, however, the regional differences *vis-à-vis* both the degree of industrialization as well as its structure are revealed as being quite large. These two points can be deduced from the change in and the level of the coefficient of variation in Table 6.1. In particular the decrease is reflected by the values for the share of value added and share of employees. The slight increase in the value for the share of establishments does not contradict this, it merely expresses the fact that relatively more smaller scale firms have been established than larger scale firms, a conclusion which can be drawn in connection with the coefficient of variation for the number of employees per establishment. As a matter of fact, it was basically the larger decrease in the disparities within several LDR states which caused this (see Table A9).

With regard to the level of the disparities, this is best viewed keeping the dispersion of population in mind: it can be easily seen that the variation for the shares (in the first three lines) is two to almost four times larger than for the population[4].

With regard to the thrust and structure of the policies carried out in this time period, Table 6.2 reveals that, when comparing the change in the correlation coefficients between location indicators and manufacturing indices, despite relatively small shifts in the coefficients they nonetheless do point to the spreading out of industries and IEs away from their initial growth locations. The extent to which this was due to the various regional industrialization policy measures, however, cannot be determined at this point.

TABLE 6.1

Indicators of the Spread of Regional Industrialization in Malaysia,[a] 1968 and 1973

	Mean[b]		*Minimum*		*Maximum*		$\frac{s}{\bar{x}}$ 100	
	1968	*1973*	*1968*	*1973*	*1968*	*1973*	*1968*	*1973*
Share of establishments (%)	1.43	1.43	.03	.04	17.86	20.43	185.09	200.35
Share of value added (%)	1.43	1.43	.00	.00	43.67	36.68	374.67	324.42
Share of employees (%)	1.43	1.43	.00	.00	31.49	26.30	288.10	253.95
Size of establishments								
value added (M$'000)	69.08	140.48	3.25	1.50	1,545.46	1,513.16	269.46	141.67
employees (number)	8.65	16.81	.67	.50	35.76	52.19	87.56	70.94
Wages/employee (M$)	1,811	1,893	555	467	5,779	7,146	40.31	45.15
Value added/employee (M$)	5,590	7,585	1,042	1,025	48,083	50,235	105.28	82.12
Wages/value added (%)	40.52	29.44	5.52	12.33	119.23	59.94	39.43	32.58
IE-acres occupied (acres)	16.71	47.50	0	0	575	818	460.29	302.23
Population[c] ('000)	119.35	136.52	15.33	17.07	797.85	1,008.97	97.44	102.54

Sources: Own calculations based on Department of Statistics (CMI, 1968, Table 4; 1973, Tables 67ff.) and MIDA.

[a]Based on district data (70 districts) whereby Georgetown and adjoining district in Penang united. See also Table A9 for a regional breakdown of one indicator: employment size of establishment.

[b]The mean of the share is always the same, i.e. 100/70 = 1.43.

[c]Estimated population based on interpolation of growth rates between population censuses 1957 and 1970.

ANALYSING THE REGIONAL FLOW OF INVESTMENTS IN MALAYSIA, 1967-1979

The approach taken in this analysis of 1,434 companies (from the DAC), in which the regional flow of these companies over time by incentives and whether inside or outside IEs is examined with respect to certain criteria on the economic suitability of a given investment, is as follows.

First of all, it was assumed that those industries settling in the LDRs would, if they were in line with the posited comparative advantage of the LDRs, i.e. if policies did not distort production structures, tend to be

(1) of the small employment size; i.e. LDRs are considered to possess comparative advantages with respect to small-scale industries;

(2) of the small value added size; i.e. given the regional distribution constraints in Malaysia and the necessity to promote entrepreneurship step by step, new companies (that is, usually those founded by nationals) will be serving relatively small markets and thus initially of small value added size[5];

(3) of the labour-intensive (or rather non-capital-intensive) type, since it is assumed that labour, and not capital, is one important comparative advantage of the LDRs[6]. It is assumed that the lower the physical capital assets per em-

TABLE 6.2
Correlation between Locational Indicators and Change in Manufacturing Indices, 1968-1973

Locational Indicators	Share of Establishment	Share of Value Added	Share of Employment	Size of Establishment Value Added	Size of Establishment Employment	Wages/Employee	Value Added/Employee	Wages/Value Added
				1968				
Location of population (per cent)								
not in town	-.605	-.391	-.507	-.037	-.427	-.162	-.012	-.086
in towns with population of								
< 5,000	-.308	-.189	-.224	-.102	-.139	-.018	-.028	-.087
5,000-15,000	.017	-.005	-.010	.104	.100	.208	.137	-.017
15,000-50,000	.024	-.009	-.003	-.020	.109	.169	-.037	.087
>50,000	.802	.533	.676	.058	.424	-.016	-.039	-.093
Capital	.627	.379	.490	-.001	.215	-.008	-.070	.027
Railway	.232	.214	.239	.202	.292	.245	.218	-.161
Airport	.452	.435	.501	.053	.304	.248	-.004	-.194
Harbour	.154	.111	.166	.383	.435	.039	.294	-.110
Population	.956	.807	.875	.082	.349	.082	.028	-.142
Number of IEs	.582	.527	.645	.103	.535	.028	.008	-.147
Acreage of IEs	.838	.951	.961	.140	.444	.144	.076	-.132
				Change 1968 - 1973				
Location of population (per cent)								
not in town	.161	.225	.261	.196	.232	.024	.107	.108
in towns with population of								
< 5,000	-.126	.052	-.099	-.018	-.061	.177	-.091	.103
5,000-15,000	-.109	-.054	-.063	-.014	-.038	-.032	.040	-.034
15,000-50,000	-.050	-.112	-.109	-.117	-.112	-.124	-.065	-.112
>50,000	-.025	-.122	-.134	-.124	-.132	-.028	-.046	-.087
Capital	-.092	-.131	-.126	-.128	-.106	-.129	-.105	-.072
Railway	-.127	-.080	-.065	-.053	-.058	-.066	.051	-.041
Airport	.402	.055	.116	.015	.032	.005	-.015	-.024
Harbour	.346	.019	.079	-.022	.002	-.009	-.062	-.008
Population	.108	.168	.140	.143	.100	-.173	-.002	-.204
Number of IEs	.208	-.063	.009	-.110	-.052	-.118	-.070	-.064
Acreage of IEs	.204	-.065	-.054	-.111	-.113	.018	-.039	-.037

Source: Own calculations based on data mentioned in Table 6.1.

[a]Coefficient of correlation.

[b]Correlated with change in population.

ployee are, the higher the labour intensity is.

Secondly, given these criteria for classifying companies corresponding (in an albeit rough a priori manner) to the comparative advantages of the LDRs, data from the 1973 CMI were collected on a 4-digit industry level, and those industries were identified which correspond to the

(1) employment size (EMP-SIZE),
(2) value-added size (VA-SIZE),
(3) capital intensity (CAPINT).

An overview of these industries (on a 3-digit level) may be seen in Table 6.3, whereby those with above (national) average values are underlined[7]. The industries corresponding to the underlined values represent those industries which are considered to be not appropriate for locating in the LDRs, given the assumptions[8] made earlier.

Thirdly, in light of the fact that the above assumptions with respect to EMP-SIZE, VA-SIZE and CAPINT could be questioned because it cannot be taken for granted that, for instance, those industries with below (above) average values for EMP-SIZE, VA-SIZE and CAPINT will actually tend to be below (above) average, the regional spread of the three indicators were examined. The results of the examination were convincing enough to allow the assumptions to be maintained (Table A12)[9].

The fourth and final point was to assure that the DAC is a (relatively) representative sample of the total population of manufacturing companies in Malaysia, despite the regulations which in essence put a lower limit on the size of companies involved (see Appendix for a description of the registry regulations). While it is obvious that such a sample will not reflect perfectly the structure and regional dispersion of the Malaysian manufacturing industry (due to the regulation distortion), a comparison of the industrial structure from the 1973 CMI with the DAC revealed that distortions, although present, were not severe (Tables A13 and A14)[10]. Assuming that the results are not significantly distorted, it seems likely that conclusions drawn from an analysis of over 1,400 companies (accounting for a major portion of the manufacturing sector[11]) would be well enough founded to be considered to be more than just indicative of the real trends.

From the first breakdown of the DAC (Table 6.3) by the general (i.e.

TABLE 6.3
Characteristics of Major Industry Groups in West Malaysia

Code	Major Industry Group	Employee Size[a]	Value-Added Size[b] (M$'000)	Capital Intensity[c] (M$)	Incentive Structure (percentage) P	OI	WI	Percentage in IEs	Incentive Structure of those in IEs (percentage) P	OI	WI
311	Food manufacturing	14.66	145.44	11,929	28.8	19.2	51.9	39.1	31.1	24.6	44.3
and 312		9.51	56.05	6,099	40.4	1.9	57.7	36.5	36.8	-	63.2
313	Beverages	43.42	838.49	14,695	22.2	-	77.8	77.8	-	-	100.0
314	Tobacco	53.92	776.31	4,785	-	-	100.0	50.0	-	-	100.0
321	Textiles	94.76	434.25	9,903	45.1	5.7	49.2	38.5	55.3	10.6	34.1
322	Wearing apparel[d]	50.05	137.41	1,698	7.9	2.6	89.5	36.8	14.3	-	85.7
323	Leather, leather prod./substitutes and fur[d]	16.42	57.75	2,105	45.5	18.2	36.4	36.4	75.0	25.0	-
324	Footwear[e]	11.70	34.32	2,804	-	-	100.0	100.0	-	-	100.0
331	Wood, wood and cork products[f]	41.65	303.03	6,518	55.6	3.0	41.4	22.2	90.9	-	9.1
332	Furniture and fixtures[g]	7.63	22.34	2,135	56.3	-	43.8	43.8	71.4	-	28.6
341	Paper and paper products	26.36	118.22	6,808	9.1	12.1	78.8	24.2	12.5	12.5	75.0
342	Printing, publishing etc.	31.12	241.16	5,961	29.6	3.7	66.7	48.1	46.2	-	53.8
351	Industrial chemicals	53.35	1,135.19	42,815	55.6	11.3	32.1	64.2	64.7	8.8	26.5
352	Other chemical products	25.89	402.08	6,862	42.7	5.6	51.7	60.7	53.7	3.7	42.6
353	Petroleum refineries	123.00	12,407.50	171,085	75.0	-	25.0	25.0	100.0	-	-
354	Misc. petroleum and coal products	19.67	375.00	6,584	75.0	-	25.0	-	-	-	-
355	Rubber products	44.70	396.52	5,707	56.6	3.7	40.7	48.1	73.1	3.8	23.1
356	Plastic products n.e.c.	30.92	148.80	5,282	26.4	2.3	71.3	39.1	44.1	-	55.9
361	Pottery, china and earthernware	23.29	128.37	45,660	-	66.7	33.3	33.3	-	100.0	-
362	Glass and glass products	45.23	346.76	27,928	41.7	25.0	33.3	33.3	25.0	25.0	50.0
369	Non-metallic mineral products	33.67	313.83	12,198	19.7	6.6	73.7	35.5	25.9	3.7	70.3
371	Iron and steel (basic)	34.20	402.99	18,324	54.5	-	45.5	63.6	61.9	-	38.1
372	NF metals (basic	77.89	1,082.22	13,843	40.0	-	60.0	40.0	100.0	-	-
381	Metal products[h]	13.44	76.84	5,067	33.8	4.1	62.6	50.7	49.3	5.3	45.3
382	Machinery[i]	17.11	101.80	5,290	45.9	8.2	46.7	70.5	53.5	11.6	34.9
383	Elec. M/C, apparatus, etc.	233.03	1,729.63	7,374	67.2	3.1	29.8	74.0	74.2	4.1	21.6
384	Transportation equipment	50.91	359.54	6,403	51.9	5.5	42.6	57.4	64.5	-	35.5
385	Professional, scientific, etc.	65.92	381.92	6,009	88.2	-	11.8	88.2	86.7	-	12.3
390	Other industries	15.82	63.55	3,933	51.6	9.7	38.7	45.2	71.4	7.1	21.5
	Average	26.94	210.39	7,702	41.7	6.6	51.7	47.9	54.3	6.6	39.2

Sources: Own calculations based on Dept. of Statistics (CMI, 1973, Vol. 1, Table 3) and MIDA (DAC, 1977).

Note: The underlined figures are above national average.

[a] Total employees/establishment (i.e. total employees = unpaid + full-time + part-time) (EMP-SIZE).
[b] Value added/establishment (VA-SIZE).
[c] Physical capital assets employee (i.e. total employees = unpaid + full-time + part-time) (CAPINT).
[d] Except footwear.
[e] Except vulcanized, moulded rubber or plastic footwear.
[f] Except furniture.
[g] Except primarily of metal.
[h] Except machinery and equipment.
[i] Except electrical.

total) incentives and IE location structure of industries, and incentive structure of those in IEs, the following traits are revealed:

(1) in those industries, where incentives (either P or OI) prevailed, the size indicators were generally above average[12];

(2) out of those 13 industries overly represented in IEs, 9 exhibited above average employment size, but only 3 tended to have an above average capital intensity;

(3) industries in IEs received relatively more (pioneer) incentives than those in the economy as a whole;

(4) the industries in IEs tended to be of the non-natural resource type.

What does not become evident from this table (and unfortunately cannot be culled from the DAC data) is the impact of the incentives on VA-SIZE, EMP-SIZE and CAPINT by industry. Such data can be drawn from the CMI (1973) – at least for the pioneer industries, which, after all, account for the lion's share of the incentives (as shown earlier in Table 4.1). The full impact of such incentives on the various indicators is quite evident (Table 6.4). Generally speaking the employment size of pioneer establishments is 12 times larger than non-pioneer establishments, the value added size about 19 times and capital intensity per employee over 2 times.

In all industries EMP-SIZE and VA-SIZE for pioneer firms are above national average and are not exceeded in any industry by non-pioneer establishments. As concerns CAPINT, 70 per cent of the pioneer industries exhibit capital intensities above the national average; in only two cases are non-pioneer establishments more capital-intensive than pioneer ones. While a breakdown of the pioneer industries by regions and industries is not possible, it can be shown that the average figure on PIs by region exceeds the non-PIs by similarly large (to some extent even larger) amounts as on an industry basis (Table 6.5). Of particular interest in the framework of this study is the fact that the variance[13] between the various regions (or industries) is far less for the PIs than the non-PIs. This is interpreted as meaning that no attempt was made to adjust production techniques in accordance with differing regional factor endowments (see also Chapter 4). Hence, a misallocation of scarce capital occurred, at least to the extent that pioneer companies settled in LDRs, thereby causing a lower employment level (for a given capital input). Furthermore, an increase in the private benefits accruing from the investment can be con-

TABLE 6.4
Selected Statistics on Pioneer and Non-pioneer Establishments by 3-Digit Industries,[a] 1973

Code	Major Industry Group	Comparison of Pioneer and Non-pioneer Establishments: Employees/Establishment		Value Added/Establishment[b]		Fixed Assets/Employee[c]	
		Pioneer	Non-pioneer	Pioneer	Non-pioneer	Pioneer	Non-pioneer
311+312	Food manufacturing	164.59	12.09	2,551.49	117.55	14,767	8,860
313	Beverages[d]	-	43.42	-	838.49	-	14,695
314	Tobacco	-	53.92	-	776.31	-	4,785
321	Textiles	441.56	37.51	2,279.68	129.67	10,724	8,233
322	Wearing apparel[e]	-	50.05	-	137.41	-	1,698
323	Leather, leather prod./substitutes and fur[e]	-	16.42	-	57.74	-	2,105
324	Footwear	-	11.70	-	34.32	-	2,804
331	Wood, wood and cork products	310.92	31.35	1,961.14	239.59	11,171	4,752
332	Furniture and fixtures	-	7.63	-	22.34	-	2,135
341	Paper and paper products	127.17	22.22	901.50	86.04	9,616	6,148
341	Printing, publishing etc.[e]	-	31.12	-	241.16	-	5,961
351	Industrial chemicals	102.63	26.60	2,515.79	385.83	45,765	36,637
352	Other chemical products	119.83	17.19	1,675.29	284.12	7,295	6,582
353	Petroleum refineries[f]	161.67	-	16,539.00	-	173,529	-
354	Misc. petroleum and coal products	28.00	11.33	653.67	95.67	7,012	5,529
355	Rubber products	172.88	42.84	4,694.50	334.35	25,061	4,577
356	Plastic products n.e.c.	215.00	19.82	961.88	99.77	6,336	4,593
361	Pottery, china and earthernware[e]	-	23.29	-	128.37	-	45,660
362	Glass and glass products	330.67	17.61	2,138.33	173.26	36,481	12,390
369	Non-metallic mineral products	213.69	23.23	2,338.00	231.34	9,850	13,392
371	Iron and steel (basic)	239.67	16.48	3,891.60	102.16	27,056	7,377
372	NF metals (basic)[d]	-	77.89	-	1,082.22	-	13,843
381	Metal products	161.75	10.18	1,304.28	49.88	9,018	3,688
382	Machinery	175.71	13.90	1,847.88	66.46	15,148	2,769
383	Elec. M/C, apparatus etc.	457.47	49.73	3,410.63	356.77	3,810	7,341
384	Transportation equipment	101.92	47.11	703.25	333.93	14,604	5,080
385	Professional, scientific, etc.	254.67	9.30	1,470.83	55.00	6,382	2,957
	Total	250.96	19.49	2,425.60	136.72	12,040	5,844

Source: Own calculations based on Dept. of Statistics (CMI, 1973, Vol. 1, Tables 2, 54).

Note: The underlined figures are above national average.

[a] Based on CMI. - For definition of employment see Table 6.3.

[b] M$'000.

[c] M$.

[d] Non-pioneer data contains two pioneer establishments not otherwise specified.

[e] Non-pioneer data contains one pioneer establishment not otherwise specified.

[f] Data on one non-pioneer establishment not included due to inconsistencies.

TABLE 6.5

Selected Statistics on Pioneer and Non-pioneer Industries by Region, 1973

Region/State	Share of Establishments (Percentage)		Share of Value-Added (Percentage)		Value Added/ Establishment (M$'000)		Employees/ Establishment		Fixed Assets/ Employee (M$)	
	Pioneer	Non-pioneer	Pioneer	Non-pioneer	Pioneer	Non-pioneer	Pioneer	Non-pioneer	Pioneer	Non-pioneer
Northern states	2.8	15.1	1.4	6.0	1,226.8	54.0	260.3	13.8	9,854	4,943
Trengganu Kelantan }	1.1	7.0	.9	2.7	1,905.8	53.8	433.5	17.1	11,991	2,816
Perlis	-	.8	-	.3	-	52.1	-	15.8	-	31,702
Kedah	1.7	7.4	.5	2.9	773.8	54.2	144.8	10.5	5,588	3,838
Southern states	19.1	21.7	12.0	20.9	1,525.1	131.5	306.0	19.7	7,909	5,355
Pahang	2.5	4.7	2.3	4.8	2,200.0	140.3	350.2	18.8	12,380	8,194
Melaka	3.1	3.9	1.3	1.6	1,041.5	55.8	438.0	13.5	3,628	2,956
Johor	13.5	13.1	8.4	14.5	1,504.3	150.5	267.4	21.8	8,416	4,917
Western states	78.1	63.1	86.6	73.1	2,689.0	158.4	237.2	20.8	13,430	6,147
Perak	11.2	17.8	8.5	11.8	1,839.2	90.5	288.0	16.2	10,414	5,787
Selangor	48.6	28.8	51.2	49.2	2,554,3	250.8	173.1	26.2	13,727	6,778
Negeri Sembilan	2.0	4.1	6.4	3.4	7,910.0	113.2	143.9	17.1	111,039	3,771
Penang	16.3	14.5	20.5	8.8	3,046.9	83.2	404.6	17.5	9,065	5,458
Total (actual number or average)	356	10,704	863,515[a]	1,463,144[a]	2,425.6	136.7	251.0	19.5	12,040	5,844

Source: Own calculations based on Dept. of Statistics (CMI, 1973, Vol. 1, Tables 4, 55).

Note: The underlined figures are above national average.

[a] M$'000.

TABLE 6.6

Regional Distribution of Establishments[a] by Selected Characteristics, 1967-1979

Region/Period	*Establishments* Number	*Percentage of Total Economy*	*Percentage of Total by Type of Incentive* P	OI	WI	*Percentage of Total in IEs*
Northern states						
- 1967	8	3.2	25.0	-	75.0	-
1968-1970	4	2.4	75.0	-	25.0	-
1971-1973	15	4.2	26.7	20.0	53.3	6.7
1974-1976	32	6.3	43.8	25.0	31.3	34.4
1977-1979	12	8.2	16.7	33.3	50.0	75.0
Total	71	5.0	35.2	21.1	43.7	31.0
Southern states						
-1967	45	17.7	55.6	4.4	40.0	6.7
1968-1979	40	24.1	42.5	7.5	50.0	10.0
1971-1973	73	20.3	42.5	8.2	49.3	26.0
1974-1976	102	20.1	42.2	5.8	52.0	45.1
1977-1979	33	22.5	33.3	30.3	36.4	54.6
Total	293	20.4	43.3	9.3	47.4	30.7
Western states						
-1967	201	79.1	51.7	1.0	47.3	54.7
1968-1970	122	73.5	43.4	3.3	53.3	48.4
1971-1973	271	75.5	48.0	3.3	48.7	60.2
1974-1976	374	73.6	36.6	4.9	58.3	51.3
1977-1979	102	69.4	21.6	18.6	59.8	50.0
Total	1,070	74.6	41.7	4.7	53.6	53.7
Total						
-1967	254		51.6	1.5	46.9	44.9
1968-1970	166		44.0	4.2	51.8	38.0
1971-1973	359		46.0	5.0	49.0	51.0
1974-1976	508		38.2	6.5	55.3	49.0
1977-1979	147		23.8	22.5	53.7	53.1
Total	1,434		41.7	6.6	51.7	48.0

Source: See Table 6.3.

[a]Based on DAC. The underlined figures are above national average.

strued as having taken place at the expense of social benefits.

In turning now to a closer look at the regional breakdown of the data from the DAC (Table 6.6)[14], the following can be seen:

(1) The share of establishments moving into the northern states (i.e. those states with the lowest level of income and industrialization) has increased continuously in the four time periods following the base year 1967 (which covers the stock of investments in existence at that time). Analogously, the share moving into the western states (i.e. those states with the highest level of income and industrialization) has generally decreased. In other words, at first

glance, the impact of the policies on the regional dispersal of new firms would seem to have been in favour of the LDRs.

(2) The share of firms without incentives in the less developed areas has decreased over time; in the more developed states the opposite was true[15]. However, on the whole the importance of the PI incentive has shrunk considerably in all regions and in the four time periods. These aspects combined with the above-mentioned increase in the share of those moving into the MDRs allow no definite interpretation with respect to the impact of the policies, as either new firms were attracted by the additional incentives or firms that would have been established anyway merely took advantage of the incentives offered.

(3) The share of firms in IEs has increased throughout the period, particularly in the northern and southern states. This can hardly be surprising in light of the above-described policies (where industries were perhaps directed into IEs), and it would thus be premature to conclude that the IEs were responsible for the increased flow of establishments into the LDRs.

While this breakdown has allowed some characteristics in the trend of regional flows of investments to be identified, still little is known in respect of the industries, incentives and industrial estates and whether development followed expected paths.

In turning to the industries[16] (Table 6.7), the extent of the spread of the industrialization process becomes quite evident – the vacant cells in 1967 have in the meantime been filled to a large degree. It can be seen that in the second period (i.e. from 1973 to 1979, during which time regional industrialization activities were accelerated) the dispersal process made particular progress. It can also be determined that generally speaking the establishments moving into the various areas did seem to be in rough, although not complete, agreement with the crude a priori indicators set up (Table 6.8). To be specific, in the case of the northern region, those industries seemingly not in agreement with the crude indicators were generally of the resource-based type[17]. It might also be noted that in most of these cases the share of incentives granted to these industries not only exceeded national averages but also exceeded the share for other industries in the region. This might well be considered as an indication of the fact that such industries, to the extent they did not correspond to the factor intensities in the region, were only able to be made competitive by receiving incentives. Should this actually have been the

TABLE 6.7

Regional Spread of Industries in West Malaysia, 3-Digit Industrial Classification,[a] 1967-1979 (per cent)

Major Industry Group	≤1967			1968-1972			1973-1979			As of 31.12.1977		
	N	S	W	N	S	W	N	S	W	N	S	W
311*	-	7.7	92.3	-	18.9	81.1	12.7	19.4	77.9	5.8	17.3	76.9
312	-	14.2	85.8	-	36.4	63.6	25.9	29.6	44.5	13.5	26.9	59.6
313*°+	-	-	100.0	-	-	100.0	-	25.0	75.0	-	11.1	88.9
314°+	-	-	100.0	-	-	100.0	-	-	100.0	-	-	100.0
321*°+	-	50.0	50.0	-	40.0	60.0	8.3	21.9	69.8	4.9	30.3	64.8
322°	-	-	100.0	-	42.9	57.1	-	38.4	61.6	-	34.2	65.8
323	-	33.3	66.7	-	100.0	-	14.3	28.6	57.1	9.1	36.4	54.5
324	-	-	-	-	-	100.0	-	-	100.0	-	-	100.0
331°+	11.2	61.1	27.7	18.4	41.9	39.7	8.0	44.0	48.0	12.1	46.5	41.4
332	-	-	-	-	66.7	33.3	-	7.7	92.3	-	18.8	81.2
341	-	-	100.0	10.0	-	90.0	4.8	28.6	66.8	6.1	18.2	75.8
342°+	-	20.0	80.0	-	33.3	66.7	-	9.1	90.9	-	18.5	81.5
351*°+	-	10.0	90.0	-	10.0	90.0	8.6	17.4	74.0	3.8	13.2	83.0
352	3.4	6.9	89.7	-	12.5	87.5	6.8	18.1	75.1	4.5	13.4	82.1
353*°+	-	-	100.0	-	-	100.0	-	-	100.0	-	-	100.0
354	-	50.0	50.0	-	-	100.0	-	-	100.0	-	25.0	75.0
355°+	-	36.4	63.6	11.1	22.2	66.7	14.7	20.6	64.7	11.1	24.1	64.8
356°	-	40.0	60.0	-	22.6	77.4	-	15.2	84.8	-	20.6	79.4
361*	-	-	-	-	-	-	33.3	-	66.7	33.3	-	66.7
362*°+	-	100.0	-	-	50.0	50.0	11.1	22.2	66.7	8.3	33.3	58.4
369*°+	21.1	5.3	73.6	7.7	7.7	84.6	11.4	13.7	74.9	13.2	10.5	76.3
371*°+	-	-	100.0	-	-	100.0	-	21.4	78.6	-	9.1	90.9
372*°+	-	-	100.0	-	-	-	-	-	100.0	-	-	100.0
381	-	6.1	93.9	0	23.3	76.7	1.4	19.5	79.1	.7	17.6	81.8
382	-	-	100.0	-	-	100.0	5.6	16.7	77.7	3.2	9.8	87.0
383°+	6.3	18.8	74.9	-	15.8	84.2	2.6	18.2	79.8	2.3	17.5	80.2
384°+	-	-	100.0	6.7	13.3	80.0	2.9	20.5	76.6	3.7	16.7	79.6
385°+	-	-	100.0	-	25.0	75.0	-	16.7	83.3	-	17.6	82.4
390	-	50.0	50.0	-	-	100.0	8.0	12.0	80.0	6.4	12.9	80.7
Average	3.2	17.7	79.1	2.7	21.5	75.8	6.6	20.8	72.6	5.0	20.4	74.6

Source: Own calculations based on MICA (DAC, 1977).

*Capital-intensive industry as determined by above average physical capital assets/employee (CAPINT).
°Size as determined by above average employees/establishment (EMP-SIZE).
+Size as determined by above average value added/establishment (VA-SIZE).

The underlined values represent those industry shares in a region which exceed the share of the region in total economy (i.e. an indication of industrial concentration).

[a] For names of 3-digit industries see Table 6.3. N, S and W designate the regions North, South and West.

case, then the thrust of regional policies has strayed from a course laid down by the posited economic guidelines.

A closer look at the three indicators set up (CAPINT, EMP-SIZE and VA-SIZE), this time not on an industry base but rather by region and time period by type of incentive and whether in IEs, reveals the following (Tables 6.9 - 6.11):

(1) Whereas the predominance of CAPINT industries in the northern states drastically decreased throughout the period under investigation (that is after 1967 and neglecting the total), a sizeable reduction can be noted in the southern states (Table 6.9). In the western states, however, a definite increase is observed. This can be interpreted as meaning that the flow of new industries

TABLE 6.8

Change in Regional Industrial Shares,[a] 1967-1977

Major Industry Group	*Northern Region*	*Major Industry Group*	*Southern Region*	*Major Industry Group*	*Western Region*
361*	→ 33.3	322°	→ 34.2	324	→ 100.0
312	→ 13.5	332	→ 18.8	332	→ 81.2
355°+	→ 11.1	341	→ 18.2	361*	→ 66.7
323	→ 9.1	385°+	→ 17.6	362*°+	→ 58.4
362*°+	→ 8.3	384°+	→ 16.7	390	30.7
390	→ 6.4	312	12.7	354	25.0
341	→ 6.1	381	11.5	356°	19.4
311*	→ 5.8	313*°+	→ 11.1	321*°+	14.8
321*°+	→ 4.9	382	→ 9.8	331°+	13.7
351*	→ 3.8	311*	9.6	383°+	5.3
384°+	→ 3.7	371*°+	→ 9.1	369*°+	2.7
382	→ 3.2	352	6.5	342°+	1.5
352	1.1	369*°+	5.2	355°+	1.2
331°+	.9	351*°+	3.2	314°+	.0
381	→ .7	323	3.1	353*°+	.0
383°+	-4.0	383°+	- 1.3	372*°+	.0
369*°+	-7.9	342°+	- 1.5	351*°+	- 7.0
		355°+	-12.3	352	- 7.6
		331°+	-14.6	371*°+	- 9.1
		356°	-19.4	313*°+	-10.1
		321*°+	-19.7	381	-12.1
		354	-25.0	323	-12.2
		390	-37.1	382	-13.0
		362*°+	-66.7	311*	-15.4
				385°+	-17.6
				384°+	-21.4
				341	-24.2
				312	-26.2
				322°	-34.2

Source: Own calculations based on MIDA (DAC, 1977).

[a]Expressed as a percentage of the number of establishments in the respective industry on a national level. In those cases where the change in shares is designated with a → the share was zero in 1967. For an explanation of *, ° and + see Table 6.7.

TABLE 6.9
Regional Distribution of CAPINT Establishments
by Selected Characteristics, 1967-1979

Region/Period	Number	Percentage of Total Economy	Percentage of Total in Region	CAPINT Establishments: Percentage of Total by Type of Incentive: P	OI	WI	in IEs
Northern states							
- 1967	5	5.4	62.5	50.0	-	66.7	-
1968 - 1970	-	-	-	-	-	-	-
1971 - 1973	5	5.6	33.3	50.0	100.0	-	100.0
1974 - 1976	10	7.4	31.3	28.6	50.0	20.0	18.2
1977 - 1979	1	2.5	8.3	-	-	16.7	11.1
Total	21	5.3	29.6	28.0	46.7	22.5	22.7
Southern states							
- 1967	12	13.0	26.7	63.6	-	33.3	33.3
1968 - 1970	11	28.2	27.5	24.0	33.3	15.0	50.0
1971 - 1973	15	16.7	20.5	19.4	33.3	19.4	31.6
1974 - 1976	19	14.1	18.6	16.3	66.6	15.1	15.2
1977 - 1979	6	15.0	18.2	9.1	40.0	8.3	27.8
Total	63	15.9	21.5	21.3	40.7	18.0	23.3
Western states							
- 1967	75	81.5	37.3	48.1	-	26.3	40.9
1968 - 1970	28	71.8	23.0	26.4	75.0	16.9	32.2
1971 - 1973	70	77.8	25.8	29.2	22.2	22.7	24.5
1974 - 1976	106	78.5	28.3	35.0	36.8	23.4	28.6
1977 - 1979	33	82.5	32.4	27.3	36.8	32.8	39.2
Total	312	78.8	29.2	35.7	35.8	24.0	31.4
Total							
- 1967	92		36.2	43.5	-	29.4	40.2
1968 - 1970	39		23.5	25.8	57.1	16.3	33.3
1971 - 1973	90		25.1	29.5	38.9	21.0	25.7
1974 - 1976	135		26.6	30.4	45.5	21.7	25.7
1977 - 1979	40		27.2	20.0	33.3	27.8	33.3
Total	396		27.6	31.8	38.9	22.8	29.8

Source: Own calculations based on MIDA (DAC, 1977).

Note: The underline figures are above national average.

TABLE 6.10

Regional Distribution of EMP-Size Establishments by Selected Characteristics, 1967-1979

Region/Period	Number	Percentage of Total Economy	Percentage of Total in Region	Percentage of Total by Type of Incentives P	OI	VII	in IEs
	EMP-SIZE Establishments						
Northern states							
1967	6	3.3	75.0	50.0	-	83.3	-
1968 - 1970	4	3.1	100.0	-	-	100.0	-
1971 - 1973	13	4.7	86.7	100.0	100.0	75.0	100.0
1974 - 1976	19	5.2	59.4	71.4	37.5	60.0	72.7
1977 - 1979	8	7.0	66.7	100.0	25.0	83.3	77.8
Total	50	4.7	70.4	76.0	46.7	74.2	77.3
Southern states							
- 1967	35	19.4	77.8	76.0	100.0	77.8	100.0
1968 - 1970	32	24.6	80.0	70.6	66.7	90.0	100.0
1971 - 1973	60	21.5	82.2	83.9	66.7	83.3	73.7
1974 - 1976	76	20.7	74.5	60.5	83.3	81.1	71.7
1977 - 1979	28	24.3	84.8	81.8	90.0	83.3	94.4
Total	231	21.5	78.8	74.0	81.5	82.7	78.9
Western states							
- 1967	139	77.2	69.2	63.5	100.0	74.7	68.5
1968 - 1970	94	72.3	77.0	78.6	100.0	78.5	78.0
1971 - 1973	206	73.8	76.0	76.2	66.7	76.5	77.3
1974 - 1976	273	74.2	73.0	74.5	73.7	72.0	75.0
1977 - 1979	79	68.7	77.5	81.8	47.4	82.0	80.4
Total	791	73.8	73.9	72.7	69.8	75.3	75.3
Total							
- 1967	180		70.9	65.6	100.0	75.6	70.2
1968 - 1970	130		78.3	77.1	60.0	81.4	79.4
1971 - 1973	279		77.7	78.2	72.2	77.8	77.0
1974 - 1976	368		72.4	72.2	66.7	73.3	74.3
1977 - 1979	115		78.2	82.9	63.6	82.3	83.3
Total	1,072		74.8	73.2	77.6	76.7	75.8

Source: Own calculations based on MIDA (DAC, 1977).

Note: The underlined figures are above national average.

TABLE 6.11
Regional Distribution of VA-Size Establishments by Selected Characteristics, 1967-1979

	VA-SIZE Establishments						
		Percentage	Percentage	Percentage of Total			
				by Type of Incentives			
Region/Period	Number	of Total Economy	of Total in Region	P	OI	WI	in IEs
Northern states							
- 1967	6	3.5	75.0	50.0	-	83.3	-
1968 - 1970	4	3.9	100.0	-	-	100.0	-
1971 - 1973	14	6.2	93.3	100.0	100.0	87.5	100.0
1974 - 1976	17	5.8	53.1	71.7	25.0	50.0	72.7
1977 - 1979	8	8.3	66.7	100.0	25.0	83.3	77.8
Total	49	5.5	69.0	80.0	40.0	74.2	77.3
Southern states							
- 1967	34	19.7	75.6	72.0	100.0	77.8	66.7
1968 - 1970	24	23.5	60.0	64.7	33.3	60.0	50.0
1971 - 1973	48	21.2	65.8	74.2	66.7	58.3	52.6
1974 - 1976	60	20.4	58.8	58.1	66.7	58.5	54.3
1977 - 1979	25	26.0	75.8	72.7	80.0	75.0	83.3
Total	191	21.4	65.2	66.9	70.4	62.6	60.0
Western states							
- 1967	133	76.9	66.2	67.3	50.0	65.3	68.5
1968 - 1970	74	72.5	60.7	62.3	100.0	56.9	61.0
1971 - 1973	164	72.6	60.5	67.7	55.6	53.8	63.8
1974 - 1976	217	73.8	58.0	71.5	63.2	49.1	64.1
1977 - 1979	63	65.8	61.8	72.7	42.1	63.9	68.6
Total	651	73.1	60.8	68.4	56.6	55.3	65.0
Total							
- 1967	173		68.1	67.9	75.0	68.1	68.3
1968 - 1970	102		61.4	67.1	50.0	58.1	60.3
1971 - 1973	226		63.0	69.7	66.7	56.3	62.8
1974 - 1976	294		57.9	68.6	54.5	50.9	62.7
1977 - 1979	96		65.3	74.3	51.5	67.1	73.1
Total	891		62.1	68.6	64.7	57.5	64.8

Source: Own calculations based on MIDA (DAC, 1977).

Note: The underlined figures are above national average.

generally coincided with Malaysia's regional comparative advantages - a conclusion also drawn from Tables 6.7 and 6.8. Furthermore, to the extent that CAPINT industries did settle in LDRs, they generally took greater advantage of incentives (in recent years of the non-pioneer type) and more often located outside of IEs (i.e. tended to be of the resource-oriented type).

(2) With regard to EMP-SIZE and VA-SIZE (Tables 6.10 and 6.11) the direction for the northern states is the same as CAPINT above, but the actual impact is considerably less; for the southern and western states a more stationary development is shown. With respect to the incentives it would seem to be indicated that the predominance of incentive-supported activities in the LDRs, as was the case for CAPINT, does not hold. As a matter of fact the regions indicate a fairly equal distribution of above average incentive-supported companies. Definite trends are discernible with respect to OI in the northern and western states (downward) and in the southern states (upward); with respect to P, only the western states exhibit a noticeable (upward) change. As opposed to CAPINT, an above average share of EMP-SIZE and VA-SIZE in the northern states is located in IEs, a fact which can probably be interpreted as showing the importance of IEs in LDRs in providing industrial infrastructure and perhaps some agglomeration economies otherwise lacking in the less developed regions.

In light of these last observations it would seem appropriate to focus in a little more on the IEs. It can be seen in Table 6.12, that (obviously) their importance is far greater in the MDRs than in the LDRs, and in looking more closely at the structure of industries and incentives in IEs and NIEs it is revealed that[18]:

(1) in the northern states a smaller than average amount of the industries in IEs is of the CAPINT type, while a greater than average proportion is NIEs. The latter is no doubt due to the capital-intensive raw material based industries. The share of EMP-SIZE and VA-SIZE tends to be above average in the IEs, a fact which could be interpreted, ceteris paribus, as an indication of the possible impact of the IEs on the structure of industries they attracted;

(2) in the western states the share of CAPINT is higher both inside and outside IEs[19], but for EMP-SIZE and VA-SIZE the shares vary. Assuming that the MDRs have a greater comparative advantage in the more capital-intensive lines of production, then the high CAPINT is in line with expected economic crite-

TABLE 6.12
Some Status Characteristics[a] of Manufacturing Establishments by Regions and States

Region/State/Status		Establishments							
				Percentage of Total in IEs or NIEs					
			Percentage of	by Capital-intensity and Size[b]			by Type of Incentive		
		Number	Given Area	CAPINT	EMP-SIZE	VA-SIZE	P	OI	WI
Northern states	IE	22	31.0	22.7	77.3	77.3	45.5	9.1	45.5
	NIE	49	69.0	32.7	67.4	65.3	30.6	26.5	42.9
Trengganu	IE	1	7.7	-	-	-	-	100.0	-
	NIE	12	92.3	8.3	75.0	75.0	33.3	8.3	58.3
Kelantan	IE	-	-	-	-	-	-	-	-
	NIE	9	100.0	22.2	44.4	44.4	22.2	55.6	22.2
Perlis	IE	-	-	-	-	-	-	-	-
	NIE	7	100.0	42.9	85.7	71.4	14.3	28.6	57.1
Kedah	IE	21	50.0	23.8	81.0	81.0	47.6	4.8	47.6
	NIE	21	50.0	47.6	66.7	66.7	38.1	23.8	38.1
Southern states	IE	90	30.7	23.3	78.9	60.0	51.1	16.7	32.2
	NIE	203	69.3	20.7	78.8	67.5	39.9	5.9	54.2
Pahang	IE	13	33.3	15.4	61.5	53.9	46.2	46.2	7.7
	NIE	26	66.7	11.5	88.5	80.8	46.2	15.4	38.5
Melaka	IE	35	71.4	11.4	80.0	51.4	68.6	5.7	25.7
	NIE	14	28.6	21.4	50.0	42.9	57.1	-	42.9
Johor	IE	42	20.5	35.7	83.3	69.1	38.1	16.7	45.2
	NIE	163	79.5	22.1	79.8	67.5	37.4	4.9	57.7
Western states	IE	575	53.7	31.1	75.3	65.0	55.1	4.9	40.0
	NIE	495	46.3	26.7	72.3	56.0	26.1	5.1	72.9
Perak	IE	59	39.6	35.6	74.6	57.6	50.8	8.5	40.7
	NIE	90	60.4	23.3	76.7	58.9	35.6	5.6	58.9
Selangor	IE	337	53.5	31.5	74.5	65.3	52.5	3.3	44.2
	NIE	293	46.5	26.6	70.3	53.6	22.9	4.8	72.4
Negeri Sembilan	IE	27	69.2	37.0	77.8	63.0	70.4	14.8	14.8
	NIE	12	30.8	50.0	66.7	66.7	58.3	8.3	33.3
Penang	IE	152	60.3	27.6	77.0	67.8	59.9	5.3	34.9
	NIE	100	39.7	28.0	75.0	59.0	23.0	5.0	72.0
Total	IE	687	47.9	29.8	75.8	64.8	54.3	6.6	39.2
	NIE	747	52.1	25.6	73.8	59.7	30.1	6.7	65.9
Total		1,434	100.0	27.6	74.8	62.1	41.7	6.6	34.3

Source: Own calculations based on MIDA (DAC, 1977).

Note: The underlined figures are above national average.

[a]IE = in industrial estate; NIE = not in industrial estate.

[b]For definitions see pp. 121ff.

ria. It can also be stated that, as opposed to the northern regions, the share of CAPINT in IEs is generally greater than in NIEs, once again an indication of a possible impact of IEs on the industrial structure[20];

(3) the incentive structure of the IE status in the northern states leans more heavily towards OIs and PIs (compared with national averages) in the case of NIEs. Furthermore, an above average share of establishments in the northern states in IEs can do without incentives, but for those outside of IEs, where locational disadvantages are no doubt much larger, a figure far below average can be perceived. This would seem to underline the regional incentive content of IEs as such, even though the specific regional designing of the IE policy mix did not include anything except possible differences in land prices.

THE IMPACT OF INDUSTRIALIZATION POLICIES AND LOCATIONAL FACTORS ON FACTOR INTENSITY - AN ECONOMETRIC ANALYSIS

From the evidence presented so far it would seem that the impact of Malaysian industrialization policies on the regional flow and structure of investment was, generally speaking, in accordance with the economic efficiency criteria. However, since evidence on the policy package impact on factor intensities has been presented in a less than adequate fashion, a set of firm-level micro-data has been analysed with econometric techniques. The data set utilized contains information on industry, employment, capital intensity, domestic share of capital, location, type of incentive and start of production[21]. Given the fact that this data allow a quantification of various policy and non-policy factors to be carried out, it is intended to attempt to isolate the relative impact of policy measures, location and production aspects, as well as ownership conditions on the capital intensity of selected 3-digit industries. The results of this analysis will then be interpreted with respect to the question as to whether the entirety of the policy package, given economic environment variables, was structured in accordance with comparative advantages in Malaysia.

The method chosen is cross-sectional OLS regression analysis, relying on the standard battery of statistics to check the significance of the results. The process by which industries were selected was carried out entirely on the condition that sufficient observations for each industry (out of the data set which contained a total of 616 observations/firms) existed.

TABLE 6.13
Summary Statistics on Investment Data

Major Industry Group[a]	Number of Establishments in Sample	Capital-intensity (M$) CMI	Capital-intensity (M$) Sample	Capital-intensity Coefficient of Variation[c]	Percentage of Respective Industry in IEs	Percentage of Respective Industry with INCEN	Percentage of Respective Industry in MDRs	Average MALSHR	Percentage of Respective Industry Existing in 1968	Percentage of Respective Industry Set-up 1969-73	Percentage of Respective Industry Set-up After 1973	Average Employment Size[b] CMI	Average Employment Size[b] Sample	Average Employment Size[b] Coefficient of Variation[c]
311	56	11,929	22,059	37.47	41.1	30.4	42.9	73.5	17.9	26.8	55.4	14.7	67.6	20.07
312	19	6,099	18,176	48.06	31.6	36.8	52.6	88.3	26.3	26.3	47.4	9.5	42.6	21.07
321	30	9,903	6,798	43.50	50.0	46.7	53.3	77.8	13.3	16.7	70.0	94.8	68.9	30.15
322	13	1,698	3,922	36.52	53.9	23.0	69.2	83.9	7.7	38.5	53.9	50.1	105.2	25.99
331	65	6,518	6,922	47.10	20.0	21.5	43.1	82.2	29.2	35.4	35.4	41.7	68.0	20.48
332	13	2,135	5,123	46.48	30.8	23.0	69.2	74.8	30.8	30.8	38.5	7.6	93.5	19.24
342	18	5,961	8,390	41.86	44.4	11.1	88.9	87.6	33.3	44.4	22.2	31.1	84.3	23.41
352	24	6,862	16,738	30.02	75.0	20.8	75.0	42.6	33.3	37.5	29.2	25.9	75.6	20.81
355	14	5,707	8,481	44.51	64.3	21.4	71.4	78.6	42.9	7.1	50.0	44.7	50.9	28.06
356	14	5,282	14,509	37.68	50.0	42.9	64.3	88.0	28.6	21.4	50.0	30.9	65.7	14.60
369	34	27,928	18,185	39.15	23.5	26.5	79.4	89.2	38.2	26.5	35.3	33.7	65.6	25.44
371	20	18,324	10,896	45.23	40.0	30.0	85.0	92.3	60.0	10.0	30.0	34.2	66.5	25.85
381	42	5,067	9,367	39.43	50.0	31.0	73.8	80.1	16.7	38.1	45.2	13.4	58.9	23.95
382	30	5,290	8,358	40.76	53.3	23.3	86.7	79.2	43.3	26.7	30.0	17.1	47.4	23.34
383	38	7,374	9,908	41.01	60.5	50.0	60.5	58.9	10.5	13.2	76.3	233.0	93.3	21.97
384	10	6,403	8,143	46.81	70.0	20.0	80.0	54.4	40.0	40.0	20.0	50.9	89.7	27.48
Total	440	7,702	10,738	45.05	43.8	29.7	63.7	77.5	27.4	27.7	44.9	26.9	68.1	23.26

Source: Own calculations based on data provided by MIDA.

The underlined figures are above national average.

[a] For names of 3-digit industries see Table 6.3.

[b] Number of employees/establishment.

[c] (Standard deviation/mean) · 100.

TABLE 6.14

Overview of Simple Correlations between LNCAPIN and Independent Variables

Major Industry Group[a]	IEDUM	INCENDUM	MDRDUM	MALSHR	68DUM	73DUM	77DUM	LNEMP
311	.050	- .093	.293*	- .374*	.119	- .226*	.109	.057
312	- .387	.014	.200	- .338	.236	- .370	.119	- .433*
321	.218	- .109	.373*	- .236	- .055	- .216	.216	- .207
322	.216	.159	- .110	.125	.278	- .653*	.489*	- .206
331	.035	- .146	.155	.062	- .144	.110	.027	- .499*
332	- .323	- .104	.580*	- .109	.033	.134	- .159	- .473*
342	.063	.487*	- .176	- .449*	- .169	.378*	- .261	.243
352	.311*	.086	.311*	- .089	.216	- .035	- .186	.330*
355	.384	- .087	.323	- .279	- .293	.580*	- .009	- .436
356	.132	.426	- .344	- .413	- .089	- .525*	.512*	.061
369	.127	- .050	- .080	- .084	.386*	- .053	- .343*	.081
371	.481*	.546*	- .375*	- .500*	- .311	- .264	.505*	.198
381	.385*	.160	.013	- .300*	- .171	.288	- .154	- .268
382	.353*	.037	.121	- .418*	- .545*	.096	.496*	- .171
383	.282*	.178	- .389*	- .061	.017	- .260	.194	.120
384	.543*	- .172	.068	- .045	.479	- .485*	.008	.704*
Number of times significant	6	2	6	5	2	6	5	5
most significant	1	2	3	1	2	3	-	4

Source: See Table 6.13.

*Correlation coefficient statistically significant at 10 per cent level.

[a]For names of 3-digit industries see Table 6.3.

[b]Only if two or more variables significant.

TABLE 6.15
Summary of Regression Results

Dependent Variable CAPINT in Major Industry Group[a]	Coefficients of Independent Variables										
	IEDUM	INCENDUM	MDRDUM	MALSHR	68DUM	73DUM	77DUM	EMP	Constant	$\bar{R}^2$	F-Value
					non-log form						
311		8.825	6.917				8.548*	.3223*	12.334	.088*	2.20
312	-18.021	36.215*		- .407*	26,569*				58.902	.258*	2.47
321		4.046	8.036*	- .187*			7.829*	-.008*	7.829	.262*	3.06
322	.701					-2.644			5.016	.296*	3.52
331	3.866*	-6.907*			-3.145*		3.402	-.025*	12.162	.101*	2.42
332			9.716*	- .156*			-5.465*		14.084	.616*	7.40
342		32.768*	9.165*	- .107*		7.663*		.007	6.606	.724*	9.93
352	16.594*							.112*	-993	.176*	3.46
355		4.177			-6.026*	43.332*			11.243	.811*	14.95
356		-28.598*	-37.827*	- .650*			29.494*	-.317	118.592	.689*	6.77
369		13.972	-11.629	.463*			-18.922*	.059	-9.869	.220*	2.75
371		-31.263*	-15.739	-1.083*		-11.984	3.687	-.018*	138.962	.546*	4.81
381	3.539*			- .116*		2.677*		-.009	18.652	.184*	3.42
382	-3.358	-6.358*	11.519*	- .130*		6.108*	17.155*	-.013	8.636	.556*	6.20
383	7.083					-6.186			9.695	.082*	2.64
384	20.542*		-2.269	- .336*		-3.492		.068*	-28.439	.864*	22.21
					log form						
311		- .705*		- .017*			.956*		4.017	.200*	5.60
312				- .027*				-.870*	8.525	.272*	4.36
321			.643*	- .014*			.688*	-.193*	2.990	.314*	4.32
322	.272					- .671*			1.478	.408*	5.13
331					- .359*			- .540*	4.316	.258*	12.13
332	- .440*	- .922*	1.016*	- .028*				- .442*	5.456	.807*	11.01
342		1.187*				.724*		.227	.667	.310*	3.54
352	.735*							.373*	.654	.181*	3.54
355	.727*					1.305*		- .326*	2.859	.380*	3.66
356			-1.222*	- .034*		.065	1.118*	- .615*	8.448	.587*	4.69
369					.888*				2.561	.122*	5.59
371	1.269*	.108		- .045*				- 339*	7.411	.431*	4.60
381	.770*			- .011*				- .454*	4.571	.354*	8.40
382			.693*	- .009*	- .543*		.649*		2.301	.467*	7.35
383	.333		- .632*						2.474	.132*	3.82
384							.859	.682*	1.141	.495*	5.41

<u>Source:</u> See Table 6.13.

*Regression coefficient or equation statistically significant at 10 per cent level.

[a]For names of 3-digit industries see Table 6.3.

TABLE 6.16
Contribution of the Individual Variables to Explained Variance[a] (Percentage)

Major Industry Group	IEDUM	INCENDUM	MDRDUM	MALSHR	68DUM	73DUM	77DUM	EMP
				non-log form				
311		22.37	22.24				28.29	27.09
312	19.99	31.78		20.21	28.03			
321		7.93	23.10	31.76			20.67	16.54
322	21.36					78.64		
331	16.30	26.28			15.06		17.11	25.25
332			37.87	39.40			22.46	
342		40.79	15.65	14.09		20.69		8.78
352	43.42							56.58
355		12.80			18.73	68.47		
356		14.12	25.58	17.88			20.81	21.61
369		11.67	12.14	21.69			23.13	31.43
371		22.54	13.51	37.79		8.64	4.06	
381	23.51			40.42		16.93		19.14
382	6.93	8.93	16.18	18.95		11.16	32.49	5.36
383	62.34						37.66	
384	24.99		2.39	32.46		4.59		35.07
				logform				
311		24.39		39.88			35.73	
312				45.45				54.55
321			24.89	31.87			24.45	18.79
322	29.34					70.66		
331					26.07			73.93
332	8.91	17.04	20.56	37.23				16.25
342		38.79				37.41		23.80
352	49.23							50.77
355	50.13							49.87
356			26.68	30.14		1.22	25.47	16.49
369					100.0			
371	37.00	2.94		38.74				21.32
381	34.87			25.47				39.66
382			20.82	29.05	23.79		26.34	
383	34.50		65.50					
384							30.05	69.95

Source: See Table 6.13.

Note: The underlined figures are above average.

[a] Calculated from share of each beta weight in total sum of absolute values of all beta weights in given regression.

[b] For names of 3-digit industries see Table 6.3.

The model used to isolate the above factors was specified as follows:

CAPIN = f (IEDUM, INCENDUM, MDRDUM, MALSHR, 68DUM, 73DUM, 77DUM, EMP)

whereby[22]

CAPIN	= capital intensity defined as invested capital per full-time worker (in M$)
IEDUM	= dummy variable indicating whether firm is in IE (IEDUM = 1) or not in IE (IEDUM = 0) (+)
INCENDUM	= dummy variable indicating whether firm is receiving incentives (INCENDUM = 1) or not receiving incentives (INCENDUM = 0) (+)
MDRDUM	= dummy variable indicating whether firm is in a more developed region (MDR = 1) or not in a more developed region (MDR = 0) (+)[23]
MALSHR	= share of Malaysian capital in total invested capital (-)[24]
??DUM	= dummy variable indicating when a firm went into operation, i.e.
68DUM	= before 1968 (68DUM = 1),
73DUM	= between 1968 and 1973 (73DUM = 1) or
77DUM	= after 1973 (77DUM = 1) (?)[25]
EMP	= employment variable inserted to ensure that possible differences in capital intensity due to employment size are adjusted for (+)

An overview of the data and a comparison with CMI data is given in Table 6.13. While it becomes obvious from this table that the data do differ from the CMI figures, actually no consideration was given to whether this was the case. Rather it was assumed that in light of the fact that about 500 firms are represented and knowing that the largest firms (with 50 or more employees) – although less than 10 per cent of the total number of firms in the Malaysian manufacturing industry (in 1973) – accounted for over 80 per cent of value added and capital assets (Table A15), conclusions drawn from this data set should be valid enough[26].

As concerns the functional form of the regressions, since no particular a priori expectations prevailed, both non-log and log forms were run. Regressions run in the log form have variables prefixed with an LN.

A first check of the strength of the possible correlations between the dependent and independent variables reveals that (Table 6.14)[27]:

(1) incentives have surprisingly few significant correlations,

(2) the industrial estates exhibit significant correlations in the less raw material-intensive industries,

(3) the hypothesized sign can be found to occur in over 50 per cent of the cases.

In turning now to the full multiple regression results (Tables 6.15 - 6.16) it can be seen that[28]:

(1) the impact of IEs (IEDUM), although in a few cases given the incorrect sign, is in accordance with a priori expectations and is also significant in five of eight cases. Its contribution to explained variance, however, is generally below average;

(2) the impact of incentives (INCENDUM) is ambiguous, as in most cases the coefficients are not significant and in those cases where they are, the wrong sign is often given. It was too, generally speaking, a variable which accounted for a below average share of explained variance;

(3) the most straight forward results are produced by the share of Malaysian capital in the total amount of invested capital (MALSHR). Not only are all coefficients significant and, with only one exception, given the expected sign, they also account for an above average of the explained variance in most of the cases;

(4) the seemingly spotty results which were generated for the regional variable (MDRDUM) could actually be interpreted as not being surprising, particularly in light of the above-mentioned reservations. It would nonetheless be hasty to draw this conclusion, i.e. little can be said, since the significant perverse results are limited to only two industries (and three equations). As a matter of fact, out of 10 significant coefficients 7 carry the expected sign. It should, of course, be noted that the fact that the MDRDUM appears in only 14 regressions can possibly be interpreted as meaning that capital intensities within most industries are not regionally different *(ceteris paribus)*. Given the evidence presented in Chapter this could well be due to the impact of incentives;

(5) with respect to the development of capital intensity over time (68DUM, 73DUM and 77DUM) it can be seen that in most cases an increase in capital-intensity, as was mentioned as being likely, has tended to take place.

CONCLUDING REMARKS

The detailed analysis of the regional flow of investments as well as the investigation of their factor intensity has shed additional light on the impact of Malaysian industrialization policies. As far as the first aspect is concerned, it could be shown that the flow of new investments into the LDRs has increased over time and at the same time the structure of these investments has been broadly in line with the respective comparative advantages. With regard to the factor intensity of these investments and in connection with the overall policy package as well as locational factors, the capital intensity bias of various measures could be substantiated (for instance the capital intensive impact of IEs as already shown in Chapter 5), although the greatest impact on factor intensities was induced by the degree of foreign ownership. To conclude therefrom that foreign investments should thus be avoided and more stress should be placed on domestically owned companies would at least be incorrect to the extent that in many cases the foreign owned companies would not necessarily have been replaced by domestic ones. It is another question, however, as to how investment incentive policies with respect to foreign direct investment should have been structured so as to induce factor intensities more in line with Malaysian comparative advantages.

1 To label it anything more than an attempt would be rather pretentious, and all forthcoming results should be regarded in this tenor.

2 This directory is a direct spin-off of the ICA (see Appendix) which contains regulations regarding the registry of companies. The DAC provides a wealth of information on location (region and whether in IE or not), type of incentive received, year in which operations began and industrial code. As opposed to the DAC, which is quite up to date, the newest CMI available was for the year 1973. Although it would have been useful and informative to have CMI data from the end of the 1970s, for the purpose of this study the 1973 census was adequate. The author sees no reason why the results, given the approach used, should be distorted because of the 1973 data.

3 This information is also a result of the ICA and is actually the primary data from which the DAC is extracted. It should be noted, however, that this data set is not the complete background for those same companies in the second section. It is rather a sample which has been made available by MIDA, and includes many of those companies in the DAC.

4 The slight increase in the coefficient of variation for the population expresses the migration to the already populated areas.

5 This does not mean, however, that larger markets cannot or should not be served by industry in LDRs, but rather that to do so at the moment would require the establishment of an extensive marketing and distributing set-up. While this type of organization was established for the agricultural sector, it did not exist for manufacturing. Thus investment in those industries where large-size (i.e. in terms of value added) establishments prevail, would, in the time period under consideration, have been a less than optimum allocation of resources. It can also be shown that those establishments with smaller value-added size are also those establishments which use a small share of outside inputs. Ergo, the smaller the dependency on others, the smaller the need for facilities to supply such inputs, be they transported from other areas or result from agglomeration economies.

6 Special consideration will, of course, be given to raw material intensive industries, which might well be capital-intensive and located in LDRs.

7 It might be noted that EMP-SIZE and VA-SIZE correspond with each other fairly well (only four exceptions).

8 What is not examined in this respect is the extent to which the companies exhibit traits not in accordance with Malaysia as a whole. Such a study would require evidence on the determinants of factor intensity in an international cross-sectional analysis.

9 Since a different source was used for the CAPINT calculation in Table A12 than other capital intensity values in this study, the figures may not be the same.

10 The examination also revealed quite clearly that in those cases where the DAC exhibited lower values than the CMI the reason for this discrepancy seemed to lie primarily in the existence of a far lower than average establishment size.

11 See Table A15 for a size breakdown of establishments; there it can be observed that although about 80 per cent of the companies in 1973 had less than 25 full-time employees, they only produced less than 10 per cent of value added, employed only 15 per cent of the full-time employees and accounted for less than 8 per cent of the physical-capital assets.

12 With regard to the structure of the 3-digit industries (from CMI) with respect to the share of pioneer establishments see Table A16. It can be noted that in almost every industry where pioneer industries in the CMI have an above average share, the DAC also reveals an above average share. Thus, even in this respect the DAC sample is quite representative.

13 This statement is made ignoring the high values in Negeri Sembilan and industries 353 and 354 (petroleum refining and products, etc.). That is, these two industries are located almost solely in Negeri Sembilan, and furthermore, in the case of 353, there is no non-pioneer counterpart.

14 Some justification would seem to be appropriate to explain the procedures and considerations which were involved in setting up and analysing the data. The time periods were selected, given the data restraints, so as to correspond roughly to various major policy developments or shifts. The year represents the year in which production began and not, as in Table 4.1, the year approval was given. In those cases where only the approval year was given, an average lead-time was applied to arrive at the year production began. Companies which were approved in 1977 were assumed to be coming on stream in 1978 or 1979, ergo, the time period designated 1977-79. The author is aware that some of these approvals will not be turned into actual investments, but this should be a minor distortion and probably does not affect the results. The author is also aware of the fact that figures on companies without information on their individual capital, employment or ownership set-up, means that adjustments to differing parameters are ignored. While such a neglect is unfortunate, since differing output or employment values cannot be specified, it must be accepted.

15 This can also be seen in Table 4.1.

16 Due to a limited number of observations in some of the industries, it was not deemed possible to disaggregate on a 3-digit basis for the same time periods as in Table 6.6. The 3-digit level was carried out only for two time periods between initial and final structures. Despite this less than optimal solution (as concerns the time periods), the industry breakdown on a 3-digit level is considered to be theoretically more adequate than referring to 2-digits just to retain the time periods.

17 The author realizes that the regional differences in employment size of firms will distort the data to the extent that comments made on, and conclusions drawn from, data based only on the number of firms might well be incorrect, i.e. with respect to the impact on employment. In order to ensure that this was not the case, the paid full-time employment size (including entrepreneurs and assuming part-time workers worked half-time) of establishments (on a 3-digit level from 1973 CMI data) was calculated for all states. This was then aggregated to the regional level and used as a basis for multiplying the change in the number of firms for two time periods, i.e. 1968-72 and 1973-77, in order to try to achieve an estimate of possible employment growth. While the results are somewhat different, it can still be stated that even with respect to employment, the LDR (the northern states) improved its share. See Table A17 for a summary of these results.

18 A more detailed breakdown of IEs and NIEs by regions by CAPINT, EMP-SIZE and VA-SIZE by incentives was also undertaken and can be provided by the author upon request.

19 The impact of the electronics industry in Penang should be noted, i.e. low capital-intensity.

20 The two major deviations, Penang and Negeri Sembilan, are actually due to 'distortions'. Penang has its (highly labour-intensive) electronics industries in IEs and Negeri Sembilan its refineries outside of IEs. Were one to eliminate these, the IE-NIE CAPINT difference would no doubt be similar to that of the other states.

21 This data stems from data submitted by firms to FIDA in compliance with the ICA.

22 The notation in brackets is the expected direction of the correlation between the dependent and the corresponding independent variable based on above-mentioned assumptions.

23 This expected sign is based on the assumption that investments were carried out in accordance with regional factor intensities, whereby the MDRs, generally speaking, are assumed to have comparative advantages in more capital-intensive lines of production than the LDRs. Contrary to prior definitions and due basically to data constraints, the MDR was defined as covering only Penang, Perak and Selangor.

24 The impact of foreign investment on the capital intensity of investment has not been discussed yet, but in light of the general consensus from the theory and based on a wealth of prior studies it can no doubt be assumed that, general speaking, a higher share of domestic ownership will mean a lower degree of capital-intensity (see Sutter (1979), Bode and Müller-Debus (1978), and Hoffmann and Tan (1980)). In 1973 foreign owned companies (including joint ventures) accounted for 6 per cent of the establishments, 47 per cent of the assets and 53 per cent of value added.

25 While it could be hypothesized that the capital intensity of production over time increases as the income level of development rises, i.e. a (+) would be called for, there are too many factors which can influence this trend to allow a definitive statement to be made. It should also be noted that the author made sure that the "dummy variable trap" was avoided, i.e. no regression was run in which all three years appeared.

26 The meticulous reader will probably have noticed that the total number of observations (which can be calculated from Table 6.13) does not coincide with the 616 observations given earlier. This is merely due to the fact that for a number of industries a sufficient amount of observations was not available. A further paring of the sample was made so as to eliminate those observations where capital intensity fell below M$1,000 per full-time employee. It was decided to do this to avoid a possible mis-specification of the regression equation.

27 This is only shown for the log form; similar results exist for the non-log form as well.

28 A regression analysis across all industries was also carried out and the results were in line with the individual industry regressions. See Table A18 for a summary of the results. It might be noted that between industries, the policy, locational and other aspects, take a back seat to inter-industry differences.

7
Summary

SUMMARY

IT has been the purpose of this empirically-oriented study to analyse the impact of Malaysia's industrialization policies, particularly with respect to their success in efficiently reducing regional economic disparities.

It can be generally stated that Malaysian macro-level and in particular regional industrialization policies over the approximately twenty years up to the beginning of the 1980s have been basically woven in such a way so as to interface best with a free-market economy. Initially, the web of government activities was thin and woven so as to improve upon social and industrial infrastructure. Explicit regional industrialization policies thus took a back seat in the initial period to macro-level industrialization measures, the basic philosophy of which was to allow for a maximum of entrepreneurial freedom. In structuring these policies the Malaysian Government placed their major stress on attracting and fostering new industries via tax havens in the form of tax exemptions (i.e. pioneer legislation) and by trying to provide an environment in which such industries could germinate (i.e. mainly tariff protection and to some extent industrial estates).

Although explicit regional industrialization measures were not introduced up to 1968, it has been shown that those measures introduced to promote industrialization on a macro-level implicitly put the less developed regions at a disadvantage. Not only were industrial estates initially limited to the more developed regions, but new investments were understandably attracted to those areas where, given the stress placed on the profit motive via pioneer industries, the highest returns could be expected, i.e. in the agglomerated areas. While this did not lead to large and ever increasing migration flows from rural to urban areas, as has been the case in other developing countries, there were enough unemployment and income distribution problems both in urban areas as well as in less developed regions to act as sparks which ignited the 1969 race riots. And it was these riots which prompted the Malaysian Government to become more deeply involved in the running of the economy, including with respect to regional industrialization.

Though in 1968 the newly formulated Investment Incentive Act contained a small regional bonus, it was not until 1973 that such incentives were given a strong regional thrust. In the meantime, however, regional policies were being carried out by dispersing industrial estates, an approach which initially was alleged as being carried out with a bit too much zealousness. Despite such contentions, it has been shown in this study that on the average the industrial estates were quickly filled, even to the point of at least providing a return on invested capital, although the rate of utilization, as well as the return on invested capital, was considerably higher in the more developed regions. In light of the fact that the revenues from such sources flow to the economic development corporation in the respective state, it has been pointed out that the greater success of industrial estates in more developed regions, if not compensated for in some other manner, means that the competitive position of the more developed regions would be strengthened. This development was furthered by the large implicit subsidies granted via underpriced plots in IEs in the MDRs. In addition, it has been shown that due to the success of the free trade zones in incorporating an increasing share of domestic inputs into the export products, which (in the electronics industry) were extremely successful in capturing world market shares, the more developed regions were given an additional boost over the less developed regions.

Regional investment incentives of the type applied in Malaysia have been shown to have caused the most capital-intensive bias of all incentives in effect. Assuming that it is not the factor capital which should be subsidized in the less developed regions (perhaps with the exception of certain raw material exploiting or intensive industries), then such policies obviously represent a severe misallocation of resources.

Although the direct impact of these shortcomings of Malaysian regional industrialization policies has not been estimated, it can be shown that, based on indicators of industries which would tend not to be suitable for locating in less developed regions, the actual development would more or less seem to be in accordance with a priori theoretical considerations. It has been shown that, in many of those cases where the industries settling in less developed regions did not correspond to a priori considerations, the share of those receiving incentive assistance was particularly large. This has been interpreted as meaning that the incentive induced a misallocation of investment, at least to the extent that these industries really did not correspond to the comparative advantage of less developed regions. It has also been shown that industrial estates do indeed seem to provide tangible benefits to companies, since in less developed regions the share of companies receiving incentives in industrial estates is less than the share of those outside of the industrial estates. On the whole it can also be established that companies in industrial estates tend to be more capital-intensive than those outside, and that in many cases companies in industrial estates are more capital-intensive in less developed regions than they are in more developed ones.

In analysing and quantifying the total impact of various policies and parameters on the capital intensity of investments it can be determined that out of all factors the participation of foreign nationals has had the greatest impact. The impact of incentives and industrial estates, although to a large extent in agreement with a priori expectations, generally accounted for a less than average share of explained variance. Of considerable interest is the evidence revealed by the fact that within industries firms in less developed regions receiving incentives do not seem to adapt their capital intensity to the changed parameters.

SOME CONCLUDING REMARKS ON POLICIES AND FUTURE PROSPECTS

Given the commitment of the Malaysian Government to expedite measures to reduce regional development disparities, it is all the more perplexing why policy-makers have not been more meticulous in structuring and effecting the appropriate policies. Since the question – what could they have done? – obviously arises, an attempt will be made here to outline alternative measures, based on partial equilibrium principles[1], with which the overriding goals might have been aimed at. Following the literature and keeping in mind the distinguishing regional characteristics in Malaysia, several basic guidelines can be established before analysing the specific policy measures instituted[2]:

(1) If regional development is not to be hampered by an ill-suited social and economic environment, then the regional distribution of social and economic infrastructure must be clearly notched into what can be perceived as the long-term development potential (see Giersch, 1965). The development potential can be best described as an all-encompassing indicator of the comparative advant-

ages of a region given the national goals of output, economic growth, employment and income distribution.

(2) In structuring such investments the relevant literature underlines the importance of ensuring that they correspond to the size and structure of the respective growth centre/agglomerations[3]. Of significance in this respect is the structuring of facilities to cater to the type and needs of those industries tending to cluster in agglomeration areas of various sizes (see Norcliffe, 1975, Townroe and Nigel, 1980).

(3) To help ensure that the economy functions as closely as possible along the lines of a market economy, measures to eliminate information disparities or deficiences need to be instituted.

(4) Likewise the promotion of a necessary ingredient for a market economy to prosper, namely the existence and nurturing of entrepreneurs and the entrepreneurial spirit (in essence producing results similar to incomes policies of the Haberler type), must be carried out in a manner corresponding to regional development disparities.

In the discussion of the impact of tax exemption measures, where the length of the exemption is determined by either the amount of capital invested or the number of jobs created, on the allocation of the factors of production, there is general agreement in the former case that they favour capital[4]. Therefore the implementation of such a measure in an economy like Malaysia's leads to a misallocation of resources, unless the specific exploitation of Ricardo goods (requiring capital-intensive methods) is to be promoted. In such a case, however, the implementation of sectoral measures would seem to be a more efficient procedure[5]. Even if the tax exemptions are based on the number of jobs created, the impact, although less unequivocal, is still seen as being biased towards substituting capital for labour. Thereby the extent of the impact depends on the assumptions made regarding the feedback of such exemptions on the share of labour in the production process[6]. Furthermore, if the length of the exemptions depends on certain employment sizes being fulfilled, then the less developed regions would be able to profit only to a small degree[7] (given a relatively widely scattered labour force), aside from the fact that small-scale establishments (and thus less developed regions) would be put at a disadvantage[8].

One possible way to induce an allocation of resources in line with the given comparative advantages (for instance, labour[9]) of the less developed regions, would be to induce an artificial 'devaluation'[10] of a region, by offering wage subsidies (see, for instance, Bird, 1966; McLure, 1971). Such a measure may be applied either with respect to the number employed or to the number trained and employed (so as to assure that human capital is developed as well). Its impact is considered in the theory to be relatively straightforward; labour will be used more intensively in those regions where subsidy is granted, and, given the above assumptions on the factor intensities in such regions, labour-intensive industries are thereby favoured (see, for instance, Buck and Atkins, 1976)[11]. The chances that regionally differentiated wage subsidies are successful in creating new employment depends, *inter alia,* on whether the factor intensity of production reflects real relative prices in a given region or whether distortions (e.g. minimum wages) in the factor market have already caused wage rates to be shifted further away from competitive conditions[12].

In structuring the wage subsidies, care must be taken to arrange a package corresponding as closely as possible to the purported comparative advantages of a region[13]. If, in addition to labour, the size factor of production establishments is also to be taken into consideration and small-scale establishments are deemed to be a comparative advantage of the LDRs, then regional wage subsidies granted on a lump-sum basis could fulfil this purpose as well. That is, since it is generally the case that small-scale establishments pay lower wages, a lump-sum payment would amount to a larger percentage share per job created than in larger firms. A straight percentage payment would on the other hand be neutral *vis-à-vis* firm size.

Additional 'leverage' can be gained if such subsidies are raised in the MDRs, thereby increasing the size of the incentive differential (i.e. the amount of 'devaluation' of the LDRs becomes larger) between the two regions. Crucial, however, to improving the competitive position of the LDRs and thus decreasing development disparities, is whether the devaluation is sufficient to outweigh the estimated locational disadvantages of such regions.

Even if wage subsidies in LDRs can attract industries and do provide an impetus to help shift the demand for the factors of production towards a structure more in line with comparative advantages, entrepreneurs responding to such measures will not just exhibit a demand for a homogeneous quantity of unskilled labour. Rather they will be interested in semi-skilled and skilled workers as well. Given the limited supply of such workers in LDRs and knowing that they do not migrate from the MDRs in sizeable numbers, the ensuing shortage of qualified workers would act as a barrier to further industrialization of the region. Although wage subsidies could be set high enough to initially attract qualified personnel from the MDRs, a longer term solution is necessary. This would entail a reform of the general and vocational educational system, which, although better than in most other developing countries (at Malaysia's income level), is failing to produce the required structure of human capital. First of all, the quality of primary education in the LDRs (i.e. in rural areas) is lower than elsewhere in the country due to poorer schools and less well-trained teachers. Secondly, the burden of keeping children at school is far higher for the poor which are mainly located in rural areas: the out of pocket costs of keeping just one child in school was 18 per cent of household income for the lowest income quintile versus 10.4 per cent for the second. Third, public subsidies are concentrated on post-secondary (55 per cent) and secondary schools (37 per cent) (Meerman, 1980, pp. 132-5). Since retention rates are lower in the rural (poorer) areas, the higher income groups received a far greater share of the subsidies. Fourth, as already noted earlier the establishment of training institutes was primarily restricted to the MDRs. Finally, the higher education system is producing more academics than the market can absorb and fewer vocationally/technically trained than needed (see Hoerr, 1973). The undersupply of the latter affects in particular the LDRs since the higher income levels in MDRs act as a magnet. All this means that only through an improvement of human-capital building measures will regional industrialization measures in the LDRs be placed on a solid foundation.

To overcome those locational disadvantages evolving from inadequate transportation (or in the widest sense communication) infrastructure and exert a positive impact on the LDRs, communication subsidies for specified regions could be considered. The impact of such subsidies can be interpreted in the same context as the impact of a tariff or subsidy in international trade theory, that is, they help induce and promote the use of the appropriate factors of production. The same theoretical argumentation can be said to apply to ensuring that non-conventional inputs, not offered by the market in LDRs but available in agglomerated areas in the MDRs, are provided to the extent that they would otherwise hinder the exploitation of the comparative advantage[14]. Such a provision could also nurture the growth of small-scale establishments since it has been shown that part of their difficulties lie in gaining access to information and services [15].

All these measures, which basically aim at shifting relative prices in such a way as to improve the competitive position of the LDRs, would do little if the necessary industrial infrastructure was either insufficient or lacking. Since infrastructure investments can be aimed at conserving capital, such undertakings can be accomplished to some extent by taking advantage of development economies of scale[16] engendered by concentrating such facilities in specific areas, for example, in the form of industrial estates (IEs)[17] or free trade zones (FTZs). The ensuing concentration of industries can in turn lead to external economies thereby improving locational competitiveness of a region (see, for instance, Lim, 1981).

The establishment of such delineated areas can also be interpreted as helping to attract and promote entrepreneurial activities. That is, the delineated areas can offer prospective entrepreneurs zones in which activities are subjected to fewer or no regulations, thereby reducing the growth-retarding bureaucratic barriers (see Olson, 1979). To the extent that barriers (e.g. tariffs) are eliminated *vis-à-vis* the outside world (as is the case to some extent in FTZs), a world market exclave has been created, from which the benefits emanating from a customs union can be reaped (see Grubel, 1983 and Spinanger, 1984).

Obviously such zones (since they are second best solutions) can only be the first step along the path to reduce restrictions throughout the entire economy. For sure they must not be used as an alibi by politicians as proof of liberal trade policies. That is, instead of inducing competitive industries, existing tariff barriers in the rest of the economy are maintained and industries are established whose competitiveness in world markets would not otherwise be given. In this connection the ongoing heavy industries plans represent a major departure from previous policies. It means that large sums of money (in essence of subsidy character) are going to be channelled past small-scale enterprises which have proved to be an important growth ingredient in the past. The economic evidence presented in this study does not lend support to following such a path.

The pricing modus by which developed tracts of land are offered and what facilities they embody depends explicitly on the estimation of regional locational disadvantages and comparative advantages – such aspects must therefore be considered together with all other measures[18]. Aside from this relative price issue, another aspect must be taken into account, namely the impact of fully developed industrial sites with all necessary utilities on the factor intensity decision of companies settling in such an area. If the impact is neutral, that is, the production structure is just as capital-/labour-intensive as it would have been without the IE, then it can be considered to be consistent with a regional policy which aims at overcoming market distortions in order to exploit the potential comparative advantage of a region. Should, however, the IE because of the presence of all utilities, attract companies which shift the factor intensity of production to more capital-intensive lines than would have been expected, based on the specific regional factor intensities, then an undesired distortion has been introduced[19]. With regard to the third factor of production, land, the extent to which it is subsidized could well cause this factor to be used more extensively. Assuming that the factor land as such is relatively abundant in the less developed regions, then policies designed to promote its use would clearly be economically justifiable. However, it is not land as such which is offered, but rather developed tracts, the supply of which might be inadequate in the less developed regions due to the large amount of capital investment necessary. Assuming that the comparative advantages of a region would remain underexploited without such investments, and knowing that economies of scale can be achieved in developing large tracts of land, it is quite conceivable that the returns reaped from IEs (on a first round basis) will exceed costs (by even more than a fair return), since the market price for alternative (individual) tracts might well be considerably higher.

Should the policy of offering developed tracts of land specifically include areas designated to be free trade zones, then certain difficulties enter into determining their possible impact. First of all, since such facilities are generally set up in areas where adequate labour supplies are available and where transportation and communication infrastructure facilities are of relatively high standard, it can be expected that they will be in the more developed areas. In light of the fact that the demand potential for (and probably also the elasticities of) products stemming from FTZs is considerably larger than the domestic markets faced by producers in other IEs, the impact of employment and income in the region (in which the FTZs are located) is, *ceteris paribus,* larger. Therefore, FTZs in the more developed areas could tend to increase regional disparities. Secondly, the extent to which FTZs prove beneficial to the region in which they are located is determined by the degree to which they are linked to the economy and exploit the comparative advantage of the country/region.

While, given an appropriate economic environment, there is little question about the positive effects of a greater integration into the international division of labour (Spinanger, 1984) and the resulting domestic multiplier effects of wage income stemming from employment in FTZs, doubt has been raised about the ability of FTZs to be integrated into the economy and also to contribute to its overall development. Some of these contentions are not of a theoretical nature, but rather stem from the viewpoint that the multinational corporation (MNC) investing in such zones profits at the expense of the host country (e.g. see Fröbel *et al.*, 1977)[20]. Others, of theoretical nature, rest on what might be considered to be limiting assumptions (see, for instance, Hamada, 1974; Rodriguez, 1976). The obvious potential regional impact of FTZs has received little attention in the literature. It can be stated that, as in the case of other policies, which at least are implicitly limited to the MDRs, if nothing

TABLE 7.1

Regional Development (Income) Differentials[a] in West Malaysia[b], 1965-1990

Year	V_{uw}	V^p_{wt}	V^p_{wo}	$V^{k^2}_w$
1965	.35955	.37621	.37621	.31744
1968	.38974	.41056	.40917	.34733
1970	.35120	.39416	.37694	.29595
1975	.32592	.35339	.33720	.27644
1980	.28860	.29715	.28400	.30204
1990	.21101	.22051	.21074	.21660

Sources: Own calculations based on L.L. Lim (1971, pp. 40-3) for 1965 and 1968; Malaysia Plan (1976, pp. 201, 204, 206-7) for 1970-90.

[a] Coefficient of variation of per capital income see footnote 21.
[b] Perlis and Kedah one observation, thus only ten states used for calculations. The four different weighting schemes used are:

V_{uw} = unweighted

V^p_{wt} = weighted with population shares in year t

V^p_{wo} = weighted with population shares in base year 1965

$V^{k^2}_w$ = weighted with area shares

is done to ensure that the increased wealth is allowed to feed through to the less developed areas, development disparities will increase.

To conclude, it would seem appropriate to ask: How large is the task which lies ahead for the Malaysian authorities to meet the regional development goals put forth in the Malaysia Plan? While it has been shown earlier that actual per capita income differences in Malaysia are relatively small, the projected reductions (up to 1990) are indeed quite sizeable. To be sure, an analysis of their dispersion (using various forms of a simple coefficient of variation[21] of per capita income) reveals that a reduction of about 30 per cent is foreseen (see Table 7.1)[22]. This means that the yearly percentage reduction from 1975 to 1990 will have to be about twice as large as was the case in the period 1970 to 1975. It thus becomes apparent that the Malaysian authorities will have to pay more attention to ensuring that congruent and economically efficient policies, as expounded upon above, are effected, particularly in light of probable slower overall growth rates in the world economy through the remainder of the 1980s.

1 For a general equilibrium treatment, albeit in a simplified model, see Dewees and Kotowitz (1980).

2 In connection with the following discussion two caveats should be brought to attention and stressed. First of all, nowhere is an attempt made to compare the possible impact of explicit regional policies on growth, employment, etc. with macro-orientied policies, but rather the argumentation is carried out under the condition that the decision of a government to aim at reducing regional development disparities is given and thus economic principles must be applied to provide the direction. Secondly, since the discussion is not carried under partial equilibrium arguments, any conclusion drawn is to be viewed accordingly. While the full ramification of all industrialization measures can obviously only be captured with a large general equilibrium model, it is assumed that the posited direction of the impact of a given policy measure would not be reversed. This was, for instance, true for a general equilibrium analysis of Mexico (see Fischer *et al.*, 1982) where with respect to regional policies no difference resulted between partial and general equilibrium conditions.

3 In a study carried out by the Stanford Research Institute it was established that the unit cost of additional infrastructure investments in cities with over 150,000 inhabitants declines very little. The study also suggests that, *ceteris paribus*, moving industry to cities larger than this size causes no significant economies of scale, but does cause increasing social costs. It consequently suggests that net social benefits will be increased if attention is paid to a decentralization of medium-size cities (see Rao, 1970).

4 Another point of criticism against such methods is that they basically favour firms where profits are expected to be particularly high during the first years. Although this should not be interpreted as meaning that many (almost) fly-by-night entrepreneurs are attracted – surely not the goal of a long-termed development policy – the degree to which it does exist, *ceteris paribus*, is a negative influence, the impact of which has not been quantified in this study. Since this aspect has not been mentioned in the relevant literature, not even in World Bank reports, it is assumed to be of little significance.

5 Similar to granting tax exemptions on a regional basis would be, for instance, granting pioneer industry status only if the company was established in a desired region. Likewise, the implementation of accelerated depreciation or investment tax credits on a regional basis can be interpreted in a manner similar to the tax exemption.

6 See, for instance, Usher (1976) and references therein.

7 As Karunaratne and Abdullah note, there still exists a need to devise more productive tax exemption policies to generate employment opportunities and promote the dispersal of industries (1978, p. 274).

8 This is not to say, however, that a specific industry, for well-founded economic reasons, should not be of large scale in a given region, but rather that incentives which across the board have a bias to large-scale industries should be avoided.

9 This applies as well to the case where the natural resource endowment of Malaysia is to be tapped (i.e. in the case of Ricardo goods). Then, however, incentives favouring capital could be introduced.

10 In a study of the integration process in the EEC and regional implications of such Balassa (1975, p. 270) notes that subsidizing labour in depressed regions would conform to the resource endowments and increase employment, with corresponding improvements in income distribution. But under capital mobility, such a subsidy will be equivalent to a combination of exchange rate devaluation and transfer.

11 A counterpart to the regional wage subsidy would be a regional payroll tax. Such a tax can also be considered complementary, since it could be enacted in the developed areas to pay for the subsidies in the less developed areas.

12 It is assumed that the impact of such measures is great enough to improve the employment level in LDRs to the extent that unwanted outward migration is reduced, but not to the extent that unwanted migration from the MDRs occurs.

13 It ought to be added that for the most part incentives are meant to be of temporary nature, similar to the infant-industry tariff. There might, however, still be factors which, given the parameters, might be less temporary.

14 Whether such subsidies benefit capital or labour cannot be determined, but to the extent that the comparative advantage of less developed regions – labour – is utilized to a greater degree, then labour will benefit (see e.g. Norman, 1979, and references therein).

15 See, for instance, Bruch (1983).

16 Despite the fact that in every publication such development economies of scale are mentioned, statistical evidence is nowhere to be found. It is hoped that ongoing research will produce the posited results.

17 The term IE in this study is considered to represent a piece of fully developed property (with utilities and communication/transportation facilities), upon which companies can be set up to perform economic activities. What type of activity is irrelevant. IE is thus a general term. There are, however, specific types of IEs, e.g., a free trade zone (FTZ), which is more demanding with respect to the infrastructure (i.e. international transportation facilities are required).

18 Another possibility is also conceivable: to the extent that the capital infrastructure of an IE as well as possible agglomeration economies cause investments to be less capital-intensive than expected, then the achieving of the employment goal is given an additional push. The evidence presented in this study does not support such an assumption.

19 It should also be remembered that the establishment of IEs must be accompanied or preceded by a number of other social and infrastructure investments in order to ensure that they are a viable part of the economy as a whole, particularly with respect to their role (minute as it might be) in the international division of labour.

20 Such feelings are further strengthened, since above the usual exemptions from customs duties other exemptions (e.g. tax exemptions) are also granted.

21 The various forms of the coefficient of variation are as follows:

$$V_{uw} = \frac{\sqrt{\Sigma\ (y_i - \bar{y})^2/(N-1)}}{\bar{y}}; \quad V^p_{wt},\ V^p_{wo},\ V^{k^2}_w = \frac{\sqrt{\Sigma\ ((y_i - \bar{y})^2 \cdot w)}}{\bar{y}}$$

where

V_{uw} = unweighted and V_w = weighted; y_i = income in state; $\bar{y}$ = mean income of all states; N = number of states; and w = weight in period t or o (base period).

It might be added that although the author is aware of the shortcomings of this disparity index, since there is no such index without shortcomings, the author's discretion prevailed. It is not contended, however, that the results presented here are unequivocal as other indices could well produce other results, not only regarding the level, but also (and particularly important for the conclusions drawn here) regarding the change over time.

22 For the projected trend with regard to the dispersal of the manufacturing industries, see Table A19.

Appendices

APPENDIX 1

LEGISLATION

General Development/Industrialization Measures

(a) Pioneer Industries Ordinance (Relief from Income Tax), 31 July 1958

Pioneer status may be granted by the Minister of Commerce to manufacturing companies fulfilling the following conditions:

1. The given industry either does not exist or only produces on a scale not suitable for the economic or development requirements of the Federation of Malaysia.

2. The prospects for the future potential of the given industry are favourable.

3. The given industry is considered to be expedient with respect to the public interest and should therefore be assisted.

If all these conditions are met and there is more than one company applying for pioneer status in an industry where only one industry is considered necessary, and all other aspects are equal, then preference will be given to applicants with the greatest amount of local capital.

Once production is begun, the extent of exemption from the income tax (which was 40 per cent at the time of the Ordinance) depends on the amount of initial fixed capital expenditure as follows:

M$	< 100,000	2 years
M$ 100,000	- 249,999	3 years
M$ 250,000	≥	5 years

Any income received in a reasonable period of time after expiration of the pioneer status but accountable to this period is treated as having occurred during the period as a pioneer company. Likewise any expenses incurred within one year after the expiration of the tax exemption, but which could be attributed to the pioneer period, is considered to have occurred during said period.

If the pioneer status has been granted for a three-year period and by the end of the third year capital expenditures amount to more than M$250,000 then an additional two-year tax holiday may be granted. In addition to these tax holidays, any losses incurred during the period of pioneer status may be carried over beyond this period. Once the pioneer status expires, all existing fixed assets (capital equipment) may be depreciated as if they were new and at a rate of 20 per cent for a period of 5 years (thereby exceeding the usual much lower rate).

Dividends paid out by pioneer companies are exempted from further taxes only to the extent that a direct shareholder in the pioneer company receives said dividend.

(b) Pioneer Industries (Relief from Tax) (Variation) Act, April, 1965

The extent of exemption from the company tax is redefined as follows:

M$	< 250,000	2 years
M$	250,000 - 499,999	3 years
M$	500,000 - 999,999	4 years
M$	1,000,000 ≥	5 years

Provision is also made to allow dividends from pioneer companies passing through holding companies to be treated as tax exemptions.

(c) Industrial Coordination Act, 1975[1]

The Industrial Coordination (Amendment) Act, 1977 is enforced as of 1 February 1978.

The Prime Minister appoints the Secretary General of the Ministry of Trade and Industry as the Licensing Officer who is the authority to issue manufacturing licences.

Any person engaging in manufacturing activity as defined by the Act is required to obtain a licence from the licensing officer in respect of such manufacturing activity. In issuing the licence, the licensing officer is empowered to impose conditions in furtherance to the objective of the Act, and he may vary such conditions at the request of the licence holder or on his own motion, but after consultation with the licence holder. Licences issued by the Minister under the principal Act before the coming into effect of the Amendment Act will remain valid subject to the terms and conditions attached to such a licence.

The following manufacturing activities are exempted from all provisions of the Act:

i) Manufacturing activities with:
(a) shareholders' funds of less than M$250,000 and
(b) less than 25 full-time paid employees;

ii) Milling of palm oil fresh fruits into crude palm oil;

iii) Producing and processing of raw natural rubber of all types including latex, skim, sheets, crepe, scrap, technically specified rubbers, non-standard and modified rubber or any other unvulcanized form of natural rubber prepared by any patented or technically specified procedure;

iv) The milling of padi into rice.

A manufacturer is not allowed to manufacture any product other than those specified in a licence without the prior approval of the licensing officer. However, a manufacturer may suspend or discontinue the manufacture of a product that is specified in a licence after notifying the licensing officer in writing of his intention to do so.

The amended Act also provides for appeal by any manufacturer who is aggrieved by the decisions of the licensing officer in respect of a refusal to grant a licence, the revocation of a licence and a refusal to approve the transfer of a licence, and any appeal should be lodged within 30 days and in such manner as is prescribed in the rules.

The Ministry of Trade and Industry also reviewed the conditions to be imposed on manufacturers as well as the application procedure for manufacturers to apply for their licences. A major feature of the revised conditions was the exemption given to manufacturers having fixed investments of less than M$ 500,000 from the equity condition such as a certain fixed percentage of a Malaysian/bumiputra participation in the equity ownership. This revision is considered at length by the Cabinet Committee on Investment, which took into account the views and suggestions of the private sector.

[1]Ministry of Finance (1978, p. 197).

(d) Pioneer Industries/Products Declared Eligible to Receive Special Investment Incentives, 1971

Pioneer Industry	Electronics industry (in respect of projects the investment plans of which have been approved by Government prior to 31 January 1973).
Pioneer Product	Radios - all types, television sets, tape recorders, electronic calculators, electronic computers, weather communication equipment, hearing aids, walkie-talkie sets, amplifiers - all types, radiograms/stereograms, gramophones/record players/record changers, fish finders, testing meters and instruments, telephone and telegraph line system, teleommunication equipment including radio and TV broadcasting equipment, X-ray apparatus, semiconductors (transistors and diodes), integrated circuits, valves, television picture tubes, carbon film resistors, fixed composition resistors, wirewound resistors, volume/tone controls, potentiometers, polyester capacitors, mica capacitors, electrolytic capacitors, ceramic capacitors, paper capacitors, variable tuning capacitors, IF transformers and coils, tuners for TV sets, antenna and oscillating coils, peaking coils, magnetic head coils/recording heads, input, output, vertical and horizontal transformers and chokes for radios, TV sets and amplifiers, various types of switches used in electronic equipment (rotary type and piano type), connectors - all types, memory planes/units, earphones, modules, power relays, ferrite core-rods, magnetic audio tape cassette reels, parts for hearing aids, printed circuit boards, speakers, microphones, circuit packers, telephone amplifiers, matrix planes, memory core arrays and its components, digital heads, magnetic device for digital and other computer memory system, plastic moulded cabinets, plastic knobs, radio chassis, coil formers, TV aerials, radiograms/stereogram chassis.

(Government Gazette (1971, A 89)).

(e) Pioneer Industries/Products Declared Eligible to Receive Special Investment Incentives, 1973

The following industries/products are included under Schedule I of Section I 3(A) which allows pioneer companies approved for the manufacture of these items to enjoy between 4-10 years of tax relief. Only projects that are more than 90 per cent export-oriented qualify for this additional incentive.

Manufacture of electronic and electrical components and products[a]	Electrical components, television sets, electronic calculators, weather communication equipment, radiograms/stereograms, testing meters, telephone and telegraph line systems, X-ray apparatus, electronic measuring equipment, timers, transducers, counters and card readers, A-D/D-A converters, annunicators, sequence programmers, automatic traffic control systems, automatic parking fee collection systems, fans, vacuum cleaners, cooking and kitchen ware, hair dryers, radios - all types, tape recorders, electronic comp0uters, walkie-talkie sets, amplifiers - all types, gramophones/record players, telecommunication equipment, television picture tubes, electronic heaters, computing scales, digital clocks, miniature motors, gatexes, scanners, shift registers, automatic fare collection systems, automatic vending systems, automatic cytological analysers, floor polishers, shavers, fractional horsepower motors
Manufacture of machinery and parts[b]	Refrigerators, typewriters, dictaphones, accounting machines, power driven handtools, air conditioners, calculators, cash registers, machine tools and mechanical precision measuring equipment
Other industries/products[b]	Surgical and dental instruments and equipment, cameras - all types, lenses, telescopes, magnifying glass and microscopes, musical instruments (all types), hearing

aids, scientific gauges of all types, projectors - all types, binoculars, watches and clocks (all types)

[a]To qualify for the additional incentive companies must have obtained approval before 31 December 1973. - [b]To qualify for the incentive approvals must be obtained prior to 31 July 1974.
(Source: Malaysia Industrial Digest (1973, Vol. 6, No. 1)).

Development Industrialization Measures with Explicit Regional Content

(a) Investment Incentives Act[1], 26 September 1968

Regulations regarding pioneer industries:

The conditions on the length of tax holidays, depreciation, dividends and treatment of losses have been adopted from the prior PIOs. Additional exemption from the income tax is provided for under the following conditions:

1.	production of priority product	1 year
2.	establishment in a designated development area	1 year
3.	incorporation of a specific (i.e. government specifies) amount of domestic inputs into product	1 year

The designation 'pioneer status' is extended to non-manufacturing industries.

Note: Companies not granted a pioneer status are now eligible to qualify for the above exemptions.

(b) Investment Incentives (Amendment) Act, 1 October 1971[2]

Special Provisions relating to the Hotel Industry

Investment incentives are granted to hotels as follows:

Area A	Kuala Lumpur and Penang Island	Pioneer status or income tax abatement on 15 per cent of chargeable income over 12-year period and accelerated depreciation allowance[3]
Area B	Selangor (except K.L.), Perak, Negeri Sembilan, Melaka, Johor and Kota Kinabalu	Pioneer status or income tax abatement on 20 per cent of chargeable income over 12-year period and accelerated depreciation allowance Industrial building allowance
Area C	Pahang, Trengganu, Kedah, Kelantan, Perlis, East Malaysia (except Kota Kinabalu)	Pioneer status or income tax abatement on 25 percent of chargeable income over 12-year period and accelerated depreciation allowance Industrial building allowance
Area D	Islands, hill resorts and other designated areas	Pioneer status or income tax abatement on 30 percent of chargeable income over 12-year period and accelerated depreciation allowance Industrial building allowance

The approval of investment incentives subjects the investment throughout the period to the conditions that

[1]Beginning in 1968 the PIO is incorporated into the IIA with other investment incentives. These included the Investment Tax Credit and export incentives.

[2]This act is deemed to have come into force with the Investment Incentives Act (1968), excepting, however, the Labor Utilization Relief.

[3]Only applies to hotels already completed and operating in period 1 January 1968 to 31 December 1973.

- the approved standard of hotel complex or parts thereof improved is maintained;

- the approved standard of management and service in the hotel is maintained;

- approved rates for rooms and services are charged;

- business operations - other than those approved - shall not be carried out without prior consent of respective authority.

Failure to abide to these conditions (or others deemed fit and imposed by respective authority) can lead to withdrawal of approval.

Labor Utilization Relief (LUR)

For any project which is deemed as serving the interests of the industrial development of Malaysia, the following exemptions from the income tax legislation - based on the number of full-time employees created by a given investment - are applicable[1]:

51 - 100 employees	2 years
101 - 200 employees	3 years
201 - 350 employees	4 years
351 - employees	5 years

Special Investment Incentives to Electronics Industry[2]

For the electronics industry (now designated as a pioneer industry[3]) and for specified (mainly electronic) products (designated as pioneer products[4]) the following special tax holidays - based on the corresponding size of the capital investment - are available if the project receives government approval before 31 January 1973[5]:

M$ < 250,000	4 years
M$ 250,000 - 499,999	5 years
M$ 500,000 - 999,999	6 years
M$ 1,000,000 ≥	7 years

(c) Investment Incentives (Amendment) Act, 20 March 1973

A company may apply for income tax exemption based on the locational incentive if

(a) it is located in an area newly designated as a locational incentive area and already receiving tax relief under the LUR or as a PI or has been receiving an investment tax credit and if it retroactively surrenders all benefits gained therefrom;

---

[1]The additional (three) extensions to the exemption period - as specified in the 1968 IIA - also applied to companies qualifying for either the Labour Utilization Relief or the Electronics Industry Incentives.

[2]Based on the powers invested in him by the IIA, the Minister of Trade and Industry decreed that these extended incentives would also be available for the manufacture of certain electronic and electrical components and products (if approved by 31 December 1973), certain machinery and parts (if approved by 31 July 1974) and selected other industries/products (if approved by 31 July 1974); the additional condition is made that the project had to be 90 per cent export oriented. Companies approved after these dates would only receive normal pioneer status. See Malaysia Industrial Digest (1973, First Quarter, p. 5).

[3]For listing see pp. 226 ff.

[4]Ibid.

[5]The additional (three) extensions to the exemption period - as specified in the 1968 IIA - also applied to companies qualifying for either the Labour Utilization Relief or the Electronics Industry Incentives.

(b) it has started production of a product in 'marketable quantities' in a given area one year prior to its being designated as a locational incentive area;

(c) it is outside a designated area and has started production before the location incentive amendments but has re-sited to a designated area for the purpose of expansion or modernization;

(d) it is already in an area newly designated as an LI area and if it either expands or modernizes.

The tax relief granted in accordance with above shall not exceed period specified for industries in designated area. The general conditions under which exemption from the income tax is granted - based on capital investment or employment categories are as follows:

	M$ < 250,000	5 years
or	- 100 employees	
	M$ 250,000 - 499,999	6 years
or	101 - 200 employees	
	M$ 500,000 - 999,999	7 years
or	201 - 350 employees	
	M$ 1,000,000 -	8 years
or	351 - employees	

Additional years of exemption (up to a maximum of 10) are possible under the following conditions:

1. if product of industry is designated as priority	1 year
2. if Malaysian content meets specified requirements	1 year

The Minister of Trade and Industry (in concurrence with the Minister of Finance) has the right to designate areas eligible for the locational incentive, specify the type of industries, the length of the exemption period and the period during which applications for said location incentive will be approved.

APPENDIX 2

STATISTICAL APPENDIX

TABLE A1
Per Capita Income and Production Shares of Major Primary Activities by Regions, 1965 (per cent)

Region/State	*GDP/ Capita*[a]	*Manufac- turing*	*Rubber*	*Mining and Quarrying*	*Oil Palm*	*Coconuts/ Copra*	*Rice*
Northern states	59.6	6.6	16.5	8.5	–	27.4	66.3
Trengganu	62.7	.8	1.6	6.0	–	2.7	4.0
Kelantan	49.2	1.7	3.7	1.2	–	19.9	13.4
Perlis	69.3	.3	.2	.1	–	.4	8.2
Kedah	64.9	3.8	11.0	1.2	–	4.4	40.7
Southern states	94.0	20.2	36.6	16.2	44.4	23.5	6.6
Pahang	116.0	3.6	6.1	10.7	3.3	2.1	2.8
Melaka	76.7	2.4	6.2	.2	–	1.8	3.0
Johor	92.2	14.2	24.3	5.3	41.1	19.6	.8
Western states	122.5	73.2	46.8	74.9	55.5	49.2	27.0
Perak	101.8	12.0	15.8	48.7	22.2	24.7	11.1
Selangor	166.3	42.3	14.4	25.2	31.1	17.4	6.2
Negeri Sembilan	108.1	9.1	13.7	1.0	2.2	.8	4.1
Penang	96.3	9.8	2.9	–	–	6.3	5.6
West Malaysia							
GDP	848[b]	10.24[c]	14.8[c]	8.7[c]	1.3[c]	1.1[c]	2.3[c]
Exports	–	–	39.0[d]	23.3[d]	3.1[d]	1.1[d]	–

Sources: Export shares: Malaysia Plan (1971, pp. 22-5). Primary production activities: L. L. Lim (1971, p. 40).

[a] Per capita income in given regions as per cent of West Malaysian per capital income.

[b] Per capita income in M$.

[c] Share of given activity in total GDP of West Malaysia.

[d] Share of exports of given activity in total export of West Malaysia.

TABLE A2
Regional Population Distribution by Ethnic Groups,
1947, 1957, 1970 and 1980 (per cent)

	Malays				*Chinese*				*Indians and Others*			
Region/State	*1947*	*1957*	*1970*	*1980*	*1947*	*1957*	*1970*	*1980*	*1947*	*1957*	*1970*	*1980*
Northern states	43.3	40.5	38.1	36.8	8.8	8.9	8.4	8.1	11.3	11.2	9.5	11.2
Trengganu	8.6	8.2	8.1	8.2	.8	.8	.7	.7	.4	.4	.2	.4
Kelantan	17.0	14.8	13.6	12.8	1.2	1.2	1.2	1.2	.9	.9	.5	1.2
Perlis	2.3	2.3	2.0	1.9	.6	.7	.6	.6	.4	.3	.2	.5
Kedah	15.5	15.2	14.4	13.9	6.2	6.2	5.9	5.6	9.6	9.6	8.6	9.1
Southern states	23.8	24.5	25.7	26.6	29.0	29.6	26.3	27.0	17.0	16.7	16.5	17.3
Pahang	5.6	5.7	6.6	7.5	5.1	4.6	5.1	5.6	2.8	3.2	4.0	4.4
Melaka	4.9	4.6	4.5	4.4	5.1	5.2	5.1	4.9	3.8	3.3	3.4	3.7
Johor	13.3	14.2	14.6	14.7	18.8	16.8	16.1	16.5	10.4	10.2	9.1	9.2
Western states	32.8	34.9	36.2	36.6	62.0	64.5	65.3	64.9	71.6	72.3	73.8	71.5
Perak	14.9	15.5	14.4	13.6	23.6	23.1	21.3	20.3	26.4	25.7	23.9	21.9
Selangor	7.7	9.3	12.0	13.5	19.3	21.0	24.2	25.6	27.3	28.9	32.0	31.4
Negeri Sembilan	4.6	4.8	4.7	4.8	6.0	6.4	5.9	5.6	7.2	7.8	8.4	8.2
Penang	5.6	5.3	5.1	4.7	13.1	14.0	13.9	13.4	10.7	9.9	9.5	10.0
Actual Population (,000)	2,428	3,125	4,868	6,182	1,885	2,334	3,122	4,065	531	696	933	1,308

<u>Source</u>: See Table 1.2.

TABLE A3
Industrial Distribution of Employment by Ethnic Groups, 1947, 1957, 1970 and 1980 (per cent)

	Malays				*Chinese*				*Indians and Others*			
Industry	*1947*	*1957*	*1970*	*1980*	*1947*	*1957*	*1970*	*1980*	*1947*	*1957*	*1970*	*1980*
Agriculture												
Rubber cultivation	20.0	25.5	25.3	18.5	23.4	26.0	17.7	11.4	47.1	41.5	33.4	24.4
Padi cultivation	48.4	37.3	29.5	14.9	6.2	1.2	1.3	2.2	2.7	2.0	2.9	3.4
Other activities	6.7	6.3	4.0	9.6	16.8	10.4	7.3	5.5	8.0	5.7	6.4	9.3
Fishing and hunting	4.8	4.1	2.6	2.2	2.5	2.5	2.1	1.9	.2	.2	.2	.2
Mining and quarrying	.5	1.0	.9	.7	4.3	5.2	3.6	1.9	1.4	2.2	1.5	1.2
Manufacturing/construction	5.1	4.7	5.7	14.1	12.9	16.8	20.1	29.1	4.0	6.8	5.4	11.4
Transport/communication	3.0	2.6	2.8	2.9	3.3	3.8	4.0	4.6	5.6	5.1	5.2	4.5
Commercial/financial services	3.0	3.1	4.3	8.0	14.4	16.4	17.4	24.4	7.3	9.8	9.2	11.4
Public sector/other services	8.5	15.4	24.9	29.3	16.2	17.7	26.8	19.0	23.7	26.7	36.0	34.1

Source: See Table 1.2.

TABLE A4

West Malaysia - Public Development Expenditure, 1956-1985 (M$m.)

Sector	*First Malaya Plan 1956-1960*	*Second Malaya Plan 1961-1965*	*First Malaysia Plan 1966-1970*	*Second Malaysia Plan 1971-1975*	*Third Malaysia Plan 1976-1980*	*Fourth Malaysia Plan 1981-1985*
	M$ m.	*M$ m.*	*M$ m.*	*M$ m.*	*M$ m.*	*M$ m.*
Agriculture/rural development	227.5	411.1	911.2	1,747.0	3,901.9	7,654.5
Mining	n.a.	.9	.4	.4	2.0	42.0
Industrial development	12.1	59.1	137.0	1,542.3	1,600.8	5,253.5
Transport	230.1	588.5	355.9	1,215.6	2,071.4	2,898.8
Communications	51.6	113.3	159.5	467.4	1,051.3	1,287.8
Utilities	238.6	527.4	646.8	770.2	1,823.2	2,227.8
Social services	138.8	520.5	644.7	1,132.6	2,511.3	5,639.0
Government administration	65.0	123.6	109.0	227.3	418.9	698.8
Total development expenditures	963.7	2,344.4	2,964.5	7,131.9[a]	13,405.7[a]	25,738.2[a]

Source: See Table 1.4.

n.a. = not available

[a]Includes M$28.9 m., M$36.0 m. and M$36.0 m. respectively for feasibility studies.

TABLE A5
Electrical Power Tariffs for Industrial and Commercial Purposes[a] in West Malaysia, 1977

Net Work/Tariff[b]	*Units (kw)/Month*	*M$/kw*
Western Network		
D (minimum 10,000 kw/month)	the first 10	.20
	next 150	.0775
	next 150	.06
	next 150	.055
E (minimum 10,000 kw/month)	the first 50,000	.08
	rest	.0535
P (minimum 500,000 kw/month)	each kw of maximum demand	8.00
	each kw used	1.00
	all units	0.36
Q[c] (Western Network and Johor Bahru)	each kw of maximum demand	8.00
	all units	0.535
Q[c] (Ipoh)	each kw of maximum demand	9.00
	all units	0.55
R (minimum 500,000 kw/month)	each kw of maximum demand up to 1,000	15.00
	over 1,000	10.00
	all units	.02
East Coast (Kelantan, Pahang, Trengganu)		
C (connected to Western Network)	all units	.08
F (minimum 10,000 kw/month)	peak load (6:30 pm.-9:30 pm.)	.21
	off peak	.075

<u>Source:</u> FIDA (Power, 1977, pp. 1-6).

[a]Rates for general lighting higher.

[b]Special provisions are included to penalize for not maintaining average power factor.

[c]Minimum charge: M$500.

TABLE A6
Water Rates in West Malaysia, 1977 (M$/1,000 gallons)

Region/State	Domestic		Trade/Domestic		Trade/Industry	
	Gallons/ Month	M$/1,000 Gallons	Gallons/ Month	M$/1,000 Gallons	Gallons/ Month	M$/1,000 Gallons
Northern states						
Trengganu	no limit	1.50	.	.	no limit	2.00
Kelantan	.	.	.	.	.	.
Perlis	.	.	.	.	.	.
Kedah	no limit	1.20	.	1.50	no limit	2.00
Southern states						
Pahang	.	.	.	.	no limit	2.00
Melaka	up to 2,200	2.50	.	.	up to 2,200	7.50[a] (5.00)[b]
	next 4,400	1.36	.	.	over 2,200	2.60[a] (2.00)[b]
	next 6,600	1.50	.	.		
	over 13,200	1.64	.	.		
Johor	.	.	.	.	no limit	2.00
Western states						
Perak	.	.	.	.	for first 5,000	1.70
					for next 5,000	1.60
					over first 1,000,000	1.50
Selangor	no limit	1.20	no limit	1.70	no limit	2.00
Negeri Sembilan	.	.	.	.	no limit	2.00
Penang					up to 5 mill.	1.30
					next 5 mill.	1.10
					next 30 mill.	.90[c]
					over 40 mill.	.80

Source: FIDA (Power, 1977, pp. 7-10), and various SEDC publications.

[a]Outside industrial estates.

[b]For industrial estates.

[c]Trade ordinary; trade special: 2.00/1,000 gallons.

TABLE A7

Industrial Structure of Industrial Estates in West Malaysia

Region/State/Industrial Estate	*Industries Represented*
Northern states	
Kelantan	
Pengkalan Chepa I	Light
Pengkalan Chepa II	Light and medium
Jeli	Wood-based
Tanah Merha	Wood-based
Trengganu	
Jakar	General
Gong Badak	General
Kuala Ibai	Clean and light
Perlis	
Kedah	
Mergong	General: rubber based products (noodles, cables electrical telephone)[a]
Bakar Arang	General: textiles, saw mill, electronics, candles, surgical appliances
Kuala Kedah	Marine: fish products
Tikam Batu	General
Kulim	General
Tikam Batu	General
Southern states	
Melaka	
Ayer Keroh	General: food products, textiles, metal products, engineering, footwear
Alor Gajah	General: rubber ware, textiles, animal feed
Batu Berendam FTZ	Electronics
Tanjong Kling	General/soyabean oil meal, synthetic yarn
Tanjong Kling FTZ	Shoes, textiles: footwear, pins, garments
Bukit Rambai	Wood based: metal containers, wood products/mills
Merlimau	General: cotton and synthetic yarn/cloth
Johor	
Larkin and Tampoi	General
Tanjong Agas	Wood-based
Tonkang Pecah	General
Pasir Gudang	General
Senai FTZ	Export oriented
Seramat	General
Perit Rajei	General: light
Bandar Tenggara	General
Bandar Penawar	General
Pahang	
Peramu	Wood; agro-based: wood products (ice storage, paper)[a]
Semambu	General: electronic components, tractors, vehicle assembly, TV
Songsang	Wood based, engineering: wood products, furniture, electrical motors
Maran	Electricity & water non-intensive: ratton products
Jerantut	Light (power non-intensive)/engineering
Gebeng	General
Mu'adzam	Agro-based, wood-based, clay-based
Western states	
Negeri Sembilan	
Senawang	General
Kampong Dich	General (no telex)
Chempang	General (non-polluting and water nonintensive)
Gadut	Sawmills
Simpang Pertang	General
Perak	
Tasek	General: cement, textiles, garments, wood products, steel
Kamunting	General: textiles, garments, electrical appliances, wood products, food processing
Jelapang	Light
Kuala Kangsar	General: textiles
Parit Buntar	General: stainless steel, solder wire, electrical wire, food products,textiles
Tupai	Light
Penang	
Mak Mandin	General: electrical appliances, food canning, lamin, plast sheets, textiles
Bayan Lepas FTZ	Industries with air-cargo needs: electronics, textiles
Prai	General: bike parts, glass lenses/frames, adhesive tape, food products
Prai FTZ	General: textiles, precis. optics; TV, radio, rubber products
Prai Wharves FTZ	General: textiles
Pulau Jerejak FTZ	Shipbuilding, repair
Seberang Jaya	Agro-based
Bayan Lepas	General: supporting industries for FTZ
Selangor	
Petaling Jaya	General
Shah Alam	General: electric organs, tires, plastics, car assembly, mint
Pandamaran	General
Sungei Way/Subang FTZ	Export oriented: electronic components
Ampang/Ulu Klang FTZ	General: electronic components, lamps, garments
Batu Caves	General: engineering, timber-based
Telok Panglima Garang FTZ	Export-oriented: electronic components, chemicals
Ampang/Ulu Klang	General
Telok Panglima Garang	General: agro-based
Selat Klang Utara	General
Setapak	General
Bangi	
Bukit Ragai	Light and heavy

Source: See Table 3.6.

[a]The industries in parentheses were under construction.

TABLE A8
Actual Cost of Developing Selected Industrial Estates in Penang, 1972, 1973 and 1974

Industrial Estate	1972		1973		1974		1972-1974		Cost/Acre (M$'000)
	Acres Development	Cost (M$ m.)	Acres Development	Cost (M$ m.)	Acres Development	Cost (M$ m.)	Acres Development	Cost (M$ m.)	
Bayan Serai	82	.01	10	.86	31	1.42	123	2.29	18.62
Bayan Lepas	-	-	18	.19	1	.07	19	.26	13.68
Bayan Lepas FTZ	43	.26	124	2.85	122	2.36	289	5.47	18.93
Prai	165	2.14	92	2.67	219	2.94	476	7.75	16.28
Pulau Jerejak	-	.03	-	.11	-	.11	19.6	.25	12.76

Source: Based on own calculations from SEDC (Annual Report, 1972 ff.).

TABLE A9
Summary Statistics on Employment Size[a] of Establishments in Malaysian Districts, 1968 and 1973

Region/State[b]		Mean[c]		Minimum		Medium		$\frac{\hat{s}}{\bar{y}}$ 100[d]	
		1968	1973	1968	1973	1968	1973	1968	1973
Northern states	(24)	4.89	12.28	.71	.91	13.87	41.24	75.49	66.95
Trengganu[o]	(6)	6.36	14.10	2.09	4.71	13.87	21.17	81.09	41.55
Kelantan[o]	(8)	4.04	18.78	.71	6.98	12.70	41.24	97.06	61.80
Perlis[o]	(1)	3.49	14.15	-	-	-	-	-	-
Kedah[o]	(9)	4.82	6.83	1.09	.91	7.94	17.00[x]	52.93	68.08
Southern states	(19)	10.79	19.94	.67	.50	35.76[x]	43.00	74.96	65.69
Pahang[o]	(8)	7.05	19.83	.67	.50	11.79	43.08	57.74	66.92
Melaka[o]	(3)	6.49	15.36	4.68	9.89	7.45[x]	23.35[x]	24.23	46.05
Johor	(8)	16.15	21.79	5.75	7.32[x]	35.76[x]	43.08[x]	60.17	70.86
Western states	(27)	10.47	18.64	1.38	4.79	32.42[x]	52.19[x]	82.59	69.78
Perak	(9)	6.41	13.26	1.38	4.79	14.52[x]	41.60[x]	72.81	87.57
Selangor	(7)	11.91	22.22	1.71	6.03	32.42[x]	52.19[x]	97.15	77.28
Negeri Sembilan	(6)	13.93	16.29	3.12	10.83	31.44	29.14	69.58	42.00
Penang	(5)	11.64	26.12	3.00	12.53[x]	24.03	42.08[x]	68.91	48.94
Total	(70)	8.65	16.81	.67	.50	35.76[x]	52.19[x]	87.56	70.94
No IEs	(63/51)[e]	7.31	14.33	.67	.50	31.44	43.08	82.00	70.71
IEs exist	(7/19)[e]	20.70	23.48	11.51	7.00	35.76	52.19	48.27	59.60

Source: Own calculations based on Dept. of Statistics (CMI, 1968, Table 4; 1973, Tables 67 ff.)

[x] = IE(s) in given district.

[o] = State covered by LI.

[a]Full-time employees/establishment. Based on district data, whereby Georgetown and adjoining district in Penang were combined into one district.

[b]The number in () = number of districts in region/state.

[c]Unweighted mean of number of employees in each district within a state.

[d]Coefficient of variation. $\hat{s}$ = standard deviation. $\bar{y}$ = mean.

[e]Number of districts in 1968/1973 in which there are IEs or no IEs.

TABLE A10
Capital Intensity and Employment Density in Selected Industrial Estates or Free Trade Zones in West Malaysia, 1977

Region/State/ Industrial Estate	*Capital Intensity (M$/Employee)*	*Employment density (Employees/Acre)*
Northern states	12,981	5.15
Trengganu	12,981	5.15
Jakar	16,634	8.30
Gong Badak	879	1.37
Southern states	9,343	10.25
Melaka	8,822	29.62
Ayer Keroh	5,222	20.70
Alor Gajah	5,408	31.69
Batu Berendam FTZ	1,989	82.12
Tanjong Kling	41,152	24.30
Tanjong Kling FTZ	20,234	57.73
Bukit Rambai	6,742	5.11
Johor	8,736	7.51
Larkin and Tampoi	9,138	12.47
Tangjong Agas	3,015	21.31
Tonkang Pecah	14,163	12.59
Pasir Gudang	12,772	3.83
Pahang	15,366	5.25
Peramu	23,123	16.04
Semambu	13,819	1.88
Songsang	4,952	5.89
Western states	8,037	23.92
Negeri Sembilan	9,678	14,97
Senawang	9,839	15,89
Kampang Dioh	5,917	6.35
Perak	7,729	16.06
Tasek	6,595	11.25
Kamunting	8,163	23.88
Jelapang	5,452	7.70
Kuala Kangsar	19,231	9.30
Parit Buntar	4,237	31.05
Penang	7,010	50,66
Mak Mandin	6,536	27.87
Bayan Lepas FTZ	2,985	139.97
Prai	14,082	31.15
Prai FTZ	7,019	51.93
Pulau Jerejak FTZ	8,095	5.36
Seberang Jaya	11,374	25.20
Bayan Lepas	13,843	99,00
Selangor	9,186	17.00
Petaling Jaya	11,942	13.42
Shah Alam	12,341	11.45
Pandamaran	9,485	11.22
Sungei Way/Subang FTZ	5,514	76,30
Ampang/Ulu Klang FTZ	1,178	87.81
Batu Caves	9,629	7.75
Telok Panglima Garang FTZ	5,432	46.80
Ampang Ulu Klang	25,688	6.41
Telok Panglima Garang	13,889	21.05
Total	8,265	21.60

Source: Own calculations based on unpublished MIDA data.

The underlined figures are above national average.

TABLE A11

Capital Intensity (CI)[a] and Employment Density (ED)[b] in Industrial Estates or Free Trade Zones in Penang, 1969-1977

Industrial Estate/FTZ		*1969*	*1970*	*1971*	*1972*	*1973*	*1974*	*1975*	*1976*	*1977*
Bagan Serai	CI	-	-	-	-	-	15,748	13,380	15,472	22,472
	ED	-	-	-	-	-	7.23	8.28	7.16	8.30
Bayan Lepas	CI	-	-	-	-	-	-	727,272	666,667	533,333
	ED	-	-	-	-	-	-	5.50	6.00	7.50
Bayan Lepas FTZ	CI	-	-	891	2,967	1,338	3,698	3,725	2,944	2,681
	ED	-	-	317.00	132.51	196.74	127.36	137.80	166.84	175.47
Mak Mandin	CI	8,036	-	12,154	10,406	11,086	12,630	12,103	11,308	11,368
	ED	35.00	48.13	50.00	51.58	55.57	49.09	44.60	50.99	42.10
Prai	CI	-	-	13,167	16,200	26,770	24,840	22,531	21,962	23,379
	ED	-	-	15.21	28.19	32.40	35.28	32.09	34.99	24.31
Prai FTZ	CI	-	-	-	-	28,000	26,426	18,876	17,190	22,779
	ED	-	-	-	-	12.50	18.58	17.97	19.73	21.12
Prai Wharves FTZ	CI	-	-	-	-	28,000	26,426	18,876	17,190	22,779
	ED	-	-	-	-	12.50	18.58	17.97	19.73	21.12
Pulau Jerejak	CI	-	-	-	53,125	16,981	10,067	10,309	15,464	31,713
	ED	-	-	-	.57	1.89	10.64	10.39	6.93	7.71
Total (average)	CI	8,036	-	12,944	8,003	6,631	9,059	9,520	8,396	9,356
	ED	35.00	48.13	39.79	61.16	77.34	59.79	48.77	55.50	49.82

Source: Own calculations based on data from Penang SEDC.

[a] M$/employee.

[b] Employees/acre.

TABLE A12

Employment and Value Added Size of Establishments for Selected Industries by Regions and States, 1973

Region/State	Major Industry Group[a] 311+312	321	331	352	355	381	383	383	385	Total
	Employees per establishment									
Northern states	7.13	23.27	50.39	10.20	41.53	4.27	8.14	-	-	15.32
Trengganu	3.64	65.00	73.68	-	12.40	3.05	6.57	-	-	15.52
Kelantan	5.38	18.93	61.90	-	22.67	5.27	7.69	-	-	22.25
Perlis	22.37	-	8.33	-	-	-	3.67	-	-	15.78
Kedah	7.41	2.50	37.21	10.20	47.84	4.29	9.14	-	-	11.50
Southern states	17.54	87.53	61.10	25.03	55.49	9.19	9.06	262.18	67.00	27.76
Pahang	6.80	10.33	80.41	-	16.12	6.67	11.09	-	-	24.64
Melaka	21.27	2.50	37.78	5.00	32.89	5.56	7.00	766.00	-	24.20
Johor	21.43	120.26	53.03	26.92	64.06	10.69	9.19	154.20	67.00	29.89
Western states	14.29	118.74	30.73	26.48	45.26	16.27	19.80	227.64	65.60	29.36
Perak	14.65	182.72	31.36	13.56	31.40	6.87	20.97	114.85	-	16.68
Selangor	21.70	66.08	36.67	49.66	53.33	25.66	18.95	151.25	36.67	34.51
Negeri Sembilan	10.32	13.75	53.47	7.40	29.33	4.65	11.33	-	-	19.36
Penang	15.97	176.89	10.14	10.39	51.97	9.74	26.22	484.55	118.75	31.44
Total economy	12.99	94.76	41.65	25.89	44.70	13.44	17.11	233.03	65.92	26.94
	Value added per establishment (M$'000)									
Northern states	39.69	29.66	283.60	22.00	230.30	8.62	28.75	-	-	50.15
Trengganu	11.31	41.17	481.03	-	-22.20	7.90	16.86	-	-	60.94
Kelantan	35.82	31.97	297.75	-	59.30	9.23	31.06	-	-	65.86
Perlis	73.31	-	51.67	-	-	-	5.67	-	-	52.06
Kedah	49.22	7.00	199.34	22.00	285.78	8.78	33.21	-	-	59.63
Southern states	116.26	478.93	489.97	143.09	417.46	43.41	34.25	867.88	326.00	170.74
Pahang	38.57	2.00	703.23	-	76.53	23.07	49.22	-	-	176.60
Melaka	94.21	5.60	112.80	16.20	326.78	29.85	22.65	1488.67	-	80.47
Johor	157.17	671.33	437.86	115.06	642.87	51.65	33.60	734.86	326.00	195.25
Western states	163.02	533.91	219.94	479.00	431.41	98.60	124.22	1888.87	398.70	261.15
Perak	87.13	1036.48	185.48	45.29	308.40	16.91	79.737	619.23	-	126.49
Selangor	339.50	274.79	271.97	1225.46	496.16	180.77	163.98	1434.51	500.44	381.71
Negeri Sembilan	85.21	16.75	509.75	48.20	121.54	22.49	37.97	-	-	239.91
Penang	176.89	713.39	56.41	43.15	439.77	32.68	75.84	3935.50	422.25	190.28
Total	139.82	434.25	303.03	402.08	396.52	76.84	101.80	1729.63	381.92	210.39
	Fixed capital assets per employee (M$)									
Northern states	12,240	988	9,124	2,219	4,954	3,470	3,672	-	2,733	6,926
Trengganu	9,440	1,427	9,355	2,314	5,344	4,163	2,938	-	-	6,652
Kelantan	7,070	502	11,194	2,195	6,109	2,831	4,394	-	-	4,632
Perlis Kedah	13,711	5,368	7,293	2,494	4,506	3,599	3,583	-	2,733	8,885
Southern states	14,115	9,969	9,118	4,674	7,711	7,175	4,491	3,284	4,451	7,692
Pahang	24,524	1,649	9,998	1,075	13,304	5,442	6,335	1,757	-	10,441
Melaka	6,314	1,050	6,750	2,298	9,948	2,874	3,630	1,848	-	4,735
Johor	9,052	10,046	8,579	4,769	6,646	8,007	3,878	5,143	4,451	7,564
Western states	10,874	13,107	7,850	9,389	8,730	9,950	5,621	5,252	6,040	10,036
Perak	9,532	15,945	7,613	2,507	6,943	3,261	2,833	6,073	3,699	10,802
Selangor	14,457	9,244	8,712	11,871	9,181	11,938	7,917	7,143	6,429	11,340
Negeri Sembilan	7,357	1,153	6,742	3,118	8,863	5,124	4,185	6,552	-	9,968
Penang	8,068	13,682	6,144	3,756	9,079	4,147	2,812	3,562	5,972	6,640
Total	10,850	11,920	8,566	7,979	8,108	9,320	5,455	4,868	5,646	9,249

Source: Dept. of Statistics (CMI, 1973).

[a]For names of 3-digit industries see Table 6.3. The underlined figures are above national average for specific industry.

TABLE A13
Comparison between the Regional Distribution of Establishments in the Directory of Approved Companies (DAC) and the Census of Manufacturing Industries (CMI)[a], 1973

Region/State	Share of Establishments (per cent) Based on DAC	CMI	Employees per Establishment
Northern states	3.5*	14.8	15.32
Trengganu	1.0*	3.1	15.52*
Kelantan	.4*	3.8	22.25*
Perlis	.3*	.8	15.78*
Kedah	1.8*	7.2	11.50*
Southern states	20.4	21.7	27.76
Pahang	2.1*	4.6	24.64*
Melaka	2.1*	3.9	24.20*
Johor	16.2	13.2	29.89
Western states	76.1	63.6	29.35
Perak	10.5*	17.6	21.83*
Selangor	47.5	27.5	34.48
Negeri Sembilan	1.0*	4.0	19.36*
Penang	17.2	14.5	31.44
Total (average)	779	11,060	26.94

Sources: Own calculations based on DAC and CMI (1973, Table 4).

[a]The * is used to note the regions/states in which the smaller than average establishment size (employees per establishment) corresponds with a smaller share of establishments in a given region/state based on DAC data as compared with CMI data.

TABLE A14
Comparison between the Industrial Distribution in the Directory of Approved Companies (DAC) and the Census of Manufacturing Industries (CMI), 1973
(per cent)

Major Industry Group[a]	*DAC Share of Establishments*	*CMI Share in respective Total by*			
		Establish-ment	*Value Added*	*Employees*	*Assets*
311	10.4*	19.56	13.52	10.65	16.49
312	3.5*	8.04	2.14	2.66	2.11
313	.6	.66	2.63	1.06	2.03
314	.5	1.52	5.60	3.04	1.89
321	8.0	2.17	4.48	7.63	9.82
322	2.2	1.95	1.28	3.63	.80
323	.6*	.48	.13	.29	.08
324	.1*	1.53	.25	.66	.24
331	8.5	9.08	13.07	14.04	11.88
332	.8*	7.80	.83	2.21	6.10
341	1.7	1.37	.77	1.34	1.19
342	2.4	4.29	4.92	4.96	3.84
351	4.2	.49	2.63	.97	5.38
352	7.1	2.56	4.89	2.46	2.19
353	.3	.04	2.13	.17	3.67
354	.4*	.05	.10	.04	.03
355	2.8	5.07	9.56	8.42	6.24
356	6.7	2.70	1.91	1.00	2.13
361	-	.44	.27	.12	.29
362	.6	.31	.51	.17	1.87
364	4.9	3.00	4.48	1.21	5.94
371	2.8	1.71	3.27	.70	5.16
372	.3	.08	.42	.08	.42
381	11.0*	13.76	4.92	2.16	4.42
382	4.4*	7.75	3.75	1.59	3.38
383	9.1	.99	8.10	2.75	4.68
384	3.7	1.56	2.67	.95	2.46
385	1.2	.24	.43	.19	.45
390	1.3*	1.09	.33	.21	.33
Total	779	11,060	2,326,929[b]	297,934[b]	2,294,646[b]

Source: Own calculations based on Dept. of Statistics (CMI, 1973, Table 2).

[a]For names of 3-digit industries see Table 6.3.
[b]M$'000.
* = Industry where employment size (employees per establishment) is less than 20; national average = 26.94, see Table A13.

TABLE A15

Distribution of Full-time Employees in the West Malaysian Manufacturing Industry, 1968 and 1973 (per cent)

Number of Full-Time Employees	1968 Estab-lish-ments	1968 Added Value	1968 Full-Time Employees	1973 Estab-lish-ments	1973 Added Value	1973 Full-Time Employees	1973 Assets
0	37.14	1.40	-	28.46	.62	-	.48
1 - 9	41.00	6.46	10.19	41.79	4.05	6.12	2.75
10 - 19	8.19	5.08	8.39	9.76	3.64	5.52	2.54
20 - 29	4.37	4.70	7.85	5.10	3.76	5.09	2.80
30 - 49	3.71	7.96	10.52	5.33	6.64	8.32	6.74
50 - 99	3.05	13.62	15.48	4.55	14.01	13.00	12.36
100 - 199	1.48	21.65	15.27	2.60	16.41	14.47	16.92
200 - 499	.85	21.46	18.67	1.72	24.73	21.50	31.06
≥ 500	.22	17.69	13.65	.69	26.13	25.99	24.35
Total (actual figures)	9,013	873,851[a]	120,807	11,060	2,326,929[a]	268,162	2,294,646[a]
Average establish-ment size	-	96.95	13.40	-	210.39	24.25	207.47

Sources: Own calculations based on Dept. of Statistics (CMI, 1972, Table 7, p. 37; 1978, Table 8, p. 18).

[a]M$'000.

TABLE A16

Selected Indicators of Shares of Pioneer Establishments in 3-digit Industries,[a] 1973 (per cent)

Major Industry Group		*Share of Pioneer Establishments in Total*			
		No. of Establishments	*Value Added*	*Employees*	*Assets*
311+312	Food manufacturing[b]	1.41	30.11	16.16	24.48
313	Beverages[b]	2.74	-	-	-
314	Tobacco	-	-	-	-
321	Textiles	14.17	74.37	66.01	71.75
322	Wearing apparel[c]	..46	-	-	-
323	Leather, leather products and substitutes and furniture[c]	1.89	-	-	-
324	Footwear	-	-	-	-
331	Wood, wood and cork products	3.69	23.85	27.51	47.15
332	Furniture and fixtures	-	-	-	-
341	Paper and paper products [c]	3.95	30.10	19.04	26.89
342	Printing, publishing etc.[c]	.21	-	-	-
351	Industrial chemicals	36.54	77.97	67.68	72.35
352	Other chemical products[d]	8.48	35.33	39.25	41.72
353	Petroleum refineries[d]	100.00	100.00	100.00	100.00
354	Misc. petroleum and coal products	50.00	87.23	71.19	75.80
355	Rubber products	1.43	16.88	5.37	24.22
356	Plastic products n.e.c.	5.69	36.76	39.53	47.43
361	Pottery, china and earthenware[c]	2.04	-	-	-
362	Glass and glass products	8.82	54.43	64.50	84.25
369	Non-metallic mineral products	3.92	29.17	33.72	27.23
371	Iron and steel (basic)[b]	7.94	76.66	55.62	82.13
372	NF metals (basic)[b]	22.22	-	-	-
381	Metal products	2.15	36.48	25.87	46.04
382	Machinery	1.98	36.01	20.37	54.47
383	Electrical machinery, apparatus, applicances and supplies	44.95	85.51	88.25	79.58
384	Transportation equipment	6.94	13.57	13.89	31.67
385	Professional, scientific, etc. equipment n.e.c., photo/optical goods	23.08	88.92	89.15	94.66
Total		3.22	37.11	29.99	46.88

Source: Own calculations based on Dept. of Statistics (CMI, 1973, Vol. 1, Tables 2 and 54).

[a]Based on CMI.

[b]Non-pioneer data contains two pioneer establishments not other-wise specified.

[c]Non-pioneer data contains one pioneer establishment not otherwise specified.

[d]Data on one non-pioneer establishment not included due to inconsistencies.
The underlined figures are above national average.

TABLE A17

Estimated Growth of Employment by Region and Industries, 1968-1977

Major Industry Group[a]	*Firm Size*[b] *1973*	*No. of New Firms*[c]		*Estimated Employment*[d]		*Firm Size*[b] *1973*	*No. of New Firms*[c]		*Estimated Employment*[d]	
		1968-72	*1973-7*	*1968-72*	*1973-7*		*1968-72*	*1973-7*	*1968-72*	*1973-7*
		Northern states					Southern states			
311+312	9.10	-	16	-	146	14.93	11	26	164	239
313	11.43	-	-	-	-	44.73	-	1	-	45
314	33.58	-	-	-	-	14.25	-	-	-	-
321	27.04	-	6	-	162	43.11	14	16	604	690
322	2.25	-	-	-	-	41.54	3	10	125	415
331	44.55	6	4	267	178	56.52	13	22	735	1,243
332	3.99	-	-	-	-	4.53	2	1	9	5
342	16.72	-	-	-	-	14.61	2	1	29	15
352	8.20	-	3	-	25	12.01	2	8	24	96
355	27.14	1	5	27	136	36.42	2	7	73	255
356	13.67	-	-	-	-	62.00	7	7	454	454
369	23.81	1	5	24	119	22.37	1	6	22	134
371	4.80	-	-	-	-	21.56	-	3	-	65
381	3.44	-	1	-	3	6.94	10	14	69	97
382	6.76	-	2	-	14	8.03	-	6	-	48
384	23.26	1	1	23	23	22.59	2	7	45	158
Total	16.23	9	43	341	806	26.93	69	135	2,353	3,959
Share in national total	-	3.10	6.90	3.62	4.11	-	23.79	21.66	24.99	20.20
		Western states					Total			
311+12	14.00	37	78	518	1,092	12.47	48	120	682	1,477
313	39.90	2	3	80	120	31.48	2	4	80	165
314	71.26	1	2	71	143	46.97	1	2	71	143
321	109.13	21	51	2,292	5,566	64.69	35	73	2,896	6,418
322	35.69	4	16	143	571	39.42	7	26	268	986
331	31.80	12	24	382	763	43.18	31	50	1,384	2,184
332	7.48	1	12	7	90	5.41	3	13	16	95
342	27.29	4	10	109	270	20.31	6	11	138	285
352	17.93	14	33	251	592	14.85	16	44	275	713
355	41.35	6	22	248	908	35.61	9	34	348	1,299
356	25.41	24	39	610	991	35.65	31	46	1,064	1,445
369	30.90	11	33	340	1,020	26.22	13	44	386	1,273
371	40.21	11	11	442	442	24.26	11	14	442	507
381	11.03	33	57	364	629	7.15	43	72	433	729
382	18.14	19	28	345	508	11.69	10	36	345	570
384	43.40	12	26	521	1,128	31.99	15	34	589	1,309
Total	35.31	212	445	6,723	14,833	36.82	290	623	9,417	19,598
Share in national total	-	73.10	71.43	71.39	75.69	-	-	-	-	-

Sources: Own calculations based on FIDA (DAC, 1977) and Dept. of Statistics (CMI, 1973, Vol. 1, Table 69 ff.).

[a] For names of 3-digit industries see Table A16.

[b] Number of full-time employees per establishment (part-time employees are included with a weight of 50 per cent; entrepreneurs also included).

[c] Based on DAC.

[d] Estimated by multiplying firm size with number of new firms.

The average of total are calculated on a state level.

TABLE A18
Regression Results Across all Industries[a]

Independent Variable	CAPIN b_i	CAPIN Beta-weight Share[b]	LNCAPIN b_i	LNCAPIN Beta-weight Share[b]
IEDUM	.5626	.18	.2817*	3.69
INCENDUM	.3389	.10	.5065	.61
MDRDUM	.8041*	2.51	.2043*	2.60
MALSHR	-.3718*	7.74	-.8223*	6.97
73DUM	-.1131*	3.28	-.1230	1.45
77DUM	-.6026	1.94	.8870	1.17
EMP	-.1781*	2.34	-.1794*	4.65
DUM312	-.1316	1.73	-.1860	1.00
DUM321	-.4187*	6.74	-.1259*	8.38
DUM322	-.4384*	4.81	-.1497*	6.69
DUM331	-.3754*	8.64	-.9975*	9.34
DUM332	-.4802*	5.27	-.1384*	6.19
DUM342	-.3915*	5.03	-.8951*	4.68
DUM352	-.4440*	6.54	-.6718*	4.03
DUM355	-.4351*	4.95	-.1145*	5.31
DUM356	-.2832*	3.22	-.4228*	1.96
DUM369	-.1897*	3.28	-.1170	.82
DUM371	-.3392*	4.58	-.5607*	3.08
DUM381	-.3698*	7.05	-.9345*	7.25
DUM382	-.4519*	7.39	-.1127*	7.50
DUM383	-.4297*	7.83	-.1040*	7.71
DUM384	-.5016*	4.85	-.1249*	4.91
Constant	.8513		.4261	
$\bar{R}^2$	.123		.224	
F-value	3.81		6.77	

[a]New variable: e.g. DUM312 = Dummy variable for industry 312. If industry = 312, DUM = 312 = 1, otherwise = 0.

[b] See Table 6.17 for explanation.

* Significant at 10 per cent level.

TABLE A19
Regional Concentration Ratios[a] of Manufacturing in West Malaysia, 1965-1990[b]

	1965	1968	1970	1975	1980	1990
Northern states	.45	.27	.44	.56	.76	.83
Trengganu	.29	.17	.37	.70	.86	.80
Kelantan	.44	.39	.41	.48	.73	.82
Perlis	.31	.12	.47	.54	.74	.85
Kedah	.54	.27				
Southern states	.86	.74	.83	.95	1.02	.96
Pahang	.62	.39	.56	.79	.97	.88
Melaka	.65	.63	.45	.62	.70	.77
Johor	1.02	.93	1.05	1.11	1.13	1.06
Western states	1.18	1.28	1.19	1.14	1.06	1.08
Perak	.61	.60	.67	.80	.88	.92
Selangor	1.55	1.76	1.61	1.31	1.14	1.02
Negeri Sembilan	1.40	1.21	1.17	1.05	.98	.84
Penang	1.14	1.18	.96	1.23	1.33	1.40
West Malaysia total[b]	10.24	11.97	13.30	15.70	18.26	27.28

Source: Own calculations based on sources in Table 7.1.

[a]Share of manufacturing industry in region's GDP/Share of manufacturing industry in total economy.

[b]Share of manufacturing industry in total economy.

APPENDIX 3

Maps of Industrial Estates

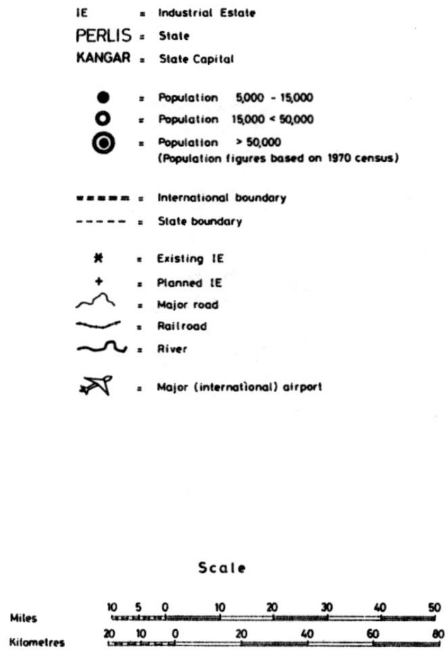

MAP A1

Industrial Estates in Kedah, Penang and Perlis

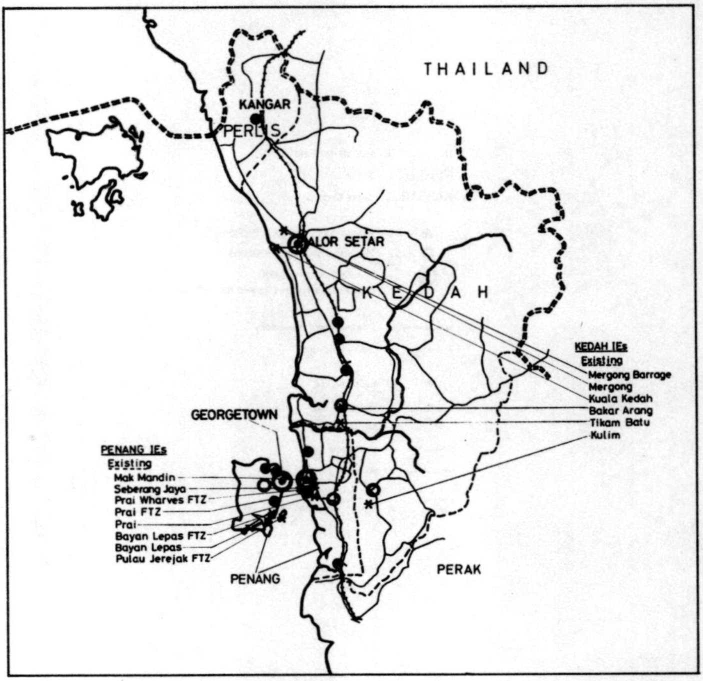

MAP A2
Industrial Estates in Perak

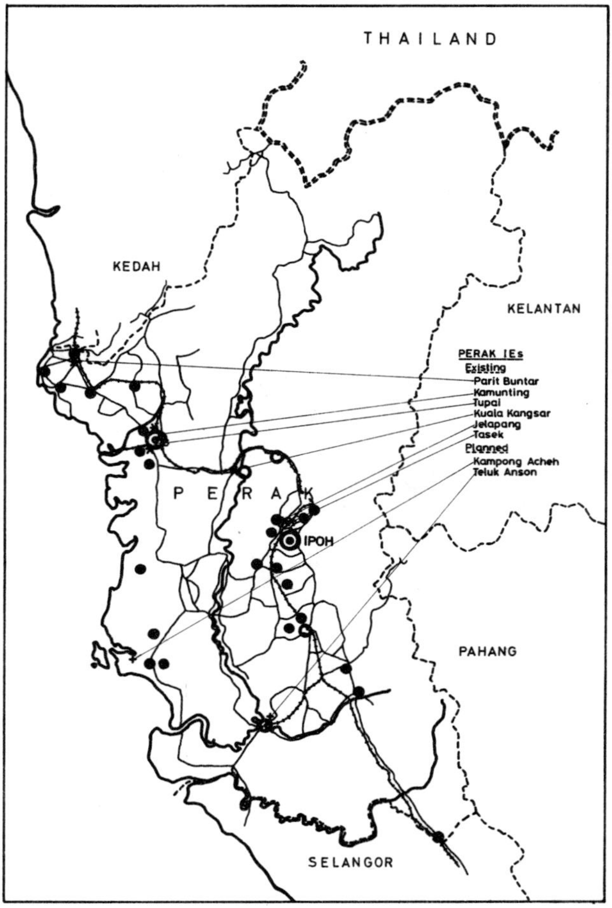

MAP A3
Industrial Estates in Melaka, Negeri Sembilan and Selangor

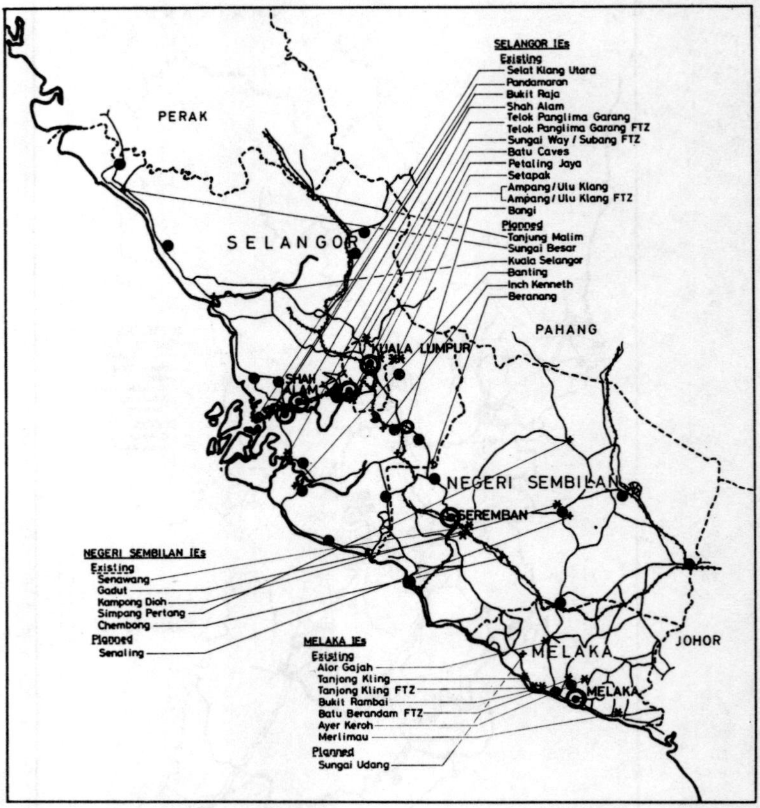

MAP A4
Industrial Estates in Johor

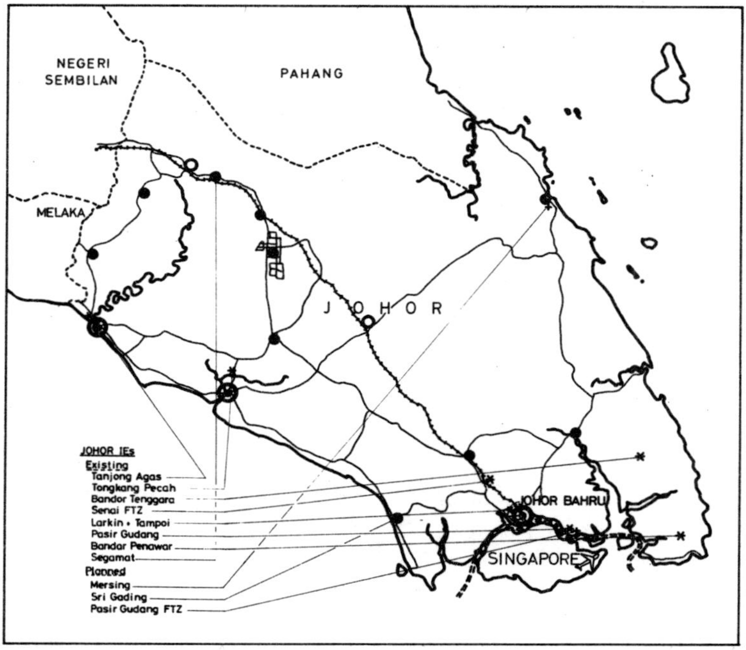

MAP A5
Industrial Estates in Pahang

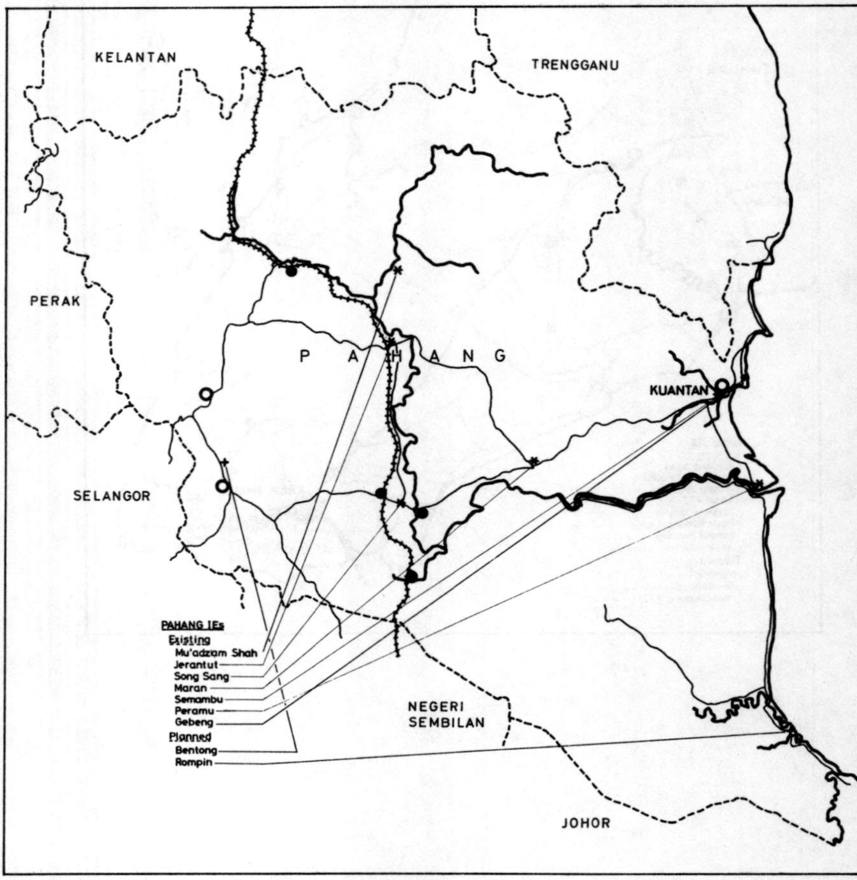

MAP A6
Industrial Estates in Kelantan
and Trengganu

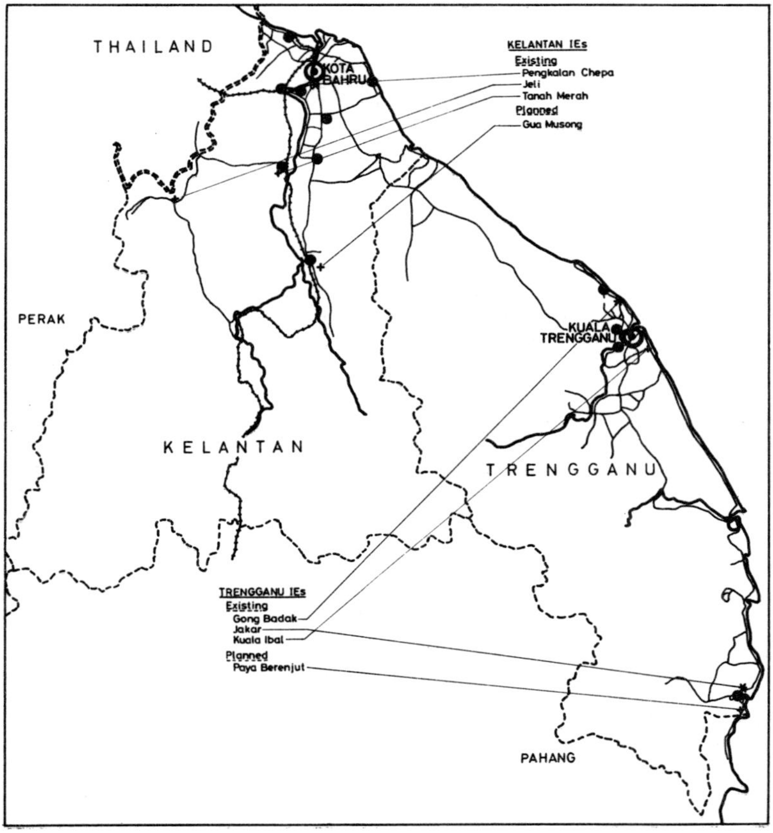

Bibliography

Adelman, Irma, Cynthia T. Morris (1973), Economic Growth and Social Equity in Developing Countries, Stanford, Stanford University Press.

Agarwal, Jamuna P. (1980), 'Determinants of Foreign Direct Investment. A Survey', Weltwirtschaftliches Archiv, Vol. 116, No. 4, pp. 739-73.

Arndt, Heinz W. (1983), 'The "Trickle-Down Myth"', Economic Development and Cultural Change, Vol. 32, No. 1, pp. 1-10.

Arrow, Kenneth J., Hollis B. Chenery, Bagicha S. Minhas, Robert M. Solow (1961), 'Capital-Labour Substitution and Economic Efficiency', The Review of Economics and Statistics, Vol. 43, No. 3, pp. 225-50.

Asian Finance, Hong Kong, various issues.

Balassa, Bela (1961), The Theory of Economic Integration, London, Allan & Unwin.

--, (1975), 'Structural Policies in the European Common Market', European Economic Integration, Amsterdam: North-Holland Publications, pp. 225-74.

--, (1977), 'Effects of Commercial Policy on International Trade, the Location of Production, and Factor Movements', in Ohlin, Bertil *et al.*, (eds), The International Allocation of Economic Activity, London: Basingstoke, pp. 230-58.

--, (1978), 'Export Incentives and Export Performance in Developing Countries', Weltwirtschaftliches Archiv, Vol. 114, No. 1, pp. 24-61.

--, *et al.* (1982), Development Strategies in Semi-Industrial Countries, Baltimore, published for the World Bank by the Johns Hopkins University Press.

Baldwin, Robert E. (1970), Nontariff Distortions of International Trade, Washington, D.C., The Brookings Institution.

--, (1971), 'Determinants of the Commodity Structure of United States Trade', The American Economic Review, Vol. 61, No. 1, pp. 8-33.

--, (1979), Beyond the Tokyo Round Negotiations, Trade Policy Research Centre, Thames Essay No. 22, London.

Banerji, Ranadev (1979), 'Employment and Growth Potential of Rural Industries, Small-Scale Industries and Medium and Large-Scale Industries in India. A Comparative Overview', Kiel Working Paper No. 64, Kiel.

--, (1978), 'Average Size of Plants in Manufacturing and Capital Intensity. A Cross-Country Analysis by Industry', Journal of Development Economics, Vol. 5, No. 2, pp. 155-66.

--, (1978), 'Small-Scale Production Units in Manufacturing: An International Cross-Section', Weltwirtschaftliches Archiv, Vol. 114, No. 1, pp. 62-84.

Becker, Gary (1975), Human Capital, A Theoretical and Empirical Analysis with Special Reference to Education, 2nd edn., New York, National Bureau of Economic Research.

Beckerman, Wilfred (1966), International Comparisons of Real Incomes, OECD Publications, No. 20,137, Paris.

Bhagwati, Jagdish N. (1978), 'Foreign Trade Regimes and Economic Development: Anatomy and Consequences of Exchange Control Regimes', National Bureau of Economic Research, Special Conference Series, Vol. 11, New York.

--, and Ranganath Bharadwaj 1967), 'Human Capital and the Indian Pattern of Foreign Trade', The Indian Economic Review, N.S., Vol. 2, No. 2.

Bird, Richard M. (1966), 'Tax-subsidy Policies for Regional Development', National Tax Journal, Vol. 19, No. 2, pp. 113-24.

Bode, Thilo, Thomas Ed. Müller-Debus (1978), Direktinvestitionen in Malaysia - Der Einfluß auf die wirtschaftliche Entwicklung, Tübingen, Erdmann.

Böventer, Edwin von (1979), Standortentscheidung und Raumstruktur, Hannover, Schroedel.

Bredo, William (1970), 'The Industrial Estate Spreads the Development Risk', Columbia Journal of World Business, Vol. 5, No. 2, pp. 19-25.

Bruch, Mathias (1978), 'Efficiency and Choice of Techniques in the Mexican Manufacturing Industry: Small Plants Versus Large Plants', in H. Giersch (ed.), International Economic Development and Resource Transfer, Workshop, Tübingen, pp. 63-95.

--, (1980), 'Small Establishments as Exporters of Manufactures: Tentative Evidence from Malaysia', World Development, Vol. 8, No. 5/6, pp. 429-42.

--, (1983), 'Kleinbetriebe und Industrialisierungspolitik in Entwicklungsländern - Eine vergleichende Analyse der ASEAN-Länder', Kieler Studie No. 182, Tübingen, J.C.B. Mohr.

Carlino, Gerald A. (1978), Economies of Scale in Manufacturing Location, Theory and Measure, Leiden, Nijhoff.

Chee, Stephen and Khoo Siew Mun (eds.) (1975), Malaysian Economic Development and Policies, Conference Proceedings Series No. 3, Kuala Lumpur.

Chenery, Hollis B., *et al.* (1974), Redistribution with Growth, London, Oxford University Press.

--, *et al.* (1980), 'Interactions between Industrialization and Exports', The American Economic Review, Papers and Proceedings, Vol. 70, No. 2, pp. 281-7.

Cheong, Kee Cheok, *et al.* (1979), Malaysia: Some Contemporary Issues in Socioeconomic Development, Kuala Lumpur, Persatuan Ekonomi Malaysia.

Chow, Steven C., Gustav F. Papanek (1981), 'Laissez-Faire, Growth and Equity - Hong Kong', The Economic Journal, Vol. 91, pp. 466-85.

Christaller, Walter (1933), Die zentralen Orte in Süddeutschland. Eine ökonomischgeographische Untersuchung über die Gesetzmäßigkeit der Verbreitung und Entwicklung der Siedlungen mit städtischen Funktionen, Jena, Fischer.

Corden, Warner Max (1974), Trade Policy and Economic Welfare, Oxford, Clarendon Press, Vol. 16.

Courtenay, Percy P. (1972), A Geography of Trade and Development in Malaysia, London, Bell.

Currie, Jean (1979), 'Investment: The Growing Role of Export Processing Zones', Economic Intelligence Unit (EIU) Special Report No. 64, London.

--, (1983), 'Special Economic and Export Processing Zones and their Role for Trans-national Corporation Investment in the 1980s', Working Paper for UNCTC workshop, UNCTC, New York, mimeographed.

Davies, Glyn (1967), 'Regional Unemployment, Labour Availability, and Redeployment', Oxford Economic Papers, N.S., Vol. 19, pp. 59-74.

Deardorff, Alan V. (1980), 'The General Validity of the Law of Comparative Advantage', Journal of Political Economy, Vol. 88, No. 5, pp. 941-57.

Department of Statistics, Census of Manufacturing Industries (CMI), West Malaysia, Peninsular Malaysia, various years, Kuala Lumpur.

--, (1970), General Report, 1970 Population Census of Malaysia, Kuala Lumpur.

--, (1971), Field Count Summary, 1970 Population and Housing Census of Malaysia, Kuala Lumpur.

--, (1971), A Preliminary Report based on Field Count Summary, 1970 Population and Housing Census of Malaysia, Kuala Lumpur.

--, (1975), The population of Malaysia, Kuala Lumpur.

--, (1976), Population Projections for the States of Peninsular Malaysia 1970-1980, Kuala Lumpur.

--, (1980, Preliminary Field Count Summary, 1980 Population and Housing Census of Malaysia, Kuala Lumpur.

--, (1982), Local Authority Areas: Population, Households and Living Quarters, 1980 Population and Housing Census of Malaysia, Kuala Lumpur.

Dewees, Donald, Yehuda Kotowitz (1980), 'A General Equilibrium Analysis of Regional Subsidies', Public Finance, The Hague, Vol. XXXV, No. 3, pp. 344-62.

Donges, Juergen B. (1978), 'A Comparative Survey of Industrialization Policies in Fifteen Semi-Industrialized Countries', Weltwirtschaftliches Archiv, Vol. 112, No. 4, pp. 626-59.

--, (1981), Foreign Trade Policies for Industrial Development, Reconsidered, Kiel.

--, Gerhard Fels, Axel D. Neu, *et al.* (1973), Protektion und Branchenstruktur der westdeutschen Wirtschaft, Kieler Studie 123, Tübingen, J.C.B. Mohr.

--, Lotte Müller-Ohlsen (1978), Außenwirtschaftsstrategien und Industrialisierung in Entwicklungsländern, Kieler Studien No. 157, Tübingen, J.C.B. Mohr.

--, James Riedel (1977), 'The Expansion of Manufactured Exports in Developing Countries: An Empirical Assessment of Supply and Demand Issues', Weltwirtschaftliches Archiv, Vol. 113, No. 1, pp. 58-87.

Drabble, J.H. (1974), 'Some Thoughts on the Economic Development of Malaya under British Administration', Journal of Southeast Asian Studies, Vol. 5, No. 2, pp. 199-208.

Esman, Milton J. (1972), Administration and Development in Malaysia, Ithaca, Cornell University Press.

Federal Industrial Development Authority (FIDA), Annual Reports 1972-1977, Kuala Lumpur.

--, (1977), Directory of Approved Companies (DAC) in Production as at 31st December 1977, Kuala Lumpur.

--, (1977), Labour and Wage Rates, Kuala Lumpur.

--, (1977), Power, Water and Telephone Rates for Industry, Kuala Lumpur.

Fei, John C.H. and Gustav Ranis (1971), 'Development and Employment in the Open Dualistic Economy', The Malayan Economic Review, Vol. 16, No. 2, pp. 91-116.

--, *et al.* (1979), Growth With Equity: The Taiwan Case, New York, published for the World Bank by the Oxford University Press.

Fels, Gerhard (1972), 'The Choice of Industry Mix in the Division of Labour Between Developed and Developing Countries', Weltwirtschaftliches Archiv, Vol. 108, No. 1, pp. 71-121.

Finger, J. Michael (1975), 'A New View of the Product Cycle Theory', Weltwirtschaftliches Archiv, Vol. 111, No. 1, pp. 79-99.

Fischer, Bernhard, Egbert Gerken, Ulrich Hiemenz (1982), Growth, Employment and Trade in an Industrializing Economy - A Quantitative Analysis of Mexican Development Policies, Kieler Studien 170, Tübingen, J.C.B. Mohr.

Fisher, Irving (1930), The Theory of Interest, New York, Macmillan.

Friedman, Milton (1953), 'The Methodology of Positive Economics', in Friedman, Milton (ed.) Essays in Positive Economics, Chicago, University of Chicago Press, pp. 39-42.

--, and Simon Kuznets (1945), Income from Independent Professional Practice, New York, National Bureau of Economic Research, Publication No. 45.

Fröbel, Folker, Jürgen Heinrichs, Otto Kreye (1977), Die neue internationale Arbeitsteilung, Reinbek, Rowohlt.

Giersch, Herbert (1965), 'The Economics of Regional Policy', The German Economic Review, Vol. 3, No. 1, pp. 13-24.

--, (1979), 'Aspects of Growth, Structural Change, and Employment - A Schumpeterian Perspective', Weltwirtschaftliches Archiv, Vol. 115, No. 4, pp. 629-652.

Gilbert, Alan G. (ed.) (1976), Development Planning and Spatial Structure, London, Wiley.

Glismann, Hans H., Frank D. Weiss (1980), 'On the Political Economy of Protection in Germany', Kiel Working Paper No. 113, Kiel.

Government Gazette (1958ff.), Ordinance Supplement, Kuala Lumpur.

Grubel, Herbert G. (1967), 'Intraindustry Specialization and the Pattern of Trade'. Canadian Journal of Economics and Political Science, Vol. 33, pp. 374-88.

--, (1982), 'Towards a Theory of Free Economic Zones', Weltwirtschaftliches Archiv, Vol. 118, No. 1, pp. 39-61.

--, (1983), Free Market Zones: Deregulating Canadian Enterprise, Vancouver, The Frazer Institute.

--, Harry G. Johnson (1971), Effective Tariff Protection, Geneva, Graduate Institute of International Studies and GATT.

Gruber, William H., Raymond Vernon (1970), 'The Technology Factor in a World Trade Matrix', in Vernon, Raymond (ed.), The Technology Factor in International Trade, New York, National Bureau of Economic Research, Conference Series No. 22, pp. 233-76.

Haberler, Gottfried von (1956), The Theory of International Trade, with its Applications to Commercial Policy, London, Hodge.

Hamada, Koichi (1974), 'An Economic Analysis of the Duty-free Zone', Journal of International Economics, Vol. 4, No. 3, pp. 225-41.

Hawley, Amos H., Dorothy Fernandez, Harbans Singh (1979), 'Migration and Employment in Peninsular Malaysia 1970', Economic Development and Cultural Change, Vol. 27, No. 3, pp. 491-504.

Hiemenz, Ulrich (1979), 'Rural Industrialization, Employment and Economic Development: The Case of Mexico', in Giersch, Herbert (ed.) International Economic Development and Resource Transfer, Workshop 1978, Tübingen, J.C.B. Mohr, pp. 3-30.

--, Kurt von Rabenau (1973), Effektive Protektion, Theorie und empirische Berechnung für die westdeutsche Industrie, Schriften zur angewandten Wirtschaftsforschung No. 32, Tübingen, J.C.B. Mohr.

Higgins, Benjamin (1968), Economic Development: Principles, Problems and Policies, New York, Constable.

Hirsch, Seev (1974), 'Hypotheses Regarding Trade between Developing and Industrial Countries', in Giersch, Herbert (ed.) The International Division of Labour: Problems and Perspectives. International Symposium, Tübingen, J.C.B. Mohr, pp. 55-82.

Hitiris, Theodore (1979), 'The Impact of Protection and Concentration of the Labor Intensity of United Kingdom Industries', Weltwirtschaftliches Archiv, Vol. 115, No. 4, pp. 653-69.

Hoerr, O. Donald (1973), 'Education, Income and Equity in Malaysia', Economic Development and Cultural Change, Vol. 21, No. 2, pp. 247-73.

Hoffmann, Lutz, Siew Ee Tan (1974), 'Employment Creation through Export Growth: A Case Study of West Malaysia's Manufacturing Industries', in Giersch, Herbert (ed.), The International Division of Labour: Problems and Perspectives, Tübingen, J.C.B. Mohr, pp. 399-433.

--, --, (1980), Industrial Growth, Employment, and Foreign Investment in Peninsular Malaysia, Kuala Lumpur, Oxford University Press.

Holzhausen, Walter (1974), Federal Finance in Malaysia, Kuala Lumpur, Penerbit Universiti Malaya.

Hoover, Edgar M. (1948), The Location of Economic Activity, New York, McGraw-Hill Book Company.

Horiba, Yutaka and Rickey C. Kirkpatrick (1976), 'Factor Endowments, Factor Proportions, and the Allocative Efficiency of U.S. Interregional Trade, Review of Economics and Statistics, Vol. LXIII, No. 2, pp. 178-87.

Horn, Ernst-J. (1976), Technologische Neuerungen und internationale Arbeitsteilung, Kieler Studien No. 139, Tübingen, J.C.B. Mohr.

Hoyle, Brian S. (ed.) (1974), Spatial Aspects of Development, London, Wiley.

Hufbauer, Gary D. (1970), 'The Impact of National Characteristics and Technology on the Commodity Composition of Trade in Manufacturing Goods', in Vernon, Raymond (ed.) The Technology Factor in International Trade, New York, National Bureau of Economic Research, Conference Series No. 22, pp. 145-221.

Hunt, Sir Joseph *et al.* (1969), 'Impact of Investment Grants on Capital Intensive Industry , in The Intermediate Areas, A Report of a Committee under the Chairmanship of Sir Joseph Hunt, London, Her Majesty's Stationery Office.

International Bank for Reconstruction and Development (IBRD) (1955), The Economic Development of Malaya, Baltimore, Johns Hopkins University Press.

--, (1963), Report on the Economic Aspects of Malaysia (Rueff-Report), Kuala Lumpur.

Isard, Walter (1956), Location and Space-Economy, New York, MIT Press and Wiley.

Jan, Jamil (1975), 'The Chairman's Column', Malaysia Industrial Digest, Vol. 8, No. 2.

--, (1978), 'The Chairman's Column', Malaysia Industrial Digest, Vol. 11, No. 1.

Johnson, Harry G. (1968), 'International Trade: Theory', in International Encyclopaedia of the Social Sciences, New York, Macmillan, Vol. 8, pp. 83-95.

--, (1975),'The Problem of Economic Development', in Johnson, Harry G. (ed), On Economics and Society, Chicago, University of Chicago Press, pp. 282-302.

Kaldor, Nicholas (1970), 'The Case for Regional Policies', Scottish Journal of Political Economy, Vol. 17, No. 3, pp. 337-48.

Kanemoto, Yoshitsugu (1980), Theories of Urban Externalities, Amsterdam, North Holland Publication.

Kapoor, Ashok, with the assistance of James E. Cotten (1973), Foreign Investments in Asia. A Survey of Problems and Prospects in the 1970s, Princeton/N.J., Darwin Press.

Karunaratne, Neil Dias, Abdullah, Mohamed B. (1978), 'Incentive Schemes and Foreign Investment in the Industrialization of Malaysia', Asian Survey, Vol. 18, No. 1, pp. 261-74.

Keesing, D.B. (1966), 'Labour Skills and International Trade: Evaluating Many Trade Flows with a Single Measuring Device', The Review of Economics and Statistics, Vol. 56, pp. 287-94.

--, (1968), 'Labour Skills and the Structure of Trade in Manufactures, in P.B. Kenen and R. Lawrence (eds.), The Open Economy, New York, Columbia University Press.

--, (1971), 'Different Countries' Labour Skill Coefficients and the Skill Intensity of International Trade Flows', Journal of International Economics, Vol. 1, pp. 443-52.

Kenen, Peter B. (1970), 'Skills, Human Capital and Comparative Advantage', in Hansen, W. Lee (ed.), Education, Income and Human Capital, Conference on Research in Income and Wealth, Studies in Income and Wealth, Vol. 35, New York, Columbia University Press, pp. 195-230.

Kojima, Koyoshi (1964), 'The Pattern of International Trade among Advanced Countries', Hitotsubashi Journal of Economics, June, pp. 16-36.

Kravis, Irving B., *et al.* (1978), 'Real GDP per Capital for More than One Hundred Countries', The Economic Journal, Vol. 88, No. 350, pp. 215-41.

--, (1984), 'Comparative Studies of National Incomes and Prices', Journal of Economic Literature, Vol. XXII, No. 1, pp. 1-39.

Krueger, Anne O. (1970), 'Comment on P.B. Kenen', in Hansen, W.Lee (ed.), Education, Income and Human Capital, Conference on Research in Income and Wealth, Studies in Income and Wealth, New York, Columbia University Press.

--, (1978), 'Alternative Trade Strategies and Employment in LDCs', The American Economic Review, Vol. 68, No. 2, pp. 270-4.

--, (1978), Foreign Trade Regimes and Economic Development: Liberalization Attempts and Consequences, Ballinger Publishing Co. for National Bureau of Economic Research, Special Conference Series, Vol. 10, New York.

--, *et al.* (1981), Trade and Employment in Developing Countries: Individual Studies, University of Chicago Press for the National Bureau of Economic Research, Chicago.

Krüger, Klaus (1982), 'Regional Policy in Malaysia', Geoforum, Vol. 13, No. 2, pp. 133-49.

Kühne, Dietrich (1976), Urbanisierung in Malaysia - Analyse eines Prozesses, Wiesbaden, Harrassowitz.

Lary, Hal B. (1968), Imports of Manufactures from Less Developed Countries, National Bureau of Economic Research, Studies in International Relations, No. 4, New York, Columbia University Press.

Lee, Hock Lock (1978), Public Policies and Economic Diversification in West Malaysia. 1957 - 1970, Kuala Lumpur, Penerbit Universiti Malaya.

Lefeber, Louis, Mrinal Datta-Chaudhuri (1971), Regional Development. Experiences and Prospects in South and Southeast Asia, Paris, Mouton.

Leinbach, Thomas R. (1975), 'Transportation and the Development of Malaya', Annals of the Association of American Geographers, Vol. 65, pp. 270-82.

Leontief, Wassily W. (1953), 'Domestic Production and Foreign Trade: The American Capital Position Re-Examined', in Leontief, W.W. (ed.), Input-Output Economics, New York, from: Proceedings of the American Philosophical Society, Vol. 97, No. 4, pp. 68-99.

Lim, David (1973), Economic Growth and Development in West Malaysia 1947-1970, Kuala Lumpur, Oxford University Press.

--, (ed.) (1975), Readings in Malaysian Economic Development, Kuala Lumpur, Oxford University Press.

Lim, Kok-Cheong (1981), Problems and Prospects of Industrialization in Less Developed Regions: A Case Study of Three States in Peninsular Malaysia, Kuala Lumpur, University of Malaya (mimeograph).

Lim, Lin Lean (1971), Some Aspects of Income Differentials in West Malaysia, Kuala Lumpur, University of Malaya.

Lim, Sow Ching (1976), Land Development Schemes in Peninsular Malaysia: A Study of Benefits and Costs, Kuala Lumpur, Rubber Research Institute of Malaysia.

Linn, Johannes F. (1982), 'The Costs of Urbanization in Developing Countries', Economic Development and Cultural Change, Vol. 30, No. 3, pp. 625-48.

Lipsey, Richard G. (1970), The Theory of Customs Unions: A General Equilibrium Analysis, London, Weidenfeldt and Nicholson.

Little, Ian M.D., Tibor Scitovsky, Maurice Scott (1970), Industry and Trade in Some Developing Countries, London, Oxford University Press.

Lo, Fu-Chen, Kamal Salih (eds.) (1978), Growth Pole Strategy and Regional Development Policy: Asian Experience and Alternative Approaches, Oxford, Pergamon Press.

Malaysia (1950), Draft Development Plan of the Federation of Malaya, Kuala Lumpur.

Report of the Industrial Development Working Party (1957), Kuala Lumpur, Government Printers.

--, (1960), Second Malaya Plan 1961-1965, Kuala Lumpur, Government Printers.

--, (1963), Interim Review of Development in Malaya under the Second Five Year Plan, Kuala Lumpur, Government Printers.

--, (1965), First Malaysia Plan 1966-1970, Kuala Lumpur, Government Printers.

--, (1969), Mid-term Review of the First Malaysia Plan 1966-1970, Kuala Lumpur, Government Printers.

--, (1971), Second Malaysia Plan 1971-1975, Kuala Lumpur, Government Printers.

--, (1973), Mid-term Review of the Second Malaysia Plan 1971-1975, Kuala Lumpur, Government Printers.

--, (1976), Third Malaysia Plan 1976-1980, Kuala Lumpur, Government Printers.

--, (1979), Mid-term Review of the Third Malaysia Plan 1976-1980, Kuala Lumpur, Government Printers.

--, (1982), Fourth Malaysia Plan 1981-1985, Kuala Lumpur, Government Printers.

--, (1984), Mid-term Review of the Fourth Malaysia Plan 1981-1985, Kuala Lumpur, Government Printers.

Malaysia Industrial Digest, various issues, Kuala Lumpur.

State (Economic) Development Corporation (SEDC), Annual Report of the Free Trade Zones in Penang, various issues, Penang.

--, (1976), Industrial Development in Selangor, Selangor.

--, (1976), Investment Prospects in Kedah, Alor Setar.

--, (1976), Malacca, New Centre of Industrial Development, Malacca.

--, (1977), An Investment Guide to North Malaysia, Kedah, Penang, Perak and Perlis, Penang.

--, (1977), Investment Potentials in Trengganu, Kuala Trengganu.

--, (1977), Potential Investments in Johore, Johore Bahru.

--, (1978), Investments in Pahang, Kuantan.

Mansfield, Edwin *et al.* (1971), 'Foreign Trade and U.S. Research Development', The Review of Economics and Statistics, Vol. LXI, No. 1, pp. 49-57.

Marris, Robin (1979), 'A Survey and Critique of World Bank Supported Research on International Comparisons of Real Product', World Bank Staff Working Paper 365, Washington, D.C.

--, Some New Results on "Catch-up", unpublished paper, Kiel, 1979.

Marshall, Alfred, Principles of Economics, London, MacMillan, 1936.

Mathur, Om Prakash (1978), 'The Problem of Regional Disparities: An Analysis of Indian Policies and Programmes', in Lo, Fu-Chen, Kamal Salih (eds.), 'Growth Poles and Regional Policy in Open Dualistic Economies: Western Theory and Asian Reality, in Lo Fu-chen, Kamal Salih, Growth Pole Strategy and Regional Development Policy: Asian Experience and Alternative Approaches, Oxford, Pergamon Press, pp. 121-46.

Mazumdar, Dipak (1981), The Urban Labor Market and Income Distribution, New York, published for the World Bank by the Oxford University Press.

McLure, Charles E. (1971), 'The Design of Regional Tax Incentives for Colombia', in Gillis, Malcolm (ed.), Fiscal Reform for Colombia, Cambridge, Mass., Harvard Law School, pp. 545-56.

McMeekin, Robert W. jr. (1975), Educational Planning and Expenditure Decisions in Developing Countries. With a Malaysian Case Study, New York, Praeger.

McTaggart, W. Donald (1975), 'The Distribution of Ethnic Groups in Malaya, 1947-57', The Journal of Tropical Geography, Vol. 26, pp. 69-81.

Meade, James Edward (1955), The Theory of Customs Unions, Amsterdam, North-Holland Publication.

Meerman, Jacob (1980), 'Public Services to Meet Basic Needs', in Young, Kevin et al. (eds.), Malaysia: Growth and Equity in a Multiracial Society, published for the World Bank by the Johns Hopkins University Press, Baltimore, pp. 127-53.

Mehden, Fred R. von der (1973), Industrialization in Malayisa: A Penang Micro-Study, Paper No. 45, Houston/Tex., William Marsh Rice University.

Ministry of Finance, Malaysia, Economic Report, various years, Kuala Lumpur.

Moroney, John R. (1975), 'Natural Resource Endowments and Comparative Labor Costs: A Hybrid Model of Comparative Advantage', Journal of Regional Science, Vol. 15, No. 2, pp. 139-50.

Morrall, John F. (1972), Human Capital Technology and the Role of the United States in International Trade, Gainesville, Florida: University of Florida Press.

Myint, Hla (1967), 'The Inward and Outward Looking Countries of Southeast Asia', Malayan Economic Review, Vol. 12, No. 1, pp. 1-13.

Ness, Gail D. (1967), Bureaucracy and Rural Development in Malaysia, Berkeley, Los Angeles, University of California Press.

Norcliffe, G. (1975), 'A Theory of Manufacturing Places', in Lyndhurst Collins, David F. Walker (eds.), Locational Dynamics of Manufacturing Activity, New York, Wiley, pp. 19-57.

Norman, George (1979), Economies of Scale, Transportation Costs, and Location, Boston, Nijhoff.

Nurkse, Ragnan (1953), Problems of Capital Formation in Underdeveloped Countries, Delhi, Oxford University Press.

Ohlin, Bertil (1952), Interregional and International Trade, Cambridge, Mass., Harvard University Press.

Olson, Mancur (1983), 'The Political Economy of Comparative Growth Rates', in Mueller, Dennis C., The Political Economy of Growth, New Haven, Yale University Press, pp. 7-52.

Ooi, Jin-Bee (1976), Peninsular Malaysia, London, Longman.

Organisation for Economic Co-operation and Development (OECD), Trade by Commodities, Series C, various years, Paris.

Palander, Tord (1935), Beiträge zur Standortstheorie, Uppsala, Almgrist and Wicksells.

Pincus, Jonathan J. (1977), Pressure Groups and Politics in Antebellum Tariffs, New York, Columbia University Press.

Posner, Michael Vivian (1961), 'International Trade and Technical Change', Oxford Economic Papers, N.S., Vol. 13, No. 3, pp. 323-41.

Prebisch, Rául (1950), The Economic Development of Latin America and its Principal Problems, Lake Success, N.Y.: United Nations Publications.

Ranis, Gustav (1978), 'Equity with Growth in Taiwan: How 'Special' is the 'Special Case'?' World Development, Vol. 6, No. 3, pp. 397-409.

Rao, D.C. (1978), 'Economic Growth and Equity in the Republic of Korea', World Development, Vol. 6, No. 6, pp. 383-96.

Rao, P. Prabhakar (1970), 'Cost of Urban Infrastructure', in Dagli, Vadilal (ed.), Infrastructure for the Indian Economy, Bombay, Vora and Co., pp. 129-35.

Reimers, Walter (1982) Determinanten regionalen Wachstums, Stand der empirischen Forschung und ein neues ökonometrisches Modell für Skandinavien und die Bundesrepublik Deutschland, München, Schriftenreihe des Institutes für Regionalforschung der Universität Kiel.

Ricardo, David (1821) On the Principles of Political Economy and Taxation, 3rd ed., London, Murray.

Richardson, Harry (1977), 'City Size and National Spatial Strategies in Developing Countries', World Bank Staff Working Paper No. 252, Washington, D.C.

Riedel, James (1977), 'Tariff Concessions in the Kennedy Round and the Structure of Protection in West Germany', Journal of International Economics, Vol. 7, No. 2, pp. 133-43.

Robertson, Dennis H. (1938), 'The Future of International Trade', The Economic Journal, Vol. 48, pp. 1-14.

Robinson, Robert D. (1977), National Control of Foreign Business Entry: A Survey of Fifteen Countries, New York, Praeger.

Rodriguez, Carlos A. (1976), 'A Note on the Economics of the Duty Free Zone', Journal of International Economics, Vol. 6, No. 4, pp. 385-8.

Rudner, Martin (1972), 'The Draft Plan of the Federation of Malaya', Journal of Southeast Asian Studies, Vol. 3, No. 1, pp. 63-96.

Rudolph, Heinz (1970), 'Der Aufbau und Arbeitsweise der Bundesbehörde für Industrieplanung und Industrieförderung (FIDA) in Malaysia', Vierteljahresberichte der Friedrich-Ebert-Stiftung, pp. 189-201.

Sabot, Richard H. (ed.) (1978), Essays on Migration and the Labor Market in Developing Countries, Proceedings of a Conference held by the World Bank, Washington, mimeograph.

Samuelson, Paul A. (1978), 'International Trade and the Equalisation of Factor Prices', Economic Journal, Vol. 58, No. 230, pp. 163-84.

--, (1951), Economics: An Introductory Analysis, New York.

--, (1953), Prices of Factors and Goods in General Equilibrium, Review of Economic Studies, Vol. 21, No. 1, pp. 1-20.

Sanghvi, Rajnikant L. (1979), Role of Industrial Estates in a Developing Country, Bombay, Multi-tech. Publishing Co.

Sen, Amartya (1979), 'The Welfare Basis of Real Income Comparisons: A Survey', Journal of Economic Literature, Vol. XVII, No. 1, pp. 1-45.

Smith, Adam (1776), An Inquiry into the Nature and Causes of Wealth of Nations, Oxford, Clarendon Press.

Snodgrass, Donald R. (1980), Inequality and Economic Development in Malaysia, Kuala Lumpur, Oxford University Press.

Songuanruang, Saeng *et al.* (1978), Development of Small and Medium Manufacturing Establishments in Thailand, Association of Development Research and Training Institutes of Asia and the Pacific, Bangkok.

Spinanger, Dean, Rüdiger Soltwedel (1976), Beschäftigungsprobleme in Industriestaaten, Bundesanstalt für Arbeit, Nürnberg.

--, (1980), Regional Industrialization Policies in a Small Developing Country - A Case Study of West Malaysia, Kiel, Institute of World Economics.

--, (1984), Objectives and Impact of Economic Activity Zones - Some Evidence from Asia, Weltwirtschaftliches Archiv, Vol. 120, No. 1, pp. 64-89.

Staley, Eugene, Richard Morse (1965), Modern Small Industry for Developing Countries, New York, McGraw-Hill.

Stern, Robert M. (1976), 'Some Evidence on the Factor Content of West Germany's Foreign Trade', The Journal of Political Economy, Vol. 84, No. 1, pp. 131-41.

Stöhr, Walter, Franz Tödtling (1977), 'Evaluation of Regional Policies - Experiences in Market and Mixed Economies', in Hansen, Niles M. (ed.), Human Settlement Systems: International Perspectives on Structure Change and Public Policy, New York, Ballinger.

Stolper, Wolfgang F., Paul A. Samuelson (1941), 'Protection and Real Wages', The Review of Economic Studies, Vol. 9, pp. 58-73.

Sundrum, Ramaswamy Meenatohi (1971), 'Manpower and Educational Development in East and Southeast Asia', The Malayan Economic Review, Vol. 16, No. 2, pp. 78-90.

Sutter, Rolf (1979), Nationale Wirtschaftspolitik und Internationale Unternehmen in Malaysia, Hamburg, Weltarchiv.

Thoburn, John T. (1977), Primary Commodity Exports and Economic Development: Theory, Evidence and a Study of Malaysia, London, Wiley.

Thoman, Richard S. (1977), Free Ports and Foreign-Trade Zones, Cambridge, Maryland, Cornell Maritime Press.

Townroe, Peter Michael, Nigel J. Roberts (1980), Local External Economies for British Manufacturing Industry, Farnborough/Hants, Gower.

Tuong, Ho Doc, Alexander Yeats (1980), 'On Factor Proportions as a Guide to the Future Composition of Developing Country Exports', Journal of Development Economics, Vol. 7, No. 4, pp. 521-39.

Usher, Dan (1976), 'The Economics of Tax Incentives to Encourage Investment, with Special Reference to Malaysia', Queen's University Discussion Paper, 219, Kingston, Ontario.

Vanek, Jaroslav (1959), 'The Natural Resource Content of Foreign Trade, 1870-1955 and the Relative Abundance of Natural Resources in the United States', The Review of Economics and Statistics, Vol. 41, No. 2, pp. 146-53.

--, (1965), General Equilibrium of International Discrimination, Cambridge, Harvard University Press.

Vernon, Raymond (1966), 'International Investment and International Trade in the Product Cycle', The Quarterly Journal of Economics, Vol. 80, pp. 190-207.

--, (1979), 'The Product Cycle Hypothesis in a New International Environment', Oxford Bulletin of Economics and Statistics, Vol. 41, No. 4, pp. 255-67.

Viner, Jacob (1950), The Customs Union Issue, New York, Stevens.

Wang, L.H. and S.L. Wong (1980), 'Urban Labour Productivity and Regional Development Strategies', Environment and Planning, International Journal of Urban and Regional Research, Vol. 12, pp. 449-61.

Weber, Alfred (1911), 'Die Standortslehre und die Handelspolitik', Archiv für Sozialwissenschaft und Sozialpolitik, Vol. XXXII, pp. 667-88.

--, (1929), Theory of the Location of Industries, Vol. 33, Chicago, University of Chicago Press.

Weiss, Frank Dietmar (1978), 'Electrical Engineering in West Germany - Adjusting to Imports from Less Developed Countries', Kieler Studien 155, Tübingen, J.C.B. Mohr.

Wheelwright, Edward L. (1965), Industrialization in Malaysia, Melbourne, Melbourne University Press.

Wilson, Paul (1980), 'West Germany in Asia', Far Eastern Economic Review, July 4-10, pp. 33-54.

Wolter, Frank (1977), 'Factor Proportions, Technology and West German Industry's International Trade Patterns', Weltwirtschaftliches Archiv, Vol. 113, No. 2, pp. 250-67.

--, (1977), 'Adjusting to Imports from Developing Countries - The Evidence from a Human-Capital Rich, Natural Resource Poor Country', in Giersch, Herbert (ed.), Reshaping the World Economic Order, Tübingen, J.C.B. Mohr, pp. 97-131.

World Bank, World Tables, Baltimore, various issues.

--, World Development Report, various issues.

Wu, Yuan-li, Chun-shi Wu (1980), Economic Development in Southeast Asia - the Chinese Dimension, Stanford/Calif., Hoover Institution Press.

Yeats, Alexander (1977), 'A Comparative Analysis of the Incidence of Tariffs and Transportation Costs on India's Exports', The Journal of Development Studies, Vol. 14, No. 1, pp. 97-107.

Young, Kevin *et al.* (1980), Malaysia, Growth and Equity in a Multiracial Society, Baltimore, published for the World Bank by the Johns Hopkins University Press.

Zehender, Wolfgang *et al.* (1978), Industrial Location Behaviour of Malaysian and Foreign Investors - The Effectiveness of the Malaysian Decentralization Policy, Berlin, German Development Institute (GDI).

Index